A LIFE:
COLLECTED POEMS

A Life:
Collected Poems

A. L. ROWSE

but a poem is not poetry—
that is a life.

T. S. Eliot

William Blackwood
Edinburgh

William Blackwood
32 Thistle Street
Edinburgh EH2 1HA

First published 1981
© A. L. Rowse

ISBN 0 85158 141 2

Printed by William Blackwood & Sons Ltd

To
N. S.

Contents

II: The 'Thirties

III: Poems of Wartime

IV: Poems of War and Peace

V: American Poems

VI: Poems Mainly Cornish

New Poems

VII

VIII

IX: Children's Verses

Preface

I am grateful to the Poet Laureate for repeatedly urging me to bring together my Collected Poems: without encouragement I might not have tackled the job. For it appears that I have been writing poetry all my life—for many years before I dared to write history. It would seem to be unwelcome for an historian also to be a poet; it certainly is rare: I can think only of Macaulay and Samuel Daniel who combined the two. But my life is in my poetry.

Looking through it all now, I see that it is an authentic record of my inner life—rather than of the external public life, given to history and (for a time) politics, though it also offers a true commentary on the history of our ruinous, tragic age. Poets are prophets—those savage poems of the 'thirties offered more truthful witness than the complacent humbug of politicians or the optimistic illusions of the liberal-minded.

Early on I was interested in exploring fear, a rare subject; many poems in those decades were the fruit of long illness, also a subject not much explored in verse. Hopkins wrote of mental anguish—no one that I can think of describes physical pain. Those poems describe both; Hopkins found consolation in religion, I had none—except the beauty of the physical world, natural and human. Then I notice an extraordinary Manichean strain as war was renewed and up to the Second War itself—tragic, but the most heroic period in Britain's long history, in which she went bravely out in fire and flame.

After the war, not during it, the poet transfers himself to America, recovering health and a new inspiration. Few

English poets have responded to American landscape, and Robert Lowell thought that permanent residence in the United States was not good for their poetry. Meanwhile I retained residence each year in Oxford, and my roots in Cornwall, with which the poems record my relations—rejection, long resentment, withdrawal, contingent reconciliation within sight of the end.

Of the poems technically there is little that I wish to say. Half-rhymes and consonantal rhymes earlier were too modern for my older friends at Oxford, who at least took poetry seriously. Even the blank verse is decorated with a good deal of rhyme, both internal and terminal, as well as alliteration that comes spontaneously to the natural poet. Verse without rhyme, or scansion, or verbal decoration, is simply not memorable. Today these things are lost, in a time when—as Kingsley Amis points out—much of the 'verse' written makes no sense in any sense of the word that makes sense. To that I should add, though it is hardly necessary to point it out, that it is also uneducated.

Much the same may be said of most criticism, in a broken-down society which has lost its standards in most fields. I do not go so far as my friend Auden as to say that 'there is something lifeless, even false, about systematic criticism'; but it is certainly a duty to ignore the kind of criticism that has lost touch with the art of literature.

What, then, is there to console us in this sad time?

I observe that these poems portray an enclosed world, an almost solipsistic life, as near as may be to self-sufficiency: a strong position, I have found, from which to confront the ruin and desolation of our time. One can at least look out from the fortress of one's mind, watch and observe, pick up fragments, cherish the relics and memories of experience—and, for consolation, there is always the constant and infinitely various beauty of the external world.

A. L. Rowse

Trenarren,
St Austell

I: Earlier Poems

Ireland

A wise-eyed solemn child, tanned gipsy, see
In solitary play beneath the elder tree

In the wild hillside garden where the hours
Go by on tip-toe over the kitchen flowers:

There's sweet potato-bloom, lavender and white,
But under the hedge, nettles and aconite;

And a border made, of thyme and saxifrage,
On a ledge pennywort, and in a bed, sage.

But he, forgotten child, content to play
With dreams for company, all summer in a day,

In his coign where the green rain-water-barrel is
Under the elder, hears stranger harmonies.

His eyes, dark sloes, follow the evening sun
Up the hill slopes, till night's shadow dun

Enfolds the garden and him. In the last rich light
He finds a secret knowledge and his delight:

For then, he knows that beyond the round hill's brim
Where no one has ever been is the world's rim;

And there, he has heard tell, is Ireland coiled
In ultimate seas and is the end of the world.

'Ireland', he whispers to the sky's blue tent—
And the waters of sleep steal over him content.

The Old Cornish Woman by the Fire

By the fire she sits
In the dusky evening of her years,
And the firelight flits
Above her head, and on her whitened hairs.

Her sorrowing face,
Like a withered lily in the gloom
Of the hearth-place,
Glimmers with light in the darkened room.

She has her thoughts,
Nor stirs if anyone should pass:
Like speckled motes
They come and go against a pane of glass.

So patiently
She bears her pain: as for a friend,
So peacefully
She waits the footfalls of her certain end.

At Duporth

Into a quiet, lonely place I come,
To a coign of cliff and a lane that drops to the sea:
The shrill voices of the winds have here
No place, nor the winds' fingers in my hair.
All that was before is strangely far,
And I have entered on a secret stillness:
A frightened hush falls on the throat that sang,
On the stream that babbled dreamily in the sun,
On whispering osier and ivied stone.
There are a thousand timid eyes that watch
In the startled silence; only the monotone
Of gathered waves that break upon the shore

Below, lulls suspense with regular beat.
A sea-bird leaves his preening by the margin,
And rising through swift air, desolately
Wheels above the deserted beach. And now,
Rousing from dreams I find my quiet nook
Ravished with innumerable sounds:
The intimate brook resumes its idle chatter,
A little wind wakes among the withies;
The ivy-leaves that gleam like pools of light
Rustle softly over the stones, and even
The mosses are astir; a robin threads
The intricate hedge, and pipes a friendly song
Ere he flits mocking up the covert lane.

The Shadows on the Glass

When far into the night I sit and work,
Within a darkened room where shadows lurk,

Still and black before me as a pond
A window is, and the deeper night beyond:

Shade of another world although it be,
The shapes of friendlier things I often see.

For there upon the mirrored deeps of space
Are the homely signs of this my chosen place:

A polished surface lit in kindly glow,
The tongues of firelight dancing in a row

On shelf and cupboard; and in far background,
The shut doors that may move, and with no sound.

Myself looks at me from the darkened glass
And holds my eyes whenever they would pass:

But if a shadow now should wake and stir
This room to movement, and my heart to fear . . .

A sudden flash of the eyes, as a bird takes cover,
The moment broken and the dread is over.

The room resumes its quiet homeliness,
And nothing stirs in the night's lone distances.

Grown-up to Child: Ten Commandments

Take a rake with ten teeth
    To hollow out the sea;
Ride astride a sea-bird's back,
    Nor ever be
Afraid to raid the nests of gulls
    In the shy places of the rocks;
Nor slow to draw music from
    The fluted comb.
Spread a bed of gathered down
    From dandelion clocks;
Scorn not the thorn whereon there grows
    The everlasting rose.
Do not you afear to spin
    A thread to catch the air,
Nor lack to pluck the golden broom
    On the high ledges where
The rare birds there do preen and plume
    Themselves above the bay.
Nor fail to sail a coral boat
    Out to meet the day
At dun of dawn: And may
    Your eye descry
    Whatever there shall lie
Between the green sea and the sky.

Paradise Square

There was a moment of fleet-foot joy
Today in Paradise Square.
Even time itself stood still,
When the obscure sun from behind a cloud came out
And darted fingers of light through the aspen trees;
The wind awoke and walked in the gardens of
Paradise Square.
Little old women looked down through lattices
Of high upper windows in windmill houses,
And laughed to see the trees blown silver and grey.
A tiny white cur sniffed at the breeze
And fell three steps down into the street.
A journeyman tinker went by under a tower,
With bag on back and apprentice lagging behind.
Today there was a moment of fleet-foot joy,
When even time stood still in
Paradise Square.

Jeremiah, the Tabby Cat, Stalks in the Sunlit Garden

While you clamber over the blue gate in the garden,
In the sunlit garden I
Already arrived am before you: while
In a flash of the eye,
You are suspended in your leap
Against the blue ground of the gate. And then,
Unconscious cinema-actor, you cross your stage,
The plot where light cuts the shade like a jewel
On what intent?
Your eyes are amber in the sun, flashing
From the cushioned tuft of harebells
And calceolarias.
Now you thread the intricate pattern

9

Of garden stems and stems of shadow,
And cross the lawn:
Your supple flanks serpentine, your tread
Stealthy and secret, of who knows
What generations of jungle cats?
And so you reach the undergrowth of the sycamore;
Nor pause to hear me calling from my window
Whence sight of you I lose,
Your dappled side lost in the camouflage of shadow;
And you have left the sunlit garden
For who knows what memories of lost generations of
    great cats?

The Snake: Homage to D. H. Lawrence

One day in childhood
Coming down the hot summer road,
The sun brilliant upon the angular elvan-stones
    polished by the horses' hooves,
Passing the triangular bed of nettles
    in the corner of the hedge:
I turned and suddenly saw
Coil upon coil, the striped and fascinated
    rings of a snake sleeping there:
Slowly he shifted and a lithe
    movement like a shudder passed
    through the shifting coils as he lifted
    them to settle himself again.

Of a sudden overwhelmed with horror
I fled spinning down the village street
    in the hot sun, nor stopped
    until the welcoming doorway of my home.

Still I have not forgotten the sudden fascination,
　　the nearness, the unexpectedness;
And I wonder if perchance I shall see
　　the snake, as tonight,
　　come slowly unwinding his coils
　　out of the dying embers, the red
　　bed of the fire, unwinding himself through the
　　bars;
Or come slowly up out of the recesses
　　of the deep blue chair,
　　or from under the stealthily moving
　　　pattern of the carpet:
The horror of it
　　if he were, as in my childhood,
　　　suddenly there!

Saturday at Truro

Because this is Saturday, and because
It is afternoon, and the day's scrubbing and cleaning
　　are over,
The neat and pictured red houses stand in their rows
Prim and tightly like aproned women; and all
The brass-rimmed doorsteps flashing in the sun,
A canary cage set above the black hollow of the door.
Suddenly I hear from a window opened to the street,
In a lull of traffic, the three quarters sprinkled
From a somnolent clock upon the oppressive air.

And because that was Saturday
And we were soon to go different ways,
We were together, child of the daydream eyes and I:
Visiting our toy cathedral town, set within green hills,
With runnels that go purling under the mirrored sky.
The selfsame chime we heard, like drowsy beads of
　　water

11

Dripping, from a tower upon the commerce of the
   market-place.
And all the belfries followed: St Mary's loosened
   tongue,
Deliberate and spare of speech;
And the Cathedral chime, a distant fine-spun web of
   sound,
That floated high overhead, out to the meadows
And over the woods and waters of the valley.
When evening came, we chose the shadow of a lime
And sat by the river-side on a spur,
Watching a tall ship, rigged and delicately sparred,
That came with proud movement, against the sunset
   hills,
Slowly up the river, with the breeze and flowing tide.
O magic hour, when the day closes its petals up
And folds itself, a flower upon the pond of the
   encroaching night.

The Fallen Tree

Walking through the fields in the eye of day
Blinded, I came upon a tree that lay

Across the accustomed path. Felled in the strife
With elemental winds, writhing for life,

The great tree bore the seals of agony.
And now, like marble or like ivory,

Immovable and still, without a breath
It lies, finding a serene peace in death.

And yet in the branches of the unfallen trees
There runs a gentle music of the breeze

12

Among the boughs, like a small stream's murmur,
An echo of the singing winds of summer.

The hedges are yellow where the sunlight lingers:
Touched to colour by the season's fingers,

They stand in regiment of gold and red.
Now over the stripped body of the dead

Tree, there creeps a gleam of mirrored white
And blue of steel, the sheath and shadow of light.

The crumpled leaves fall with scrannel cry
Over the tree's marmoreal ecstasy.

Still in the high elms, there runs a whispered dirge
Of leaves in motion, the remembered surge

Of waves within a shell, hollow and smooth,
Some far, faint song from the netherland of youth.

Ode

How many days now, how many months and years,
Since that rain-mirrored evening of the spring,
When rooted in enchantment by the shore
Suddenly I heard the song of a bird take wing,
Sweet and uncertain in the stillness, and soar
Out into the shattered silence of the bay:

So many years, so far a thing, and yet
The sea is strong within my nostrils now
As then, the wind off the sea in my hair
And in my eyes, and to my heart shall bear,
Over the remembered music of the waves,
This confident song, this ringing ecstasy.

The cup of the bay is brimmed with melody
As the calyx of a flower is filled with light.
Only the iron walls of the cliffs reject
The supplication of this throat and break
The song into a thousand petals white
That all the hollows of the sea reflect.

One last gleam of the sun lights up the rock
From whence the song comes ringing: there it rides
Mute in tongueless immobility,
Proudly over the lapse and flow of tides:
Yet like a brave doomed ship with light at mast
Has set its course out to the open sea.

If only, before the night, the song should loose
The moorings of the rock, so that it break
From its foundations, and urging the slow bark
Across the ominous ways of the fatal sea,
And triumphing should meet disaster: if only
The song should cleave the ways of the deep and wake

The dead who sleep in the valleys of the sea,
So that the sea give up her dead: if only
The stopped ears might hear music again,
And all the huddled skeletons of drowned men
Assemble their bones and throng forth from the lonely
Places beneath the waters' immensity:

The song shall pass, as we who are mortal pass
Across the margin of this translunary sphere;
And no brave ship shall be set voyaging,
Image of man's infinite loneliness,
A cry that gathers strength from nothingness;
For the world is dead and there is none to hear.

The Progress of Love

(*For A. v. T.*)

Your beauty was of such a quality
As I have seen distilled by sober light
Of day upon the surfaces of things:
The delicate touch of the sun's passing brings
A glow of life upon the palace front,
That sinks from desire to memory, and dies.

So was your passing from the shadowy room:
While you were there, the late light lingering,
All things grew sentient of your loveliness;
And here a face caught the refracted impress
Of your beauty. And when you went, you drew
Evening on, and owl-soft dusk came down.

Now is your spring, and yet will summer come
To strengthen you, and make you brave to war.
And you will follow up the hot dusty course
Of irrevocable time, nor have remorse
For him that loved you, and would have you never
Changed by contact with the harsher world.

And then will autumn lay a still cold finger
On your beauty, will dim your liquid eyes,
And suck the warm juices of your lips.
This living dream you are shall see eclipse,
And I'll not mourn you in my waking state,
Wide-eyed and in my frozen heart secure.

Many days now has your image haunted me
And set me forth upon my wonted ways:
In field and pasture you are at my side,
Impetuous, inseparable guide,
Yours is the vision that the sun informs
In cloud, in water, in every stone and leaf.

Though spring shall fade, and autumn
    summer follow,
And winter come to ravage with decay,
Something of your beauty will remain
Untouched, intangible, beyond all wane;
Nor can you altogether die, as long
As I shall live you will go on in me.

The Garden

The enchanted garden under the stillness lies,
And the dark trees that taper to the skies
Funereal are, like sombre swaying plumes.
Beneath the stars, gigantic night entombs
All that the familiar day revealed.
Only a midnight lamp that has for shield
The velvet verdurous gloom of vernal trees
Disturbs the dusk, all night unseeing sees:
This is my beacon, this solitary eye
That watches me insensate till I die.

This is my life, to watch the seasons pass
Over the garden's clear enchanted glass.
There goes by the procession of the hours,
The days, the years, nor stirs the ordered flowers.
And there as on a magic plane I see
The ceaseless flow of time away from me:
Not in my heart, but in the external world
This evidence of my weak mortal hold.

And so through change to inevitable change
The visible shadows of existence range
From the dawn to the coming of the night.
Have I not waited for the dim uncertain light
That steals into this world of mystery,
Troubling its strangeness and its intimacy?

16

And in this place, where late the loud birds sang
Before the dawn, so that the garden rang
With passion and with ecstasy, now all
Is silent upon roof and stone and wall.

Hush! the hour when all things living wake
It is: they stir the garden's dream and break
The threads of sleep. Now statuesque and still
The gathered chimneys of the palace spill
The last rays of the wheeling sickle moon.
A clock strikes the quarter: one note is soon
Dropped like a stone into that shadowy well;
The walls resound to the shrill sudden bell,
Then all is quiet, and the waters of peace
Flow in and find their undisturbed release.

So morning comes, and the turning earth spins on
Under the blue acres of the sky whereon
The white clouds flying, flaunt their candid banners;
The wind springs up like the feet of many runners,
Is rampant in the trees, then gradually
Subsides upon a low bough noiselessly
Nid-nodding in the idiotic wind.
Then in the noon, the tulips flame-quickened
Lay bare their hearts aspiring to the sun;
And later, in the coolness, when day is done
They shut their petals up and like a troop
Of driven ghosts, pale and defeated droop.

So comes the night, so vanishes the day,
So with the seasons passes life away:
Passes away, nor any impress makes
On the mind that knows not if it sleeps or wakes.
Only by the shadows on the garden's face
Changing, I follow time's unchanging pace:
By them I know the world rolls on its course,
Irrevocable, swift, without remorse.

C   17

Arctic Moon

The fingers of the moon upon the frozen world
Have caught the aloof heart in a net,
Caught and enmeshed there is no longer hold
Within this arctic region where life is not:

The fine and subtle fingers of the night
Seek out the lunar shadows that we are,
Sifting in the crevices the white
Dust fallen of the crumbling sphere:

The wind of death at the corners of the house
Is furtive behind the barren leaves;
Though we, but shadows moving in the caves,
For screen from the approaching death have these:

The frozen eagle poised still in vain for flight,
The patterned poplars and the momentary light.

Magpie Lane

How usual is the world of Spring:
The floods are out across the plain;
The punctual birds are on the wing,
Scattering the dew like grain.

Over the meadows and the fields
There blows a wind of daffodils;
Each passing year no difference yields
Upon the seasonable hills.

Yet still I think sometimes to meet
A tiger, amber in the rain;
And turning down the narrow street,
The Holy Ghost in Magpie Lane.

Small Enchantments

Here by the fence I halt, the familiar spot
Under the green shelter of the leaves in the hot

Summer afternoon, where the light makes lattices
Upon the running brook's sweet surfaces.

In the flat water-meadows, the sorrel is red
Among the golden kingcups. And overhead

A passing plane, blue and silver in the sun,
Drones and drowses nonchalantly on.

A sudden eddy of wind the long grasses
Stirs, and reveals the sedges' hidden places.

Yet all the while had I taken no notice
Of the enchanted brook, playing to entice

Me from my dream of ordinary things,
That to the subsiding pulse of motion sings.

A gentle rill of sound as it ripples over
The pebble edge makes discreet music hover

In the intimate air. Nor had I seen
A tiny splutter where a furtive wren

Bathes among the shallows, among the cresses.
O magic of this place where secret voices

Put out their strength to soothe and charm a while:
These are the small enchantments that beguile.

Hinksey

(*In memoriam Robert Bridges*)

The wind in the alders and across the marshland
    is like the plunging of many seas.
I am borne down in the heavy waters
    to where the strong tide runs by:
The trees are but fronds in the current waving,
    the long grasses leaning over.

The wind makes a furrow in my hair,
And all is stillness around me in the bent avenue
    So loud is the wind's voice.

Here on an earlier summer day were two
Lovers, kissing in the rain,
Oblivious of the wind, the trees and the eye of day.
They pass, the destroyers of my peace,
Strewing the floor of the world with broken flowers.

I, the passer-by, for consolation have only these:
The charity of brown ploughed earth,
The folded curves of the furrows,
The passing bells of raindrops
That break upon the upturned face.

There is no mystery in dying so.
Only his body that else had been lapped round
    by all this land,
One with the folds of the hills and the strong trees,
Is but ashes scattered in the wind
    upon the lips of flowers.

Boar's Hill

The wintry sun a pallid laughter yields
To the sterile slopes and the forsaken fields.

No leaf is left upon the autumnal bough;
The sabbatarian rooks go homeward now.

And homeward I, yet pause to think that here
I stood for a moment of a former year,

And watched a fox drive his purposive line
Across the snowy ploughland, in a fine

Dark streak upon the white from hedge to hedge.
Now like an ossuary at the edge

Of hill and sky, rises the skeleton
Water-tower and bleakly leans upon

The open heaven. The gathered wind forlorn
Is shrill among the trees, yet to the shorn

Pasture is temperate and nothing stirs.
Only a memory returns and whispers

To me in the willow-walk, of a child
Homeward from the wood returning with wild

Irises in his arms, and in his eyes
A fugitive fear, a sudden sweet surmise.

Now all the land, crepuscular and still,
Glides into darkness; and I follow from the hill

The last void loveliness upon the plains,
Till of the city there is nothing that remains.

II: The 'Thirties

Extempore Memorial

(For Charles Henderson)

(i)

These anemones, these snowdrops, this frail aconite,
That light with purple the dark corner of the room,
And tell me that in the west, the spring already come,
Heaves under the quickened mosses, runs along
The hedgerows and lights up the secret earth:

Speak also to me of one untimely dead,
This language of the soul for the dead soul,
This bond of hills and valleys, wind and trees,
Of all that country that by death is his.

How should my life have become so bound,
So mixed with his that by his death,
I now see never that ridge of land,
The familiar road, the stone-pines on the edge
        leaning to the wind, their driven shapes
        fantastically flanking the forsaken house;
Nor ever see the curve of hills
Encircling the lighted city
        through nocturnal mists, June night of stars,
        or by the January moon;
Nor ever walk in the funereal woods,
        the waters in my ears falling,
        letting fall their drops upon my mind,
            and in my heart:
Nor know all these in the flesh, or in the mind's eye,
        but they are his, being made so by his death?

(ii)

Now come back to me the evidence of those hills,
Those walks, the bridle-path, the gorse bright
        over Idless, and swept sky;

25

So also the December rains and the plantations
Shivering with wetness and the winter sun;

The Christmas moon above the hollow bowl
Where the city lies sleeping, lapped by the blown bells;
     the quiet house where the successor of Peter,
     sheltered within the peach-clad walls
     under the shadow of the tower,
Looks out upon his flock and keeps his hours.

O bells, O moon of Bethlehem,
O moving finger of time that writes
     upon those walls, upon the trees,
O prince of the Church, O people,
O sleeping city, O sapient bells
     that call the heart home,
     opening the casements
     upon what inner kingdoms,
     what peace forgotten,
     save in the unquiet tongues of bells
     ringing to church on Christmas Eve,
     the people waking in the steets,
     shaking themselves from sleep
     having dreamed dreams under their spell:
O Sapientia, O Radix Jesse!*

(iii)

Who is this that moves when the leaves move
Blown by the wind along the midnight road
By Tresillian Bridge, past Pencalenick and St. Clement's
     Cross?
What dear ghost is this comes revisiting his former places?
I who remain keep watch in vain
     upon the faces of the clouds that pass,
     hoping for a sign of one who has long forsaken
     the friendly woods;

* The Nine O's form part of the Christmas ritual at Truro Cathedral.

Perhaps to-night under the strong headlights
       of the passing car,
     the leaves dropping in crowds,
A falling star
     may signify
     the mystery.

(iv)

He lies not here: here you will not find him,
       but in another country, under other stars,
       not his, not ours, in stranger soil.

The stone-pines and the cypresses
       whispering the sounds and perfumes of the sea,
       take up these messages from this country
         that by death is his,
       wherein the spirit finds release;
Here circumscribed by every line and fold,
       in every blade and leaf
       at home, at peace.

How Many Miles to Mylor?

   How many miles to Mylor
      By frost and candle-light:
   How long before I arrive there,
      This mild December night?

   As I mounted the hill to Mylor
      Through the dark woods of Carclew,
   A clock struck the three-quarters,
      And suddenly a cock crew.

   At the cross-roads on the hill-top
      The snow lay on the ground,
   In the quick air and the stillness,
      No movement and no sound.

27

'How is it?' said a voice from the bushes
    Beneath the rowan-tree;
'Who is it?' my mouth re-echoed,
    My heart went out of me.

I cannot tell what strangeness
    There lay around Carclew:
Nor whatever stirred in the hedges
    When an owl replied 'Who-whoo?'

A lamp in a lone cottage,
    A face in a window-frame,
Above the snow a wicket:
    A house without a name.

How many miles to Mylor
    This dark December night:
And shall I ever arrive there
    By frost or candle-light?

The Dead Friend

Sometimes when day draws in I think I hear
The firm and friendly step upon the stair,

The door open, the long familiar form
Stooping a little, enter now the room.

He looks a little sadly as one that's lost
To life and me, that affable shy ghost,

Yet moves across to his accustomed place
In the angle of the window, looks into my face

Questioningly, as if I had some remedy
That might be sovran for this strange malady

Of being dead. But when most I think to have
Found something that might heal, a word to save,

So turn to him, he is no longer there:
A soundless movement, a sigh upon the stair,

And I remember in the empty room,
A narrow, cypress-darkened grave in Rome.

Waylaid

What face is that peering from the shadow,
Though I turn not, of the darkened window:

Who is it watches me with such loving care,
So closely, when I turn he is not there?

Wherever in this waking room I am
Reminds me that another called this home.

Silent, so still, so sleepless an eyelid,
What cover I may take, I am waylaid.

Always beyond the turning of the eye,
And when I think to follow, slipping away:

If I should turn, I know, you are not there,
Unmoving, still I know this moving fear;

And if perchance then I am listening
My inner ear shall hear the dead man sing,

Very low and soft and void of grief,
Regretful, yet having small regret for life.

This is he who formerly was here,
Who dead, forgetting not the things that were

His, lays a shadow upon all that's mine:
Poor ghost, come home then, come you in!

The Field

This quiet moment, unbroken of sound, as if
I should stand for ever at edge of cliff,

The world unmoving, the pastures of the sky
Still and harrowed by no cloud, and I

A lonely column of shadow in a field,
A long gaunt finger pointing to the mild

Plains of the sea and the translucent east.
There is a brooding quiet in the west:

The high tired voices of children: Silence again.
And all the generations of former men

Are forgotten while a bird intent darts low
Along the hedge. And now with tread more slow

From the four corners of the field they come,
So many dead men have made this their home.

The day will be when I shall be dead as they,
And the quiet land that bore me, in that day

Will know me no more then than the dust of those.
They squandered here the labour of their thighs,

The far-off, linked, inseparable lovers,
Until the moon set or sun rose. And others,

Watching a moment between the hills and sea,
Knew too a time would come and they not be.

Now all the land is silent as the dead:
I celebrate their spilled and wasted seed.

The Road to Luxulyan

Passage is opened for the sun in heaven:
A fleeting wind drives by, a way is riven

For the late reluctant gleam to light upon
The splintered granite, the road bare as bone.

The March light sudden and fitful of heart,
Mocking with faint hope the summer heat,

Explores the skeleton land and now reveals
The rifts and crannies that the rock conceals,

The secret periwinkle and parched mosses.
Now sings the keenlier in the long dry grasses

The shrill mnemonic of the scuttling wind:
The razor sound zizgags to the quarry's end,

Skimming with swift, subtle touch the edge
Of precipice and angular cut ridge,

And scurries swish-swish to the moor's rim.
Across the hollows of the pastures come

The comfortable cries of silly sheep.
And now in the distance the familiar shape

Is suddenly there, of the snakewhite road once seen
Strung with red gems of light under the moon.

A gust of wind blows out the rapid sun:
The grey wings settle on the land again.

April Landscape

The cracked bell rings to Lenten service over
The April fields, lifting the mists that hover

Across the dun distances from wood to wood.
Each quiet stroke renews the familiar mood

Of a dream that has been dreamed, and again I hear
The interior, murmuring complaint of prayer.

Now the dark woods of Duporth are pierced with late
Innumerable sweet voices, separate

And clear above the burden of the sea.
The long sea-swell rolls in its symmetry

Of surf, breaking the springwhite flowers of foam
Upon the iron rocks amid the fume

And thunder of spring upon the heaving sea.
The sheltered slope is strewn with sticks that the

April winds have sown: the trees are yet bare.
A night-moth voyages on the uncertain air,

Seeking the dizzy region of the cliffs.
Somewhere in the domed sky a gull laughs

Above the turning world, and with shrill mirth
That the sea should mumble the corners of the earth.

Trenarren Waiting

The moon at end of day
Stares at me across the bay;

The clouds scud overhead
Across the valley of the dead,

The plain where the drowned men
Rise and fall again.

Smoke for this hour ascends
From the still house, befriends

The dark and friendless grounds:
Nothing now there sounds,

Save the crack of boughs
Around the waiting house.

Under the lowering sky
The importunate seagulls cry;

The wind stirs the frieze
Of black, ancestral trees.

What if the long-drowned men
Assemble their bones again,

Since all is at an end,
The thronged cliffs ascend,

Once more themselves arouse
Against the doomed house?

Idea

Suppose the brain is turned
And, looking up from the lamplit desk,
I meet the stony glare
    of a jade-green different star,
Image of cold, ironic steadfastness,
Watching me?
(Bright star, would I were steadfast as thou art.)
But who is steadfast?
Not you. Not I.
In the dark well of the palace
The moon-lipped sill of a window
Gleams, and is withdrawn.
The leaves glitter in the wind, in the darkness
Falling. The world is falling.
Und doch ist Einer welcher dieses Fallen
Unendlich sanft in seinen Händen hält.
O vanity of desire for life and love:
The world is but a jewel, and we
The prisoned lights that lurk in hidden depths,
Shifting and insubstantial as the leaves.
I am blown to where the cliff of Spain
Draws its frozen draperies in stone
Out of the vermiculous sea.
You know the route:
That way madness lies.

Walk by the Moon

Over the hill's neck
King of the land I walk,
Under the moon.
There are those eyes that follow me,
And the curve of another's lips:

34

But in vain, but vain
    as the thunder of the sea,
    the grateful folds of the cliffs.
If a foot should stumble,
There would be an end perhaps:
The long silver leagues of surf
Leap up to receive me.
Into what hands then would I commend the spirit?

A dumb beast sheltering under a wall,
A broken gate, the faces of drowned men
Turned upwards to the innocent surface of the sea,
A lonely heron fishing in a creek,
The labouring spirit of the woods,
A roof that the wind sings through:
These would be greater content,
Less sinister than
A bruised reed.

The Dream

The dream begins to stir again
In the secret places of the exhausted brain.
(Life is difficult because quotidian.)
Yet, in the Wittenberg Platz on a summer noon,
The open balconies yawned up to catch the sudden sun,
The trees gleamed in a little wind,
And lights brushed the geraniums on the market stalls.
These moments have I stored up against the ruin
That time will bring upon us and upon our love.
But time that ruins also heals
And perhaps will lay a finger to console; or so you say:
As if this should be for consolation
In the cold gradations of decay.
What are these soft autumnal leaves
That come drifting across my tired eyes

35

Drifting, nor cease to beat
With slow insistent concatenation
Upon the brain?
For all is not yet dull
Under the different skull,
Although innumerable webs are woven
To net the vanishing dream.

Auguste Nept: 1877*

So here you are, brave soldier!
You that were young in seventy-seven.
But he has left for later ages,
For the posterity that is I,
The ineffaceable mould of feature
The form that in God's eye
You were, and still to us is you.

Did he think so to forget
The summer of seventy-seven,
And Brussels dusty under the lime trees,
And the Caserne, the bugles and the trumpets,
The watered pavements in the morning,
Your upturned face in the archway?

(O for the summer of seventy-seven,
The heat, the Exposition Universelle
And the gendarmes of the Trocadéro, the gardener
Watering the flower-beds before the heat o' the sun,
And MacMahon, and you.)

Where else then is this body,
Mauled or distorted by the years,
Scarred by fevers of the flesh,
Put out by death?

* The model for Rodin's *L'Age d'Airain* was named Auguste Nept.

Where is this dust:
Mixed into the mould of battle,
Ploughed into the fields,
Or sleeping by some quiet water
By Louveciennes or Charleroi,
Having found death late in an arm-chair by the fireside,
Or early, by the fevered waters of the Congo?

Only thus are you exempt from the body's death
And left for ever young.

The Stricken Grove

Enter now the stricken grove

W. H. AUDEN

Here in the grove that's forested with bells
They walk who know their own loves' funerals;

Two by two, though oftener one by one,
They seek their shelter from the tolerant sun:

They are but ghosts of their own discontent,
Hugging their private disillusionment,

Laying their withered fingers without heat
Upon the wounded places of the heart,

Cherishing their anguish and their pain
Till the tufted forest cry again

Adonis, Adonis!—O Adonai! O Lord,
If only we might hear the unlikely word

Spoken aloud to the world as once we heard
Each to himself alone, nor ever feared

37

The exquisite risk, the danger of despair
Nor any defeat. Now there is nothing there:

Only the sexual birds repeat their cry
And the vibrant lovely snake glides by.

This is the stricken grove: no life is here.
Too late for joy, too proud for hope or fear

They move as shadows: these are they
Who blench not when their bodies turn to clay.

The Snake

J'y suivais un serpent qui venait de me mordre
PAUL VALÉRY

In the water-meadows the young men walk,
Admire their women, stiff with sex they talk,

Self-consciousness upon their fallow faces
(Better to be private in these public places).

The young women to assert their innocence
And hide their native insignificance

Chatter like parokeets along the paths,
Whose plumes they borrow for their summer clothes.

The human scene outdoes the verdurous,
The borders lush, the birds lascivious.

The wise and hidden snake remains apart,
Unseen, unmoving, eating out his heart:

He is not deceived, but steadfast sees
With lidless and live eyes these fooleries,

38

Withdraws himself into a world remote,
With its own inner bitterness replete,

After long seasons' silence to reflect
On what is passing in the world, eject

Some suitable poison of the wounded brain
On all that's folly, human and inane.

O snake, be thou my friend, an enemy
No more, no more a living fear to me:

But let me feel amid this treachery
Your fang, your ringed and steeled fidelity.

The Apes

This is the day and this the magic hour
When apes, contemplative, now take the air.

Under the green lobes of the leafy glade
Darkling, the melancholy beasts parade:

Their native forest but a garden, whence
The velvet wallflower wind assails the sense.

Down this blind alley comes a sideling pair,
One serious green face, a vacant stare

The other, arm-in-arm they walk or run,
The eternal father with the eternal son.

Another, lithe and sinuous, long of limb,
Hangs shrinking at the water's rim,

Dripping at mouth and fessle, harshly screams
Across the river, and disturbs the drums

Of birds that startle into lyric song.
No matter: he heeds nothing: needs not to sing:

He has his girl. Behind the shifty leaves
A flash of the eyes betrays the furtive loves.

Syringa blossoms drop on the honied air;
A young ape steals the sleeping petals there.

The females, gaudy of colour, chatter and grin
And chatter, while the inane bird cries again

Cuckoo! Cuckoo! in the wood to hairy ears.
A reflective ape regards himself with tears

In the mirror of a pool, and lifts his eyes
Slowly, with what contempt, with what surmise?

Take Off Your Hat!

Take off your hat to the dead.
There is more point in the dead
    than in the live,
Their ears closed to the innumerable
    idiocies of common converse,
Their mouths stopped from adding
    to the sum:
They are the truly happy, the fortunate
As they go by on their carts, the hearses
    decked with flowers,
The mourning coaches following them
Keeping up a decent appearance of grief,
Tribute of superfluous respect.
Take off your hat as they pass,
Remove your headgear!

Vox Clamantis in Deserto

War is the supreme reality in the life of a nation. All else, even in times of peace—which are but a preparation for times of war—must be subordinated to this reality. War is not an instrument of policy: policy is an instrument of war.

LUDENDORFF

The voice of one crying in the wilderness,
Prepare ye the way of the Lord.
My mind aches, my temples throb,
    my tongue is swollen and dry,
    the seat of my reason would give way
When I behold the desolation we have made
    and called it peace.
(If there were only twenty men found in the city,
    or ten or five,
Still would I not destroy it.
Can the city be saved?
But the city does not want to be saved.)
War is not an instrument of policy:
Clausewitz was wrong: we know a thing or
    two
Today: policy is an instrument of war.
Where had we heard that before?
Ludendorff in nineteen-eighteen,
    then after the War heard no more,
    no more attended to
    than an old rag upon a stick,
    a clout upon an old clothes-line:
Now back again in place and power,
    the man of the War;
    the men of after the War now dead:
Liebknecht dead; Ebert dead
    that should have been his friend;
Rathenau dead; Erzberger dead;
the man of the trenches, of the Munich bier-halle,
the nondescript of nineteen-fourteen
    in the seat of power,

having learnt nothing and forgotten nothing by the
    War,
remaking the world to what it was before.
The men of the War come back once more,
Ludendorff and Mackensen, Göring
        the friend of Richthofen, writing
        the latter's will more largely upon the air.
My reason would give way when I observe
        the world that these have made.
Am I insane? I ask. Or am I sane?
The question that Swift often would put to himself,
Looking out upon the world's insanity.
The world concluded that it was sane, Swift mad.
Am I perhaps mad? and Ludendorff sane?
Then policy is but an instrument of war,
        war the one reality,
        the one thing certain
        in a world unreal,
        the world of a dream.
The voice of one crying,
The voice of one crying in the wilderness. Repent
        for the Kingdom
                sane
        the Kingdom
                sane sane sane
        is at hand!

1936

1937

Behold the antics of the populace:
Here in a corner in a close embrace

A loving couple without shape or grace
Front to front, vapid face to face.

A toddling father with his toddling child
Walks in the meadows in the warm mild

Weather, has no thoughts to occupy
His vacant mind, nothing to signify

Except the daily round by tube and train
And bus, from home to town and back again;

His constant one concern to earn enough
To keep his woman and his child, a roof

Over their heads and the garage: pity
Him. Behold the fresh youth of the city

Enter now the walks with unseeing eyes,
Loud of mouth, whose voices hold no surprise.

A day will come when there shall descend on them
From the skies they do not observe, some stratagem

Of fate to search and sear their flesh with fire,
Seal the eyes that are stupid with desire:

Liquid fire will rain down from the air,
Will suddenly arrive upon them there

And lick their bodies up and burn their bones,
No-one at hand to hear their mutual groans:

For these are they who warned of what's to come
Walk blindly on to their appointed doom.

Homo Rationalis

Nature I hate and what's unnatural choose
For rule of life, rather than hourly lose

The sense of separateness from the common world,
Admit a likeness which I never willed

To all that's human, similar and mean:
Rather the animal than the inane,

The rational without reason, without sense
The sensible, devoid of innocence,

The monkey-antics of the human child.
Better the native mischief and the wild

Malice of the ape, the young baboon
Or chimpanzee, than suffer with slow scorn

The usual mother's loving lunacy,
Suckling her child in human foolery.

Nor love the more the adult with his power
To greater harm, his procreative hour

Now come, yet nothing makes to justify
The sterile motions of his ecstasy.

Of the unequal I assert the sense,
The valued quality, the difference.

Not All the Multitudinous Seas

A hundred times a day I wash the hands,
Wash them of human folly, while the sands

Of time slip through the fingers and I smell
The chloroform upon the folded towel.

Everywhere the odour follows me, the scent
Of folly, death and disillusionment,

Subtly stealing into a thousand places,
Lurking in unexpected forms and poses

To come out at me with sudden sweet surprise
And ruin pleasure with a sad surmise:

The blight that lies like something infinite-
ly fine and light, a film of powder, white

Upon the covered face of everything:
The canker in the core of fruit, the sting

In the honey-bee, the poison in the heart,
The worm that gnaws the vitals and the hot

Anguish of mind denying peace.
What prophylactics are there to give release,

What instruments to sear and cauterise
This wound, the affected place to sterilise?

Not all the multitudinous seas could cleanse
The scent of folly from the human hands.

Utility of Illusion

I smell the madness of the winter world,
the patent disgust of man for man, of all that's human,
madness upon the pavement, in contiguous bodies
jostling, thrusting, waiting for a bus or a tram,
of homo sapiens or domestic animal,
the lunatics that look upon each other and,
liking what they see, play their part
persuasively a moment in the eye,
the incriminating smile, the gesture of a hand
suggests the body naked with the hair that smells,
the itching fingers, palms that sweat:
the meaningless afternoons, the tea-time hour,
the tea-table spread before the fire,
each in a confiding mood,
one watches the other for a move,
in mutual stimulation are renewed,
are fortified to face life in the nude,
stripped of illusion like the winter trees of leaves,
their trunks washed black in the rain,
the slow soft rain upon the heart that grieves,
the stimulus of madness to the brain.
There is madness in the room I feel,
in the touch, the contiguity of things,
assails the sense of taste and smell and sight,
behind the shutters, in the humble holes and corners,
in the seams and cracks of the floor:
Quick! Shut the shutters,
shut out the light!

The House of Silence

O that the world were but a quiet shell,
A house of silence within which to dwell,

Where the relentless patter of the rain
Of sound should cease upon the tired brain

And tired eyes and heart should find release,
And from the stress of life, a little peace.

So that quiet should, on a sudden, fall
Upon the world like water and run through all

The intricate channels of the vaulted mind.
O that some unseen hand would still the blind

Insane laughter of children, and lay a finger
On the throats of men: Nor should there linger

The echoes of their vanished presences
Without the empty walls and in the spaces

Of that appointed house. So that there be
A blessed silence, and the mind set free

To voyage in those conchoid halls, explores
Her utmost galleries and corridors.

Animal Afraid

Something has happened to me,
I know not what, nor how, nor when:
some interior worm
eating my body's vitality
has left me like a beaten shell

47

cast up by the sea,
the once vivid occupant
avid of life, drinking in the tide,
now absent, quite drained away:
a space vacant
where that intangible thing
having motion and colour
          and light and sensibility
has lived its life:
now gone.

What has happened I do not know,
save that some grief of the body
has stolen in unawares upon the spirit,
has sapped and seeped
and driven innumerable channels,
          honeycombed with sea foam
My will, my mind, my hair,
My teeth, my heart, my guts
      and even to the sensitive finger-tips.

What has happened that insensibility
steals over me like one already dead,
so that the hair and nails
go on living when the heart has stopped,
life receding from the organs
stage by stage, very gradually
till all is vacant, the senses fled from me
who was formerly
so greedy to drink in the air, the sea
the sun, the variety
of colour and sound and smell,
cliffs and ledges, meadow and moor and river:
all that gave pleasure
now shall I never
enjoy again, full lip, full eye:
the heart dry, the body
this animal afraid to die?

Epithalamium

Behold them standing at the altar there,
The candles clearly burning in the March air,

The yellow spring-flowers in the chaste and bare
Church, are bright in the eyes of the bridal pair:

These two have chosen each other with equal heart
In sickness and in health, till death do them part.

The congregated women crane to see
This act made sure before society

For greater warrant of security
From man to woman. Or rather say that she,

Having won her woman's victory,
Will fasten like a sea-anemone

Upon him, the female instinct to enfold
And wrap him round, nor ever loosen hold.

Or like those plants of so seductive smell
That delicately entice within their cell

Uncertain insects, frail and fluttering,
Whose petals shut upon the wounded wing,

Whose stamens search the heart and suck the brain,
Nor ever let their prisoners out again.

Or as that animal with honeyed tongue
Licks up the unwary, innocent and young:

Or spider that with hairy limbs confines
Lovingly his prey within fine lines,

Till the long forefinger strikes to paralyse
The willing victim, the fascinated eyes:

So too society, the octopus
Many-tentacled, lays wait for us,

Softly the inner core of man seeks out,
Pierces the flesh and slowly eats the heart.

Carrion Comfort

Not, not carrion comfort, I'll not feed on thee.
                                    G. M. HOPKINS

Fool, knave, idiot that I am
Not when well to leave well alone
The itch of the eye, the tongue, the ear,
The body to forgo,
But must excite the mind to new
Wantonness, further foolery:
Who will deliver me
From the body of this death?
Who
        will deliver me?
Not who, but what,
Not what, but that
Which unspecified
Is still unsatisfied.
No satisfaction had
Or possible to be had,
But this mad mind, this mind unsatisfied
That still would have
The fresh rose to fold with flame
And clothe the self with shame:
Not peace, no peace but death itself
Can stay the self
From verge of perjury,
This lived hypocrisy.

Poems for a Wedding

(i)

Open the temple gates unto my love,
Open them wide that she may enter in.

SPENSER, *Epithalamion*

A pretty thing is human happiness:
Man and girl embrace with tenderness,

Holding mouth to mouth and lip to lip,
Lest from that uncertain cup should slip

Some tepid nectar of security
To spoil the momentary certainty

With what the future holds: and she the while
Hangs loose and willing, innocent of will.

In due course an announcement will be made
In the *Times*, according to the usual mode:

Friends will be very welcome at the church;
They will be so happy: Thank you very much.

The pure young man takes to himself a wife,
Prepares to live the squalor of domestic life.

Yet I foresee a different future
In which the man grows old and changes feature,

Loses vitality and grace, while she
Retains her primal insatiety.

So they two go complaining to the grave:
No happiness remains and none to grieve.

Now is it become for them as is most just
For lovers, earth to earth and dust to dust.

51

(ii)

*Again, if two lie together, then have they
heat. But how can one be warm alone?*

Ecclesiasticus, iv. 11

The phallic crocuses are up and out
Standing on tip-toe as if to shout

Their happiness, like lovers soon to be
Locked by the law in wedded chastity.

The Church confers a blessing on the pair.
A clutch of leering women will be there

To watch each motion of the bride and groom,
How they enter, how up the aisle they come,

She very white and virginal and he
Erect, conscious of his virility.

The well-bred women silent speculate:
One more licence given to fornicate.

The tasteful honeymoon will be in France,
There will be time to dance, a time to dance—

A dance of death, for I have surely known
The bridegroom not return from honeymoon,

The bride not rise from premature child-bed,
Fruit of too eager joy, that gate of the dead.

So let me speak that have no children: I
That know not how to live nor how to die.

Poem on Marriage

'Il avait nommé cette Chimère "l'Hippogriffe".'
H. DE MONTHERLANT

The thought of marriage is enough to make men mad;
To think that in the end a man is had

Neck in the noose, foot in the trap caught fast,
Winged and brought down, snared and secured at last

By nature's forces, malign, inscrutable,
Himself no more an independent will

But only a straw, a conduit through which the power
Of human need to multiply may pour,

This parody of purpose, begetting more
Men so that all may proceed as it was before:

The end and aim of life! No wonder this
One broke his word and fled across the seas;

Or that one threw himself under a train
In the underground; or a third paid in vain

Long visits to the psycho-analyst,
Yet never found again what he had lost:

Once trapped and hostage given there's straight an end
To freedom of the body and the mind.

The Escaped Self

Twice only has this dream appeared to me in which
Lying stifled and ill at ease upon the pillows
My face has peered out at me from the darkness
Leaning so closely, so lovingly over me
With such insistent sharp reality
As of another person not myself, yet this
Self at the same time more myself
Than the self asleep upon the pillows.
This other self unsleeping watching me
So closely, so intimately as if in sleep
The soul and body had slipped connexion
And this were now the soul escaped
From bondage of the body observing the
Dead body lying there among the pillows.
But if a third occasion should come
And the escaped self not return,
Unable to re-enter the prison of the flesh,
The cord cut, the connexion severed,
The gulf now too great to be bridged,
The body asleep or dead impotent to recapture
The self escaped into the night of darkness—
Would this thing seal my doom?

I Must Forget

I must forget that there's physical beauty in the world,
must reject perfection of gesture, so easily concluded,
the fine form of the body, mould of the spirit,
eyes that are awake, awake,
awakened to beauty and to sin.
Contemplate animals: the strange world
of birds, geometrical and rare,
scattering seeds upon the air.
Contemplate cats: the low forms

54

crouching, belly to earth, ready to spring.
Avoid the green window and that form;
Withdraw the intellect into the void of its own making,
crying *Peccavi, Peccavi*—
that bitter satisfaction freed from dependence
upon all that moves in the moving world:
lust of the eye, desire of the body
here inhibited, here extinguished,
quite put out.

Pride of the Body

What pride of the body,
What lust of the eyes
    to look upon the body's strength,
Shall find defeat
And bite the dust.
When this delight
    at length be past,
Shall flower from this seed
Some fragile bloom
    of spiritual grace;
All that is earthy
    then put away,
The usual hand,
    the common face.

The Pharisee

At the point at night,
    where the copulating cars draw up,
    the lustful lovers sit huddled inside,
        dark above the soft explosion of the sea;
        or here where the beam of St. Anthony's light

55

lays a dark track across the harbour mouth
to Pendennis and envious me:
I envy their abstraction from the world,
their absorption in each other,
their self-sufficiency:
the primal couple as of ape or dog
making a fruitful unity.
They heed not the rain that patters
on the window-screen
the careful footfall of the passer-by;
at intervals the tolerant car
patiently labouring gives forth a sound,
some rhythmical motion indicative
of the generative gesture of the obscure within.
The wave breaks upon the shore below;
a solitary curlew cries;
the devout observer passes on.

Summer Gale

The midnight summer wind that stirs the blinds,
Stirs now the shutters in the village street:
The moonlit houses lift their lidded eyes
To where the risen moon, drawn anchor, sets
Her golden sail above the glow-worm bay.

O that I might set sail into this night,
Draw on my course in the teeth of the summer gale,
Divide the silver furrows of the sea,
Following the moonwake on the waves,
And at the cold hour of windfall meet with dawn.

O to be there now: the noise of the summer sea
About me, and summer scents from the land blown,
Wild thyme from the cliffs, honeysuckle and mown
Sweet hay, the rhythm of the tide to bear me
Onward, myself the wind, myself the sail.

Sunday Night: Truro

At 7.30 the cathedral town wakes up,
Wakes up and the deserted streets begin to fill
With people that an hour ago went on their way
Piously to church.
The sleepy wings of silence settled then upon the town
And the moon came out, scattering moondust on the
    roofs.

Then were we like unto them that dream.
I heard them within the lighted walls, singing
The King of love my Shepherd is,
Whose goodness faileth never.
The City Road is doorshut, blank, forgotten,
The roofs moonblanched, rigged high
Out of the shadowy waters.

Now in the streets arrive the many feet returning,
Mingled with the gay, the brave, the light of heart:
O moon that makes restless the hearts of men,
That lays an insane beam upon their mind:
Fetching up the dark southern men out of the hulks
That hug the stale brackish wharves,
To dog with subtle steps under the dark trees
The passage of light women.

This is the world's way, I say:
So passes the world away.

Then breaks a far faint surf upon the bewitched brain,
And Kenwyn bells drift late across the city
From that secure hill to the shifting margin of the river
Where the strange birds asleep there nightly cry.

Garden Episode

(For C. H.)

Here on the bank there will be crocuses
Blowing their frail horns
In the late, reluctant Spring.
Now all is bare, unfructified.
Yet on the rotting mould
One prophylactic bloom:
Flower of the night's hot copulative mood.
Was it some assignation, or a chance encounter?
Some Bloom or Sweeney among the nightjars, tasting sin,
Who shed this fleshly cerement,
Then went his way?
Only this delicate orgasmic flower remains,
Poor trampled crocus of the baffled Spring.

Spring in Grove Alley

Spring comes: the sudden ashamed sun bursts out
Over the roofs, and Grove Alley is dramatised
With ribbed shadows and lights as tangent.
The old lady with the worm-eaten fur
And tame cat obsequious, bitten of the mange,
Is at her area-gate, sniffing the morning air.
The milk-cans at the door are squalid, platitudinous.
A thrush to the imprisoning walls is eloquent.
At the bend of the road the street-lamp leans
With the times, out of joint.
The railings are there, as before:
So is the old lady of the fur,
And the mangy cat,
So is the sudden sun,
So is the Spring.

Grown-up to Child

I spun a silver penny:
    It made no sound:
I threw a copper penny,
    And it rang upon the ground.

I saw a golden apple
    High on a bough;
But only a russet apple
    Would tempt me now.

I found a little stick
    The road I came:
In two hands I took the stick
    And it turned to a flame.

Address to Tree-in-Light

O most suave and lovely light
That burns within the colonnade:
O tree, a pillar of delight
Ascending to a heaven of jade,
A fount of water aspiring to the sun:
O still anatomy when day is done:
A drooping peacock in the autumn noon,
The frozen architecture of the winter moon:

O moving light, be to me
A symbol of eternity
Across the fragile facets of the world
Where mortal shapes escape the hold
And turn to shadows; where all things pass
As on a moveless sea of glass.
O tree, be thou to me

A substant image of mortality:
Brave and secure unto the solemn
Crown of the stars you hoist your column;
Yet can you not stay the years' corrosive breath
Nor still the onward wind of death.

By Moonlight

O life within a fragile shell
O unreal world wherein we dwell
Under the shadow-light of the moon;
We are but gliding ghosts that soon
Fade insubstantial in the dew
Of the night's intenser blue;
We are the shapes that haunt the dream
And moving soundless, send a beam
From this dim region of a well,
Fronded and funereal,
Across the spaces of the night.
So magic is the changing light,
Perhaps the world is at an end,
And we the troubled ghosts that send
A message to the stars in vain
That know not of our crystal pain,
We are the prisoned lights that gleam
In the cold jewel of a dream.

Dream Sonnet (I)

(To A. v. T.)

I fell asleep and dreaming of your lips
Upon my lips, I thought that you had come
Into the unhappy twilight of this room;
And opening the door as if no lapse

Of time there were since you were here, you came
Stealthily across to where I lay,
Moving a little sadly as in a dream,
And leaning over, you smiled and went away.

Then waking, I knew you were no longer near me,
Your body from the compulsion of desire
Escaped into thin air where I might not follow;
Still I project my dream across the fallow
Spaces of illusion to where you are,
Hoping against false hope that you will hear me.

Dream Sonnet (II)

I dreamed I saw your face emaciate
Lean back exhausted on my arm's support,
The head a little sideways to create
The illusion of life that must not yet depart:
The fine and subtle fingers of the light
Creeping up the pillar of your throat,
Touching the dropped eyelids and the white
Flanges of your brow where life was not:

'Cold—O cold and lovely', then I cried,
'Onesimus, that I might bear the hope
Of April, with the gay quarrel of the birds
Unseal your frozen lips that I might shape
Them to return of spring.' But all my words
Were vain: and so I knew that you had died.

A Thrush Singing in Summer

A thrush sings
As if he would break
The strong wall.
Yet the dead should wake,
The heavens fall,
Ere such a thing
Could be.

Rather shall man see
The wall stayed,
The dead but dead:
His last word
Unspoken,
Unheard,
His heart broken.

Image

This corner of the garden, this patch of gravel,
June roses, hollyhocks and leaves of fig
Upon the wall,
A bird cheeping,
And over the wall
A bell ringing late to service:
Let this not be
Forgotten, let this be
An image and a memory,
An oasis of the mind
To return to from the wastes,
The weariness, the narrow straits.

Visit to the Office of Inland Revenue

Walking alone in the water-meadows,
The sun comes out to warm my withered wit,
Enabling my disturbed mind to forget
That gesture placing the chair carefully for me to sit,
The light behind me, shining upon official forms,
The familiar papers and upon
    the dust-gold eyelashes and hair upon the wrist:
    image of what interior harmony,
    the steadfastness and certainty.

Now already half-an-hour away
I walk, like Elijah, raging in the fields,
While the melancholy plane drones on above
    the waste of November waters
    and a solitary rook planes home
    towards Marston. Beside me pass
Upon the path the brides of Christ,
Holding up with averted faces
Their black and fustian dresses
    in the muddy places.

I take no comfort in the motley cows,
Black and white and red upon the pastures green,
Nor seen against the tapestried trees.
I take pleasure only in thought of these:
    the fidelity of the woman,
    the gentleness and strength of the man.

The Field Full of Folk

Crossing the field full of folk,
The hayfield full of the players' cries,
Whose lithe bodies twisting in the sun
Draw the shadows after them and the eyes

Of the spectators: I, pausing
A moment when the play is done,
Come upon a sickle lying in the path:
And in the honeyed voices of these men
Departing upon the heavy, seeded air
I hear the sharpening of the scythe.
The limbs that were so shapely shall be laid low
Laid level with the fallen grass.
The young men that pass, like lovers go
Down the long alley to the willow pool:
O shadows, draw close about them, lap them round,
For the day shall come and they'll lie quieter under-
        ground.
The men that stop their horses in the sorrel hay,
The horses tormented by the maddened flies,
All these that swarm together at the end of day:
    They shall all die,
    Even as I.
O let the play go on: O let it not be done:
Too soon the evening comes, night and oblivion.

Death by Drowning

'You always rise twice,' he said,
Is no consolation to a man that thinks to drown.
Fear death by drowning: For there is the sea
Never still, never the crystal stillness of a mirror,
Never that calm,
The last breath breathed upon that smooth surface,
Curdling its clearness for a moment
Then dying away, withdrawn into what realm
Whither as whence?

Not this, but the sharp indrawn breath.
The choking, the harsh battle for life,
The many waters breaking in
Along the secret channels, shifting the hidden nerves
Until all ends.

Or perchance to be drawn back to life,
Like that not-yet-forgotten love,
With slow agony in the sea-embittered eyes,
The painful voyage of the blood
Along the frozen arteries
So recently stilled, so numbed
They would not their own joy,
Their former state, resisting that rich life.

Pastoral Poem

Into the meadows that laugh with flowers I went
For May is gay and gaiety's soon spent,

Taking my wonted place upon the stile,
Here seeing all that's secret in the pool,

The lying cresses and the black frog-spawn,
The lucid light that lights a sleeping stone,

Discovering all the busy traffic there,
All that's imprisoned from the upper air

Within their world of water. Over the pool
A tall elm casts a shadow; the wind is cool,

Scattering the husks and seeded burrs
Blown upon the surface. Two lovers

Come idiotically down the road,
Fondling a moment, then turn back afraid:

Here the philosopher contented sits
Contemplative, observes a man that spits.

All That Was Most Passionate

All that was most passionate in our lives
Has been already felt: there will be no more
The first stirrings of desire,
The shoot of passion through the blood and in the veins,
The touch that sets the mind on fire,
The mating of spirits that have found themselves
Each in the other, in the body no less
Than laid up waiting in the mirror of the mind.
Such motions will be less frequent than of old,
Will move thee less, while creeping Time at thy gate
Makes stealthy move upon thee. Every moment sees us
Ageing in body as in mind. The fine finger-tips
That were so sensitive of touch become duller now;
No longer will the heart stand tip-toe
With expectancy that the stranger may turn this way:
We are ageing now, in mind and body:
The one brings strength of purpose, peace,
Confidence in action, the gathering force,
The outspread wing, the leap, security;
The other leaves keenest joy of the senses,
To run, to walk, to ride, to swim, to fly,
All these and early love foregone;
The gathered powers brought to the point
Of deliberate action, this mind
Tied to the body of the dying animal.

'Was Für Ein Leben?'

What sort of life is this,
What sort of life, I say?
Waiting on platforms at windy junctions,
Sitting in compartments perusing papers,
Or listless gazing out of breathed-on windows
Upon the country that passes with a gesture

As one passes that is not for me;
Or attendant upon doctors in the corridors
Of clinics (*This Way for In-patients*),
The smell of cleanliness thick upon the senses;
Or filling up income-tax forms, insurance-forms,
Or buying investments, surrounding premature old age
With hopeless security;
Or lingering upon last promontories
In search of health and the sun:
What sort of life is this, I say,
Was für ein Leben?

Night-Piece in Pain

'It is no less painful though poised':
So the half-sleeping mind to itself.
What is? Where?
So the waking mind becomes aware of pain,
Finishes its sentence:
Pain is no less painful though poised in the mind.

Is the mind poised amid the pain,
Or is it the pain that is poised upon the brain?

No more asleep, it is the body's pain that matters:
The dreary pathways that ache along the limbs,
The sameness, the hotness, the dryness of the bed,
The pillows hard, the crumpled linen
Giving no comfort to the limbs that long for sleep.

There is no rest to be had,
Treading the weary ways over and over again.
I know them all, each turning of the stair,
The lull, the momentary quiet, the crisis passing

And the dull return of hope for sleep,
And then the weary round, once more
The sameness, the hotness, the dryness of the mouth,
The eyes that ache:—Put out the light!
There are grey rings around the tired globe.
Put out the light.

Then to doze, and begin all over again
The weary argument with oneself,
Oneself no longer one, but several.
The pain is poised among them, one says,
Half-asleep, to the neighbour of my dream.
Here we all are: I have no pain:
The pain is outside me. It is you that have it.

And so on and on, the crisis beginning again,
The eyelids heavy with sleep, the limbs longing,
Yet sleep drawing farther and farther off, and I
Left with consciousness of pain returning.
There is no argument: I am in pain.

Turn on the light again.
Here are the weary pathways made visible:
The tossed bed, the thrown clothes,
Pillows askew, the body twisted for ease
For relief from pain, across the bed,
Coldness, numbness gathering in the limbs,
My heart, my stomach, my bowels, the pit of fire,
Pain, like the lion gnawing my reins.

What lion? What pain?
The crisis passing, sleep returns,
The eyelids closing on the grey rings of light,
The light put out, the light put out.
Darkness, greyness, flutes, the memory of music,
The music of the unseen stars,
Bringing healing in its wings.

Pain Receding

The dim memory that the body holds,
Away from me, away with the passing of the night,
So that the body hardly remembers
Its own anguish, only in the shy recesses
Lingers the phantom of that agony,
That discipline, lurking in the corners
Like dust that cleaves after the house is swept:
The house is swept, bare and sweet
The body feels unto itself in the morning,
The raw flesh inflamed now at peace
As if cool water had flushed the hidden channels,
Water, water, dripping from the rocks
Sweeping through the clean passages
To leave sharp and pure the crystal sediment of sand.
So, as the night vanishes, and the hot
Flushed theatre of this unreal dream
Passes from the confused reluctant mind
Awake-in-sleeping; as the night tires
And the exhausted body watchful
In the comfort of receding pain,
The ritual over, what was to be borne
Once through, the cup not put away;
So then come the first advancing
Fingers of the day through broken shutters,
Stealing upon the glad eyelids,
Bringing the kiss of peace and late oblivion.

Feed My Sheep

'These are they that are arrayed in white robes.'

At the lean-to corner of the windy street
The raddled harridan awaits her fate:
The heavy commercial, loose of mouth and limb,
The lean counter-jumper, lack-lustre eye, long of nose;

Smirking and lurking she makes up to them,
Leading her little dog upon a string.
Here the fat mama with no sense of sin,
Expecting commendation of the passing world,
Propels her perambulator on the much-soiled pavement.
The post-office assistant perks a cheek
To the straggling sun and the casual passer-by,
Eyeing the young man making his way across the square,
Who has an after-tea appointment
And so tilts his hat in the eye of the western sun.
    Feed my sheep. Feed my lambs.

These are the lambs at play: these are they:
The company-promoter, the professional stag,
The newsvendor, the hawker of public lies,
The good women of the streets, these Jezebels
(None so poor to do them reverence),
The young men, these fallen like Lucifer
From among the angels; the insane children
That gesticulate amid the surge of traffic,
The blind man selling matches, greasy, obese,
Sitting all day long in his chair, a slow trickle
Oozing from the corner of the twisted face:
    Feed my sheep: these are they.

'We want young blood': the election crowd
Sweats and sways and shouts. Somebody loud
Above the cat-calls: 'Give young blood a chance.'
A woman drunk throws a kiss, begins to dance
Up to the young candidate, brilliant with rosette
In the bright button-hole: her hat falling
Over her eyes, her hair straggling.
'We are so happy together': the candidate's wife
Bulletins, the shadow of the divorce-court in her eyes,
The corrupt pork-butcher wipes his lips,
The election over, count made, declared,

A triumph for democracy. The crowd is delirious:
The sovereign people can hardly stand upright,
Staggers, make a rush, assaults the citadel.
Everybody is happy.
      These are they: Feed my sheep.
      These are they: Feed them?
      Feed my hate.

Les Horreurs

Ce sont des choses qui me font horreur,
La Chair est triste, et j'ai lu tous les livres.
TRISTAN CORBIERE

These idiot human figures see:
   a priest comes round the corner
   against a gust of wind,
   reading his breviary.

Another: a woman wheeling a perambulator,
Complacently providing the cannon-fodder of the future.
A parson in his pulpit, as the medievals saw him,
   preaching to geese.
A young man enclosing a motor-cycle with his thighs,
   avid of speed and power,
   wasteful of his virility.

Or the horror of girls that expose their souls upon the
      pavement,
   that giggle in streets, that know not how to hold
      themselves,
   how to behave, or lie or stand,
   that leave litter over all the world,

cigarette ends, orange-peel, banana-skin.
    Behold the people:
These are they for whom a new world is made,
for whom a new heaven and a new earth are opened.

I tire of the old men sitting opposite me in the train
    the senile lips sagging at the corners,
    knees opening and shutting with some private pain,
    or with the rhythm of the train.

I am tired of being carried like a corpse around the
        country,
    of carrying myself, a man pregnant with pain,
    my disease, my mind;
    give me rather the steeled hand of the engineer,
    the warmth of body of the furnace-man
    in the colliery's interior glow,
    the loneliness of the aviator,
    the presence and the sense of danger.

I am tired of trees and hills and houses,
    the anonymity of scenery,
    of children taking ostentatious note of animals,
    of animals seeking to be noticed.

I am weary of women waiting with their children,
    under signposts along the bus-route.
Tout le va-et-vient de la vie humaine
    m'ennuie, et à la fin m'épuise.

I am tired of hearing about Julie de Lespinasse,
    of the fragments of Menander
    and the shards of Egypt;

of the pianist who treats the piano as his mother,
or the 'cellist her lover.
I would something have incomparably barer than before,
the whiteness of a bone
picked up on the beach
that the tide sings through
where the eyes were,
Something incomparably fine and delicate,
something more rare than ivory, than hope
or satisfaction legitimate and had.

Immediate Joy

So quiet, so immediate this joy,
So windless the evening, so still the trees
In the garden and the rectory roofs;
The impertinent small birds that tap the panes
Of the car brought to rest amid the grass
Long at the entry of the lane; the bird
That pierces the stillness of the pastures with
A cry; the silent sun beating upon
The many miles, that beats upon my head,
So apprehensive of this new-found joy,
Communicative of heart's-ease-in-things,
Too much desired to be awaited,
Too near at hand to be submitted to,
So unexpected, hardly sought, so won.

The Spring before the War

In the meadows the spring rain
Relentless as maternal love, or pain,
Forces the liquid notes
From wet birds' throats:

Raises such thoughts that I
Am glad to be alive.
It is the tea-time hour, five
o'clock: lamp-light in the windows
and in the streets. Passing by
I remark a young man within a room
standing before the fire, one hand
in pocket, the other lights a cigarette.
So stand, so let me remember
the gesture of a hand, nor forget
the firelit interior, flicker of light on things,
the warm and comfortable disarray,
a moment's imprint on the mind
before all is shattered and
each goes a different way,
and what we chiefly cherish
comes to an end.

III: Poems of Wartime

The Answer to Hate

The answer to hate is only love:
Love only, for we are involved alike
    in common suffering.
No way is there to be gained or held
By cherishing this cancer of the mind,
    eating up peace and quietude.
Nothing to be had from this unnatural
    cancerous growth, filling every nook and
    crevice with bitterness, the sterile righteousness
of vain reflection: eating away love.
Neither can I any longer live
    by this excessive clarity,
without sympathy
        for common humanity.
So little responsibility is there here,
    any more than of the animals when they lie down
        and die,
    not knowing how this should come to them or
        why.
Yet here are nobleness and sanity,
    resignation, magnanimity.
Here is one who came to die
    in a far country, fighting in another's cause.
These are they who bear their pain
    with fortitude, huddled in time of war in crowds
    in the clearings of the burning woods.
Here they die. Others survive in hospitals,
    the clean white sheets stained with their wounds
    the light of life low in their eyes
    —wars being fought in the blood of the young;
    some turn their faces to the wall, the lights
        lowered,
    screens about them, footfalls soundless as they die.
Some attend upon the sick; others make music
to seek a little distraction for the mind.

To what point unless their lives are rounded with a
    little love?
How otherwise is this grief of life to be borne?
I must some signal service then perform,
    make retribution for past bitterness,
    turn hate into love, subject the mind
        to discipline, myself prepare.

I Love Now

I love now the variety of the world
When once I admired only its unity,
Wished that all men were subjected to a like
        discipline,
    thought the same thoughts, felt the same
        sentiments,
    knit together in one insistent unison.
Now I see how things move in accord with their own
        harmonies,
I hear the Angelus upon the breeze and not object,
See two lovers upon a bench under the trees
    kissing, or walking hand in hand,
    and think no harm, am glad even that these
    are brave in their course to continue the
        generations.
I welcome the flags in the streets, floating out over the
        river,
    the noise, the clamour, the crowding of people,
    the dogs walking with their masters in the park,
    the young women astride their horses,
        their golden hair and russet and brown and
            dark
        framing their faces fresh with the wind.
Perhaps one can be in love even with the poor,
    nor mark specially the meanness of their accents,
    when they too are in love with life,
        spring in their veins, the dead winter over.

To B

I envy
    your self-sufficiency
integrity
    of bird or flower or bee
intent
    upon your purpose bent
content to be
    and not to wonder why
achieving
    beauty of body
sobriety of movement
candour of the eyes
the faithful serving hands:
the whole being
    sufficient to itself
with no dependency
    upon another.
Or like a flower
    turning to the sun
a creature at one
    with nature
not torn
    or features worn
by conflict
    of how and why
as I
seeking what satisfaction I may find
in bitter occupation of the mind
while you
    to your own self are true
nor need
    this compensation for the deed
wanted
    and by that haunted
this gap

between the impulse and the act
unknown
    to your philosophy
where soon
    what's thought is done
what begun
    is ended
what broken
    mended
not left undone
whether tying up a flower
or waiting for the hour
    to meet your girl
or getting out your car
bound
    upon your usual round
that brings you back again
    where you began.
So you and I
    that meet but day by day
pass by
    each on our different way.

To B

(ii)

I saw you in the street today
    for a passing moment;
Obligingly and with your usual courtesy
    you came my way:
Yet not without hesitation, I could see
    the delayed action for a fraction
    of a second.
Nobody else would notice save only he
    so much in need of you
    that anything you do

Can not escape the eye, the heart, the mind,
    is saved up and remembered for a day
    when you're no longer here perhaps.
Who knows now what haps
    may seize on you before your time,
    gay and alert among the chaps,
May tear the ruddy English flesh from the bone,
Expose the nerves, shatter the spine,
Making you now supple and fine
    a cripple, or something worse?

Beholding you now I seem to see the curse
    in your candid eyes questioning mine,
    that rest but for a moment
        and smile and are gone
    on some quest of no moment
    that holds you as I never can.
So you stop, stand by the roadside
    holding your bike as if at attention
    while all the while your mind
    is elsewhere on your errand,
    and the noise of the traffic goes by
    and the sky is blue as your eyes,
    the trees turning yellow and crimson
    in this solemn and ominous autumn.

When you are gone I realise
It is your life that I would share:
    that which is so closed a book to me,
    the quiet and contented round
        of work and love and sleep:
    you cultivate your garden,
    are for ever making something
        with your hands,
You go contented to the pictures with your girl,
    or take her for a ride by your side
        or down to the river for a swim;

You are erect and strong: you can run,
    drive a car, fly, strip in the sun.
While I sit here and spin these ropes of sand,
    begin again, nor ever find
    peace or content or ease of mind:
    my only gift what hurts me most,
    the faculty to see the future in your eyes,
        your ghost.

Today My Words Shall Be

Today my words shall be of love,
Love and the spirit of life in things,
Love for the fireman that passes in uniform
with rolling sailor's gait along the corridor,
for the girl knitting quietly in her corner,
the student with his book, the old man smoking his
    pipe;
the outlook from the window upon the fields,
the dun brown waste that speaks of winter,
the curve of the river by Nuneham, the trees in the
    copse,
the out-at-heel back-gardens with washing on the line,
the crowing cocks and little animals
speak to me of England and human kind.
Nothing on such a day can unlovely be:
Not the December distance with frosted trees
the horizon delicately fingering,
nor the stubbed willows holding up their crowns,
the tufted haycocks, the red and mottled cattle
scampering home across the fields,
the loquacious crows chattering of Sunday,
the fine upsurge of the downs,
the country church that fortress-like
lifts up its head above the village

82

keeping its vigil through the centuries:
On such a day all these things speak to the heart
but lately frozen, that now beats
with love of life and common humanity.

Cornish Acre

This is the field that looks to the south:
No words come to my mouth
To signify my dread
Of this field of the dead.

This is that field where on a time
Hope died in me,
Even as I looked out upon
The gay and smiling sea.

The blue and bitter southern sea
Laughed back at me and said
'Have you any recruits for me
From the field of the dead?'

Over the dark and echoing woods
I heard the bell toll nine,
And then I knew full well
The augury was mine.

O moving finger of time that writes
My name in water, on the sea,
Pause yet awhile upon this slope
Remembering me.

Duporth Camp: September 1940

They will come no more home to field and byre,
Our roads will not see them waiting at the corner for
          their girl,
     the beaches watch them stripping for a bathe
     laughing and chaffing their comrades as they
          dress
     and smoke their after-a-swim cigarette:
Their sweethearts will wait for them in vain when the
          sun goes down,
     take to bed with them an image and
     stretch out their hand in the night to a shade:
Nor the land feel the labour of their bodies,
     the coves and quiet places hear their voices
     on parade, the challenge of the sentries,
     their quick step going up and over the hill.

Yet, there are those who will not forget,
     who will remember at each turn of the day:
     at sunrise when the bugles blow *reveillé* over the
          bay,
     at midday 'Come to the cook-house door, boys';
     the silence of afternoon upon the camp
          as if everybody had suddenly gone away,
          received his marching orders, shouldered his
               kit
          and gone—as one has gone today.

When all that is far behind, and life resumes its usual
          sway,
This place for one will be a place of ghosts.
Perhaps there will come this way
     one who was here for a time and went away,
          leaving no memorial of himself,

nothing to remember him by
save that he would say, looking out to sea:
'That is a thing that I could never understand,
why anybody should break their heart about
me.'

In the Train

In the corner of the compartment
The young air-force pilot sleeps,
The lax pose of body in uniform
Drawing all eyes to his repose:
No secret, for as he sleeps he smiles,
Some thought of whom he's going to meet
Is printed on the blood-red mouth,
Lights up the corners of the lips,
Contracts the curve of the brow,
Some thought that transcends the here and now.

Outside the window the winter rages
Over level plain and Midland field,
The rivers are swollen and barely clear the bridges,
The landscape blotted out with mist and rain.
The guard comes in with his usual message
'Please pull down the blind on either side:
It's the regulation.' We obey
Now enclosed in our travelling box
We four, four lives that fall together
Roll on through the darkness towards London
And our separate dream.

Some other thought fills the sleep
Of the young pilot as he lies
Long leg outstretched, head on arm

Resting, a thought more grave, more stern.
So perhaps one day will he look
When they pick him up, arm supporting the head,
Outstretched hand upon thigh,
Upon the face an expression of gravity
And over all the overshadowing
Wings enfolding him.

Remembrance Sunday:
Coombe Church 1940

On this afternoon of mid-November
    the quiet country church is well
    filled, but today there is no bell;
    on one side the khaki ranks of the Home Guard,
    on the other the bandsmen in their uniform,
    the country people warm in their Sunday best.
    The squire is in his pew, the legion's banner laid
    to
        rest
    upon the altar where the candles burn
    in the thin light of winter afternoon.

All is as it was before. A dream, a haze, a mist
    descends upon me and obscures my eyes
    with the dear dead dust of centuries:
All is passing as it passed before
    in days of the Edwards, Henrys and Elizabeth:
    the country folk come yet once more
        to commemorate their dead,
    singing, Onward Christian soldiers, Onward as to
        war.
    So many wars, so many times
    the bells ring out their chimes
    for peace proclaimed, upon the village green
        under the elms and limes

that remember the faithful few
who in every age do not return.
There are no bells today:
the sound of a plane passing overhead
wakes me from my dream of the dead:
to find the parson ascending the pulpit,
assuring us our cause is just,
we fight because we must.
He remembers before God the names
of Bakers, Coopers, Smiths:
I see them early or late at plough
against the clean, bare world of winter,
or coming hot and sweating down the summer
lane
from harvest, stopping at the brook
among the water cresses for a drink.
Now they are where there is no thirst, I think,
nor any weariness, nor getting up from sleep
nor lying down at night beside their dear
companion.
All that they died for,
gave up the dewy morning and the scented night,
the harvest moon, the stars over the familiar hill,
All has to be fought for again—
the parson assures us their sacrifice was not in
vain—
the price to be paid in the lives of their sons:
while they sleep, those other ones,
far away from Coombe, far from their home,
from the village green, and cricket in summer
and winter games among the trees—
in France, in Palestine, under the seas.

Fight the good fight, we sing:
the young air-gunner with pursed lips
carries the cross slowly down the aisle—
Fight the good fight with all they might:
behind him crowds the slow crocodile

of bright-faced choirboys, newly washed and
   spruce:
Run the straight race, through God's good grace,
Lift up thine eyes, and seek His Face.

The people stand as the procession goes by
Singing, Faint not nor fear, His arms are near,
   He changeth not, and thou art dear.
The last light of the wintry sun lights up the cross,
   the white head of the clergyman:
   laying a loving finger upon them every one
      as they pass slowly down the church
      out of my dream, and day is done.

On Chaplin's *Great Dictator*

This little man, this common man
who suffers in himself the lot of humanity,
is lost among the millions who fight in modern war,
emerges with a sense of lost identity
into a world given up to gangsters,
where force and fraud and lack of decency
and evident brutality prevail—
a world in which he has lost his way,
is like a man fumbling at a door for a key,
cannot remember the word
but now upon the tip of the tongue,
the so familiar speech that would put all right,
enable him to get back upon the simple track
where right and wrong are not confused,
nor the cry of the most numerous unheard.

So he passes through the world,
takes upon himself the sufferings of common man,
is despised and rejected for a son of Israel,
suffers the disappointment of small hopes,

88

the defection of friends, is beaten and pursued—
yet nourishes a seed of hope within,
unconquerable spirit, that rises
yet O at the moment of our greatest misery
to offer words of consolation in defeat,
an ultimate assurance of our victory,
the singular magic of speech
that puts forth flowers in our hearts
and lays upon our lips the finger of prophecy.

Sunday Cinemas

All is well at my return
    to my native town:
I find pompous Parsifal
    beating the air as usual
    on the subject of prayer and Sunday cinemas.
The young men, it seems,
    have other things to think of
    than to attend his ministrations,
    though there are the delights
    of Faith Teas and bun-fights
    and cocoa to lure them to the word of God, or
        rather
    of pompous Parsifal, who affects to be
    Our Heavenly Father,
    and Moderator of the Free Church Council
    all rolled in one.
Lord, how he pontificates,
    lays down the law to these poor bums!

All is meetly well,
All is as it should be:
The world's about our ears,
But never mind
It's some consolation to find

89

Our Parsifal in his pulpit and
All's well with the world.
Does he ever leave his pulpit
and look at himself in the glass,
turn up the hem of self-righteousness
and underneath see
the vacancy, the smug complacency?
Sunday cinemas indeed!—
While all around
The world topples into ruin and disaster,
Men lose their lives, are bombed and drowned
that such as this
may hold forth in conscious bliss
    of the wickedness
        of Sunday cinemas.

Visit to the Dentist

Explore with me the romance of Keble Road
On a May morning: the baker's van with its load
Of sweet-smelling, new-baked loaves drawn up
At the door, the blue-print housemaid with white cap
On her knees scrubbing the sprinkled steps.
The rain-washed pavement gleams, the sun leaps
Upon the neat and decorative garden-plots
Of wall-flowers, tulips and forget-me-nots.
Above the wall a silver birch but waves
Its plumes in the wind with feminine grace, weaves
The sunlight in and out the shifting leaves.
While I wait in the swept and polished waiting-room,
Across the lugubrious bulk of the mausoleum
Of Keble and Pusey, the men of the Oxford Movement,
A thrush in the garden sings loud, triumphant.
Within, the white-coat dentist awaits his patient.
Enter now the room: the strong and surgical scent

Invades the senses. There is the vacant chair
Before the window-pane. With careful air
And delicate soft tread the dentist goes
About his preparations. I recognise
Among the smell of medicaments and salves
The pervasive, pungent odour of oil of cloves.
Now the broad, firm hands place in position
The head, the clever fingers of the physician
Explore the mouth and mould the gums. 'The tree',
He says, 'the apple-tree, bears fruit profusely,
But the pear is sterile.' The eye rests upon
Clips and needles, syringes and spittoon,
The rolls of cotton wool. All lulls the sense,
Induces apprehensive somnolence;
Hypnosis softly steals upon the brain
Absorbed in the world of sky beyond the pane
Serene, while from the region cloud there still
Approaches nearer, inexorably, the drill.

Summer Warning

Priapian gods the meadows know
Under the clouds of summer snow;
The Chinese willows droop upon
Punt and pavement, water, stone.

The blind man taps his way along
The singing street, bird at end,
Until the traffic stops the song
And lilac girls the stairs descend.

June's sweet and heavy chloroform
Climbs the slower steps of sense;
The tunnelled shades are green and warm,
And patterns of no consequence

Are made of light and leaves of sound
And petals white upon the ground.
The air is filled with wires of fear:
If you'd be happy, come not here!

The red bus runs along the road,
The pillar-box erects a warning:
In the grass, the snake, in the ditch, the toad,
At the turn the lazy lovers mooning.

With sudden shock the shut gate opens,
Upon the wall the dead fruit ripens
With subtle smell upon the air.
The world's a cage. Beware! Beware!

Days of Waiting

These are the days of waiting, when
    Crocus and aconite shoot their bud;
In the bare gardens the birds are brave,
    The spring sings early in their blood:

And in the veins of the elderly
    Ladies and petulant nurse-maids
Pushing perambulators down
    The willow-walk into the meads.

The familiar trees are still and wait
    For the sap to rise along their veins,
Put forth their bravery of leaves
    And clothe with colour the English lanes.

So the turning world moves on,
    Trees and meadows, river in flood,
Into the spring and the unknown—
    And over all the threat of blood.

The Revelation

I, who found life so difficult, so fragile a thing
    that I could hardly dare to look forward
    from day to day and hour to hour,
    dragging my weary body up the stair,
        could hardly bear
    the noise of water dripping upon
        the sensitive nerve,
    holding life and its pain in hourly horror:

This afternoon came upon a procession
        going down the street,
    the drum-major with acrobatic stick
        leading the band,
    the coloured Indian infantry, gay and smiling,
    and behind, the fresh-faced Oxford yeomen;
    and then the sea-scouts, air-cadets, engineers
        with their pontoons, searchlights, guns,
        those old Priapian gods, the guns—
    to which the land-girls paid tribute as they
        passed;
And all the people in the street happy to see them
    pass.

Suddenly I who found life difficult
    was made aware of its simplicity.
Perhaps life is simpler than I thought
(I thought), simple and promising as a smile
    from the driver of an ambulance or tank
    to the admiring girl in the street.
Then came back to mind
    the dark and passionate lad in the lane,
    the golden-haired khaki girl in the train;
And all seemed easy and effortless
    as the regular beat of the swans' wings
    that disturbs with strange exhilaration
    the swans afloat upon the surface of the water.

Maytime in Magdalen

Early May, and the scent of the earth
Nostalgic and blue like smoke
Or drift of bluebells in that woodland glade;
The hot and resinous scent of the sun;
The blue boles of the beeches,
The colour and shadow of silver coming and going.
And here at the corner where Addison walked,
The wanton flute of a thrush;
A footstep further, the memory of the summer snake
Gliding down to the water to drink.
A bird darts out and up like a fish.
Today no bells from Cotman's tower:
The fragrant, delicate eighties are buried at last;
Only the mouse-like, hooded fritillaries
Ring their bells silently in the passing wind.
The many and various scents of flowers,
Cuckoo-pint, cow-parsley and jack-in-the-hedge,
The wind-blown odour of wall-flowers from over the
    river,
Besiege the nostrils, the eyes, the heart,
The breath that comes and goes with delight,
Fills the lungs like a bellying sail;
While all day the yaffle laughs madly in the wood
That Spring's in the air and in the veins
Of the forgetful, the faithless and even the sophisticated
Has not failed to flow.

The Old Cemetery at St Austell

Cypresses, oaks, ilexes and yews
Compose the sober scene with sombre hues;
The narrow path runs down the southward slope
Among the graves, where our forefathers sleep
In the sure and certain hope of resurrection:
Head to foot they lie, looking to the east

94

Whence cometh their salvation—or so at least
They thought in former, simpler days. No such
Certainty now: all we know is that they
Are asleep hard by where they lived their useful lives;
Here they still are together, husbands and wives,
Fathers and children: in death they are not lost.

They lie in the heart of the parish, edge of the town,
On the hillside that looks to the sun going down:
On the skyline the ruined engine-house
Of Polgooth Mine, whence the town took its rise
From whose rich veins and from whose merchandise
The generations of vanished miners fed.

I see them: so many insects on the heave of hill
Scurrying about, burrowing underground;
If you listen closely you may hear the sound
Of the rumour of their toil, the dead men sing
Along their levels and hidden galleries,
A remote murmur like a hive of bees.

Yet not so: they are all fled over the seven seas:
Ruin descended on the mines and these
Men were driven forth to earn their bread
In America, Australia, Africa.
These are our exiles: they have left their bones
In foreign soil, under other stones.

There in the distance are the dark woods of Penrice,
Mysterious, aloof, funereal;
Lost in their depths lies the house of the Admiral,
The last Sir Charles: whose family did well
In the time of the Commonwealth and showed a nice
Sense of the moment, laid out their moneys with skill,

Adding acre to acre and field to field.
The squawk of pheasants now for generations
Has announced the vicinity of the squire. Yet still

Their tribute to mortality they yield,
Having come to an end with a young heir killed
In Nineteen Fourteen, in the last war of nations.

For him the white gate on the road to Trenarren
Stands open in vain, in vain the long curve of the drive
Leads across deerpark and ploughland in the wavering
Moonlight, to the wide portico welcoming
The returned, the family portraits in the hall:
He has become but a tablet on a wall.

The little chantry chapel in the church
Is filled with their memorials. Here as a boy
I used to sit in the darkling evening
Deep-ensconced in a pew, listening
To the organ's music, rapt with such extreme
Joy, my mind enchanted moved in a dream,

In which were mingled melodies and urns,
A woman weeping over a bier, coloured
Armorial bearings, glints of crimson and gold,
White marble stained with the late westering sun's
Last gleams. Heaven itself seemed to unfold
In those rich harmonies that echoing rolled

Like waves within the caverns on the coast,
And caught me up upon their crest, until
The painted roof inlaid with golden stars
Rolled back, and there revealed a miracle:
God on His throne, the Son and Holy Ghost,
Amid the beating wings of the angel host.

Now comes the shade of Mrs Arthur, that proud
Gap-toothed woman, mincing her way along
The path, turning her face upon the crowd
With authority and pride, nursing her strong
Impetuous will that was at length withstood,
Through the long unhappy years of widowhood

By an only, much-loved daugher, Margaret,
Who went over to the enemy, the man she married,
Nor ever came home again until the day
She came to see her lonely mother carried
To the grave. I see that wilful old dame yet
Holding her head erect as was her way.

Where now is the stone put up to commemorate
Those four young men drowned while crossing the bay
One day in the seventies? I used to meditate
Much on them and wonder at their fate:
What sudden squall of wind capsized their boat
That September afternoon and swept them away?

Twenty and twenty-one, twenty-seven and eighteen
They were—their names no one remembers now—
Many times have I thought of them and seen
Their little craft fighting her way through the waves,
Till rounding the point or farther out in the bay
She disappears and they are lost to their loves,

Who should have been fathers of families:
Yet now they are for ever young. Not here
Under the friendly turf, the shade of the trees
Will you find them, but out there, the whitened skulls
Washed by the tides, wedged in the crevices
Of the rocks, mouthed by fishes, eyed by the gulls.

Who are all these? Here one who lost a foot
At Inkerman and returned to keep a mill
At Tregonissey; yet another fought
In Afghanistan; a few were mariners,
But most of them were farmers, labourers
In the fields, ploughmen, small traders, carpenters.

Now are their account-books all closed up:
It has ceased to matter whether they were happy
More than a century ago, or whether

In their long absence some one else slept
With their wives, or if their children were another's:
What do these things matter in the eye of death?

I note the names: Treleaven and Rosevear,
Hobba and Jago, Hocking, Rowse and Faull,
Veale and Dunn and Drew, Trudgian and Penhall,
Sampson Borlase and his Rebecca, and here
A stranger to the parish, Abraham Dear.
Across his name the vivid ivies scrawl.

Amid so much human mutability
This walled garden is a place of rest and peace:
Death loses its horrid aspect, is seen to be
A natural term to life's unquietness:
Here all conflict is stilled, quarrels cease,
Here is neither friend nor enemy.

Yet most of them knew each other at market
And feast and fair; and some kept company
Before marrying another with whom they lie.
Here are two lovers who fell from the quay
One December night in eighteen thirty three,
And were drowned. Remember them, of your charity.

It is a Sunday morning in war-time. The bells
Are silent though it is church-time, and they
Ring out and up the hillside usually
To this garden, summoning the dead company
To worship with the living. A thrush on a grey
Headstone halts to eye me inquisitively,

Then flits away. On the road outside resound
The footsteps of people passing by to church:
You see the old superstition still has its pull
Among the old-fashioned and respectable;
If you wait, you will see the little organist
Go bustling by like a bird that hops on the ground.

The sun is on the eastern face of the tower;
Through a break in the trees you see the clock: the hour
Is close on eleven. A scented summer breeze
Lifts and lets fall again the fronds of the trees;
The grass is strown with flowers of ilexes
And early leaves, the rhododendrons blown.

What is this secret scent upon the air
So subtle it steals in everywhere? It is
The odour of resin in the cypresses
And yews, rising in the heat, a honeyed breath.
In his remote still corner a snake lies sleeping,
Emblem of wisdom, of knowledge after death.

The hours go by and now it is afternoon:
The white sail of a gull crosses the blue
Peacock sky that remembers Italy:
The sun goes round to the western face of the tower,
The majestic image of the Trinity,
The Virgin, the Angel of the Annunciation, the Flower.

There too is the holy hermit, St Austell, from whom
The parish derives its name, who lived by his well
Preaching, performed an occasional miracle.
O holy, blessed and glorious Trinity,
Three Persons and One God, One in Three:
How comparatively simple all would be

If this indeed were all. My mind returns
To the Feast-days, Trinity Sundays, of the past:
The church all breathing flowers, the white linens
Upon the altar, the stiff new surplices,
The festal air, the silver chalices,
The procession, the vague old vicar wandering, lost:

Then home through the hot, sweet-smelling summer
      lanes,
Gay with the first foxgloves and purple vetches,

Red sorrel and golden crowsfoot in the hedges,
To Sunday dinner, family round the table
Together, who now are all scattered, east and west,
And one has gone to his eternal rest.

The poets, my friends, have written learnedly
On Time Present, Time Past and Time to come,
But I do not know that they have added to the sum
Of what we knew before, and that is simply:
All creatures come by their appointed end;
Let us learn to look on death, then, as a friend.

Hark! from a field comes the comfortable sound
Of a reaper near-by harvesting his hay—
Even as these in their day were harvested.
There is speedwell growing here on the little mound
Of a child; a tiny lizard comes out to look
At the man who is strangely moved as he reads in his
        book:

'I am the Resurrection and the Life.'
So many times have these poor simple folk
Heard and taken comfort, since they must,
In these magnificent words. 'And when this mortal
Shall put on immortality': the recital
Tells nothing: we only know that dust is dust.

Yet that indeed is not all: they scattered their seed,
Before they died, like flowers upon the air.
They are our forefathers, from whom we were begotten:
Their blood runs in my veins. Therefore have I come
To fulfil my childhood's pledge and fashion this prayer.
In the place that knew them they shall not be forgotten.

Trenarren: Autumn 1941

The thunder-green sea
Brings nearer the Island
On which stood the chapel
Of Michael the Archangel.

Smoke from a chimney
In the V-shaped valley,
The voices of children,
A robin on the bough:

Familiar and cheerful
Domestic noises
Speak of contentment
About me now.

But what is to come?
I ask myself, waiting
In this burial-place
Of my ancient people:

The long-headed, dark-faced
Mediterranean
Men who drove prows
Into these inlets:

Confronting the danger
That they too awaited
In the urgent whisper,
The winter sea waiting.

Duporth Hill

The moon lies white upon the corn,
   The noisy trees are all still;
Silent are the footsteps now
   That used to ring on Duporth Hill.

Where are the Worcesters, the Gloucester lads,
   The Cornwalls and the Somersets,
Who kept their watch upon these coasts
   Where glows the light of late sunsets?

They stood on guard that bitter year
   Of our defeat, by night and day;
Over the hill the bugles sounded;
   A day came and they marched away.

The sky-line rises to the west
   A mounded form, a darker frieze;
Shades of former figures weave
   In and out the moon-blanched trees.

Where are they now who once were here?
   In Egypt, Libya, Palestine,
Scattered across the seven seas,
   Where long alone they held their line

Nor ever surrendered to despair,
   Others there are who now are still:
Silent are the eager steps
   That used to ring on Duporth Hill.

Charlestown Harbour

(To Christopher away at the War)

In the little port,
Where the ships come rarely now,
In the silence of the street
A thrush sings—you know how:

Causing the echoes to fall
Like flowers upon the quay,
Reaching over the water
To the deserted street and me,

Standing and looking down
Upon the little Dutch ship,
Her tattered flag at the mast
Fluttering by the slip.

While, at the harbour-mouth,
The wind-awakened sea
Thunders, besieges the pier,
Comes nostrilling over the quay;

And on the outer beach
With dark and sullen roar,
With regular lapse and beat
Breaks upon the shore.

Here in an inland town,
Three hundred miles away,
I hear the sound and taste
The salt rime on the spray:

See before my eye
Harbour-mouth and quay,
Hear the song of a bird,
The remembered surge of the sea.

The Ledra* at Trenarren

The white gulls gleam and disappear,
   Their cries re-echo in the caves;
The vanished ladies are all silent
   Under the blue and crystal waves.

The gathered plumage of the trees
   Sways above the familiar scene,
Resumes the life of centuries,
   The memories of what has been:

The children playing on the green
   Who now are old and mumbled bones,
The ancient lovers who took their ease
   Lying in this place of stones;

The night-long watch upon the cliffs
   When Spaniards sailed the summer seas
And made their voyage round these isles
   And home by the outer Hebrides;

The look-out kept by waiting women
   For men at sea on winter nights,
The storms and tempests of the past,
   The noontide calm upon the heights.

The places that are empty now
   Were once so full of vivid life:
Meeting of lovers, children, birth,
   Friendship and labour, springtime, strife.

* *Ledra* Cornish for slope, or cliff.

Gear

A queer place is Gear
  upon the downs
and very near to Fear
when the sun goes down
  behind the dunes,
and then you come upon
  the bare and stony places
where little skulls of animals become
  bleached and whitened bones
  that once were faces
of things that were alive like you:
the shells of snails and tiny skeletons
clean and fine, and delicate of line.
The sound of surf runs
  in your ears with the tread
  of the drowned and dead.
Here among the stones
  no one would hear the cries
  of a creature that dies.
Now the clouds rise
  no bigger than a man's finger
  to threaten the lone figure,
  spread over the land
  on either hand
  and fill the skies.
No one would hear your cries
  if you cried aloud
  to earth and cloud
No one would hear
  at Gear.

Night Scene in Wartime

Sitting at the midnight desk I observe the scene,
The surface of the window with lattice panes
My cinema screen, the suspended tassel still,
The blind drawn up. Beyond the sill, the bay.
The moon places a searchlight beam on the sea,
Lights up the golden waves that run along
The contrary coast. Or is it a searchlight
That throws a moonbeam across the headland grey,
Probing the cliffs, the coves, the caves for what
Contraband of war? There, under the hill,
Men live in danger, keeping watch; there are
The gun-sites, mines to spring, the waiting wire;
Behind the shifting haze, the enemy.
On the crest, the camp of Indian muleteers
And all that strange life of the North-West Frontier,
The alien voices hallooing in the woods,
The cat-like, khaki shadows in the glades.
The wind is rising, the trees lean together,
The weather-vane, winged helmet of Mercury,
Creaks like the swinging signboard of an inn
In novels of adventure. Within the room the clock
Ticks with an urgent regularity,
Speeds the monotonous pen, speaks of life
Passing in work to distant, measured ends.
Moonlight rests on the bars of the Sheraton chair,
As on the rims of furrows in the field outside,
On silver dish and inkstand, on pallid papers
Now emptied of writing, virginal and chaste;
White books glimmer out of the darkened shelves;
Upon the sill a bowl of daffodils,
Parchment-coloured ghosts of their sunlit selves;
The china horse crops the notional grass;
The needlework chair at angle suggests a wife.
All is in order, at peace within the room:
But light and life and movement are outside.

If I Could Say

How can one express
At once the mingled sadness
And sense of joy
In the glitter on the sea?

The pathos and regret
That stir the heart yet
When one recalls
The cries of gulls?

Or put into words
The leap of the heart
When a boy puts out in his boat
From the little port?

If I could say
All that arises in me
As I look down on the bay
From this eyrie:

The childhood vision that lay
Out between sea and sky
Beyond the horizon
Which no eye could descry;

The rounded clouds that were
The heads of angels in choir,
The sky's blue vacancies
The tents of Paradise;

The sound of water at night
Falling through the woods,
Making more solitary
The ancient solitudes:

Or stars hung over the hillside,
Snow and Christmas time,
The Blessed Virgin and Child,
The shepherds of Bethlehem.

If I understood these things
That have such power to move,
I should perhaps understand
The mystery of love:

The universe would unfold
Its secret heart to me
As a sea-flower opens and shuts
And slips into the sea.

Man and Bee: An Allegory

The angry buzzing noise the small insect makes
Fills the room: frantically he works
The mechanical propellers of his wings
Like a grounded plane, the shrill persistence sings
Its engine note against the window pane,
Where unaccountably held up, in vain
He tries to break through to the desirable, the free
World beyond, the world of greenery,
Of red-tipped stalks, of vivid leaves and flowers
To ravish of their juices through the hours.
There is the world beyond: the garden, the cornfield,
The woods of Duporth with their ponds, that hold
What mysteries within their dark-blue shades;
Behind, the headland that the sea-mist shrouds.

All invites, nor merely invites—demands
With positive, insistent urgency
He should go on his way. Necessity
Impels him to obey the clear commands

Of the inner voice that speaks the general will;
Not his to question the inscrutable
Law, but to acquit him of his burden
To the hive. There is the tantalizing garden
Voluptuous in the sun; the roses call
Their bugle-note of colour upon the wall.
What is there that prevents him breaking through,
When other insects cruising within view
Flit busily by? Why this imprisonment?
Against the invisible integument
On and on he buzzes angrily
Trying to butt his way, lowers his body
To launch a torpedo attack, rams his head
Against the glass, drops down defeated
Upon the sill, antennae quivering,
Body working with exhaustion, sting
Coming and going, then rises up again
To renew his onslaught on the window pane.

The man at the desk watches his every motion,
With mixed amusement, anger, fascination:
He too has tried to burst his way into
The world of power and beauty within view,
And been defeated by what obstacle,
What similar integument of will?
The noise in the room becomes unbearable,
Beats upon the brain: the man is moved to kill,
Crush the blind urge, the dull stupidity
That cannot rise above necessity.

Then, suddenly, by some miracle, the sound
Ceases, and all is peace within the room:
The creature, once more at one with nature, bound
On his mission round the world to roam,
A bolt of purpose, rivet of instinctive sense
Apart from which he has no real existence.

So too the man, pondering his allegory,
Having bruised his head long time in vain,
May find the barrier has ceased to be,
The membrane disappeared and all made plain
For him to enter now that world, where he
Inexplicably delivered, is made free
Of natural happiness and poetry.

Invocation for a Cornish House:
Summer 1941

A house islanded in a sea of corn,
On three sides the waves of wheat and oats,
Long-bearded barley, come up to the walls,
And all day, all night, a soft undertone
Is heard in the rooms of the house. What is it, I
    wonder?
And never cease to be surprised. Beneath
The long and lovely rustling of wind in the line
Of beeches, there is a softer, more liquid sighing,
Like a low and secret voice that sings to itself,
Is only overheard by an attentive ear.
It is the singing of the corn: so rare
A sound to live with, that yet brings home the year,
The times we live in, the necessities of war.
How often in these precarious days, looking
Out to sea, my eye follows rather
The wind's patterns in the corn, parting
The bent blades like sedges, running in rapid
Spirals and little whirlpools, as once I saw
The wind in the chestnuts in a college garden.
On the fourth side is the kitchen garden, planted
With potatoes that have finished flowering,
Spinach and peppercress and lettuces,

With three bean-rows in place of the poet's nine,
An orchard of pears and apples, bright red pollies,
Golden russets and rich Worcester pearmains.
At the green gate stands a sentinel pine.

The drive you enter is the old road to the mine,
Trodden by the feet of many vanished miners:
I often think of them when at nightfall
I come in at the gate, fancy sometimes I hear
The murmur of their manifold activity,
The wheeze of the engine, crank of the winch, chains
Clanking, the musical ring of crowbars that
Quarrymen can make chime like a peal of bells:
All subdued to a general night-murmur
Like insects in the grass, the wind in my hedge.
Hardly anything of the mine remains,
Save that, last winter, ploughing up the field
To the west, marks of the engine-house were revealed
Plain from an upper window, now lost again
Beneath the ripening corn. Perhaps it is
The voice of these former men that I hear in the voice
Of the corn. For a day came in the late seventies
When the mines were ruined and the men driven forth
To earn their bread across three continents,
In Johannesburg, and Kimberley, in Butte,
Montana, in Michigan and California,
In West Australia, Victoria and New South Wales.
Forth from our villages they went in shoals;
The cottages in neighbouring Mount Charles
Where my miners lived, were emptied of their men.

All my father's family were miners.
Out there upon the edge of the cliff I see,
Like a Rhineland castle standing boldly up,
The ruined engine-house of Appletree.
There my grandfather worked under the sea.
I never knew him. The bad air, they said,
Killed him in his forties, leaving nine

111

Sons to be brought up by his stoic wife.
Now they two lie, William and Fanny Rowse,
Among the first in the new cemetery
Upon the hillside at the back of the house.
Of their sons, six went to South Africa;
The eldest and the youngest are buried there.
The last, a lad of twenty, whom they called
Cheelie in the village, the youngest of the bunch,
A boy of irrepressible spirit, full
Of mischief, music and merriment, was killed
In a mine-accident, his body torn
In two, as he lay dying uttered these
Last remembered words: 'I've neither father
Nor mother to grieve for me; so it's all right.'

My mother's stock sprang from small farmers
About Duloe, Hessenford and Looe.
Her father's folk labourers in the fields,
Tillers of the soil, ploughmen, hinds. Yet they
Nursed a tradition that they came over from France
At the time of the Revolution: across the bay,
Along the lizard length of the Gribbin headland,
The long green limb that closes my seaward view,
Is the little fisher-place where they came in,
Polkerris with its pier and still green water,
The crab-pots and nets drying in the sun,
The air filled with fuchsias and honeysuckles,
The scent of veronica like honeycomb.
Both these simple families bore French names,
Goynes and Vanson, and had a superior way
With them, a finer sense of courtesy
Than my father's folk, who were rough fighting miners,
Quick of temper, irascible, independent,
Cornish of the Cornish; yet all of them
Loved music and played on various instruments,
Kept the village gay with their pranks and dancing.
Them I never knew but from hearsay;

But knew my mother's folk: my grandmother,
That dominating wilful old woman,
With the dark Spanish face and handsome eyes,
Who ruled her matriarchal family
With the authority of Queen Victoria
And the fear of her sharp, sarcastic tongue: who made
Cutting off her nose to spite her face
Her rule of life. That trait I get from her,
And many another, passion and pride, a quick
Unbridled tongue that runs away with me,
Loyalty to friends, an equal hate
Of all who thwart my way, no fear of the great
Nor respect of persons, but most, a fundamental
Pride, the keynote of my character.

My grandfather, of the golden voice and patient ways
(Patience he needed with so wilful a helpmate
To live so long), less generous than she,
More wise, with the wisdom of the animals
He loved, my mother used as a girl to follow,
With his team of oxen on the farm at Quintrells
Ploughing, to hear him call with that pure note,
'Whoa there, Neat and Comely, Spark and Beauty'.
When he was an old man, I would ask him to say
'Whoa there', as only he could say it, with such
Ripeness and mellow command of the animals,
So different from my father's impatient temper
And driving on the bit. Sixty years
That couple lived together, in the end
Their lives entwined like two branches of one tree:
When she died, he followed shortly after,
But nine months, not wishing to be long from her.
They lie together happily out there
In the little churchyard at St Blazey Gate,
Edward Vanson and his wife Elizabeth.
From my desk I see the spire among the trees
On the skyline, set on its old red sandstone hill.

Further along the horizon see Trenython,
The house among the woods sitting up like a hen
On her nest, home of the good Victorian bishop,
Kindly, hospitable, but so forgetful that
Many are the stories told of him, his legend
Still lives: of garden-parties, the invitations
For which were never sent, the bishop left
To entertain the band; or guests arriving
For lunch, having toiled up the hot, dusty hill
In summer and been shown into the garden where
The bishop walked among his flowers, he showed
Them round with his affable, shy courtesy,
Dismissed them at the gate at foot of hill,
To toil up again and in at the front door.
Yet a spirit of departed piety
Presided over the house: I celebrate
That vanished way of life, the daily prayers,
The house at Whitsuntide, Rogationtide,
In Lent and Advent, full of ordinands;
The visits of country clergy and their wives,
The post for ever coming and going, the affairs
Of the Church, the burden of episcopal routine;
The journeys to the Continent, visits
To Florence, the galleries and Fiesole,
The Victorian preference for Gothic; the library
With the Correggio over the mantelpiece,
The bronzes from the Summer Palace at Peking.
Then the last day of that busy life: the entry
In a book: 'The Spirit of the Lord shall give me rest.'

In those days there'd be at Tywardreath church on
      Sundays
The carriages from Trenython and Menabilly,
The coachmen with cockades and decorative whips,
Waggonettes for the servants. And there would be
That proud, impetuous woman, Mrs Sackville,
Preceded by her footman carrying cushion
And prayer-book slowly up the aisle to her pew.

114

Passionate pride of ancestry was matched
With an equal temper in her: the story went
That she boxed her husband's ears in church,
And after that lived, like Miss Haversham,
A shuttered life in her house overlooking the sea,
Point Neptune, the terraces falling to the water's edge,
Dark-shadowed by waving ilexes. When she
Came to die she was buried at top of the cliff,
In sight and sound of the sea she must have loved.

Beside her rises the forbidding figure of old
Jonathan Rashleigh, stern patriarch,
Who quarrelled with his son for marrying a Radical's
Daughter: the curse fell on them: they both died young,
Leaving an infant heir to grow up there
In evident disfavour, to inherit a hate
For the place and all that secret peninsula.
He had his revenge: in time to come he saw
Decay descend upon those gardens, the rare
Exotic plants fostered by his grandfather,
The tree-ferns in their deep green covert, the palm
Avenue, the shrubberies a wilderness.
Decay ate its way through the shut-up house
Mouldering away by moonlight or the light of day,
The broken blinds revealed the painted portraits
In the dining-room, the walls bleached, the silk
Curtains tattered, wall-paper hanging. Rot
Perished floors, wainscot and panelling.
Now some of their cherished possessions are in this
    house:
The chair I write in stood in a front bedroom
Looking out over those shaven lawns to the sea;
A writing-table—to think what flounced and frilled
Ladies wrote their faded letters at it;
A carved cedarwood chest that came from Italy
In the seventeenth century, with Venetian glass and
    finery.

Theirs was all the privacy of the Gribbin,
The full view of which I now possess:
May that gracious personality be
The spirit of this house as it informs the view:
A shape more feminine and exquisite
Than the masculine presence of the Nare, more rare
And subtle, having placidity and calm,
Something withdrawn within its own perfection,
Yet lives with the varying moods of the day and year,
Cloud-dappled, wind-folded, spring-green with corn,
Or grey with mist. I recall the crimson and blue
Confusion of campion and bluebells down to the edge
Of the rocks, when I took refuge that melancholy
Day of a wedding which took my girl away.
That vision that lies across the bay from me,
Has something of her grace and poise and secrecy.
I love to watch the sea nostrilling its way
Along the low tide-line like a ship's prow,
And, absent, observe it often in the mind's eye.
Look now! A rapid cloud moves across
The vivid green of the cliff's face; the white
Wing of a gull is caught aslant the bay.

Nearer at hand are the bushes and briars of
        Campdowns,
Where the gipsies held their convocations. And all
About, the green mounds of former mines
Covered now with vegetation, Crinnis,
Wheal Eliza, Wheal Buckler, and Pembroke Mine.
On the left the chimneys of Charlestown Foundry,
        still—
But at how different—work, the tools of war
In place of ploughshares of the long Victorian peace.
In the fold of the hill below is the tiny port
Whence the clay ships left for all parts of the world;
Now an occasional Dutch schooner with tattered flag
At mast and bullet-holes on bridge and stern.
There in the bird-haunted wood lived Christopher,

116

Friend of the green woodpecker, shy curlew and the jay,
A lad staunch of heart and hand and head,
Who'd come up across the fields, leap over the wall
To pay me a visit, before he went away to the war.
And so around the shelving curve of the bay
With, today, little white stitches in the blue sea,
To the tufted crest of Duporth, the memories
Of the camp that first summer of the war, the bugles,
The voices coming over the hill, the Scottish lad,
The fading footsteps, the Indian muleteers
Performing their strange dances on the cliffs.

So back to the house in its rose-garlanded walls;
The roses make pools of red in the window panes.
This place accumulates its loyalties,
The more precious for the tension of the time.
There were those nights of Plymouth's agony,
The upper skies fantastically criss-crossed
With searchlights, the lower a white diffusive glow
Where Plymouth burned, gun-flashes like
      sheet-lightning,
Flares descending in coveys like birds of fire
The starry points of shell-fire spreading the sky,
The roar of guns from thirty miles away:
And all a splendid, solemn spectacle seen
From my room like a box at the theatre, night after
      night,
Until I broke down and wept with utter misery
And helplessness for the fate of that dear city.
And all the while the fear that walks the house
When night falls: the noises of darkness reflect the day,
The death-rattle of machine-gun fire on the headland,
The guns at sea, the dull thud of a bomb
Somewhere nearby that prints on the sleeping mind
Inviolate England, inviolate no more!
The dreams of enemies lying in the corn
About the besieged house; everything on edge,—
If a rose-petal falls, one registers a blow.

117

The Invocation

So now tonight, when the bearded barley drinks
The moon, and the corn is stippled with night-gold,
The bent blades swaying are praying now to Venus
And Mercury to avert the blows of Mars
And spare their seedlings the ravages of wars:
So, too, I pray, preserve this house that I
May gather the fruits of so many years' dreaming,
Researches into memory's observant eye,
Achieve some signal thing before darkness falls
On these loved walls and shuttered windows, on the
    sea,
The distant headland, the ripened corn and me.

The Age of Innocence

If I might but regain the age of innocence,
Nor ever through the world's complexity
See the bare anatomy;
If I might cease for ever to pursue
The shadow of a thought into
The grave of form, the husk's substance,—
If I should see the lean face of a man,
Airman or pilot, driver or man on watch
Passing in a train or passing in the street,
Without immediate negation of desire,
Or let the lewd eye of woman rest on me
Without suspicion of the flesh;
If only these things might be,
That I should see
The fullness of the tree and not the bare tree,
The flower in bloom without the withered stalk,
The child without the ghost of age
Grinning behind the innocent eyes,
The toothless lips behind the gay talk,

Or see the sun rise without thought
Of planetary change or slow decay:
If these things might be
I should perchance see
Some comfort in the world's experience,
Content in sense,
My spirit cease from intellectual agony.

All Souls

Evening. Silence, and the questioning of birds.
A bugle blows its erotic note over the city;
The light creeps round to the north face of the tower.
The grey, stone chimneys are still and void of life,
    saying, There is no love,
Here there is neither marrying, nor giving in marriage,
No heart to hold, no limbs to cherish,
The happy birds go winging upon their business—
The soldiers in the street on theirs—
Beyond the walls, the roofs, the eaves.
Than walls of stone or bars of iron more binding
These intellectual integuments,
Because self-willed.

The mullioned windows of the Middle Age
Look blindly out upon a world they do not know;
The gargoyles that express their child-like humour,
Propitiate the powers of evil, the fear of the unknown,
Look down forlorn upon a world that no longer
Finds them funny.

There is something affecting about those windows,
Like eyes that have lost their power to see.
The figure of Christ stands isolated upon his perch,
The didactic gesture of the hand,
The spinster parting of the hair.

119

The shadow of the tower moves along the roof;
The proletarian clatter of cups and plates
That speaks of domestic contentment,
Marks the hour.

Later, the high-flying swifts,
Crying their passionate, restless, unsatisfied cry,
Aspire about the steeples of the city:
Emblem of the incurable nostalgia of the heart.

Moon, Snow, Winter Afternoon

The moon, the snow, the light of winter afternoon,
  as if one watched life going by from under the sea:
  the leafless twigs that sway in wind and light,
  the fronds and ferns that wave under the sea:
  life seen through the refraction of water,
  held at a distance, the world of closeness and desire
  held at finger's breadth, the breath of a ghost
  between the sentient man and the revelation he
      waits for.
As if it might suddenly come
and the world wake, shiver and tremble with ecstasy,
or a flower might burst out of the heart withheld
and all that but waits, breathe upon the lips,
along the nerves and into the veins,
make one this waiting, observant man
with the moon, the breath of wind upon the snow,
the leafless twigs that wave in the sun,
the chatter of birds, the drone of the plane
that swells and subsides in the neighbouring sky.

And all the talk of the real and the rational recedes
  like a wave receding upon the shore,
And all that one is aware of is life passing away
  in sun upon stone, shadows clouding the windows,
  the memory of bells uprooting the heart,

120

the evidence of time passing in the skin, or in the
   eyes, the hair,
the greater heaviness of the body,
the mind that no longer leaps as even the trees
leap to meet the spring,
but is more conscious as the years go by
that a time will come and he not be.

In the Walks

Nobody in the walks
Nobody in the walks but the wind and I,
The wind tearing the hair of the trees
Wrinkling the surface of the water
Causing the leaves to fall on the bosom of the stream,
Upon the woman with the hare-lip, painting
The Chinese perfection of the scene
The single willow by the deserted pond
And I, mad and forlorn like Christopher Smart, racing
Down the cathedral walk open
To the blue, plane-punctuated sky.
How would it be
To see
The world from the bottom of the bottle-green river,
The alders and pollarded willows leaning
Over the banks, the sticks afloat
The hair caught in the roots and sedges?
The traceried windows look out
Upon Charles and Henrietta and all their rout
The fatal scrimmage of the Civil Wars
The young men pursuing Venus and Mars.
The women's tresses of the willows
Weave and unweave over the water.
Look! There is a silver world of under-leaves
Of willow and alder and aspen,
While against the Uccello background of tree-trunks

The dark shadow of a hound
Pursues the shadows of ancestral wolves
That hunted here when Canute was king
And at Christmas heard the monks sing
Out over the wilderness of waters
And bade the boatmen row nigher
As the voices rose in choir
From the grey walls mirrored in that water-world.
Over the meadows is the odour of death and
      reawakening.

Midnight Approaches

Midnight approaches and the legion fears
Torment the sick soul with the thought
Of what is done cannot be undone,
What left undone too late to be done now
In these grey watches one knows not how
The body can waylay the mind to wantonness
The mind excite the foolish flesh
With ardent promise of proximate ecstasy
No sooner had than hated, repented
In the moment of enjoyment while these cold hours
Withdraw the veil from those delights
Search out reproaches hidden in the flowers
Awake long-stilled anxieties and fears
That stalk unnamed through the dark corridors
Of memory and forgotten association
With all that's ill, tempt with thought of suicide,
The knife on the tray, the rope from the roof,
The quivering sense of insecurity
Waiting for a knock, a knock on the door:
These suggestions evidences of failure,
The difficulty implicit in life yet to be lived.

Tea à *la Russe*

The old lady with sparse, corn-coloured hair
And fragrant courtesy of the Romanovs,
Presides now with slightly bewildered air
Over the cakes and scones, the loves
Of the refugees from Central Europe
Who have found here in war-time Oxford
Their refuge, their island.
The plates and cups are disposed;
Here a vase of tulips and grape-hyacinths.
The other occupants, middle-aged women
Armed with pince-nez and querulous brows,
From the neighbourhood of the British Museum:
Those other exiles find too their refuge here,
Discuss the incidence of bombs,
Insurance rates upon lost furniture.
Over the teas and the lost, the old lady
Presides, bewilderment in her blue eyes
Pale as northern skies in spring,
Hardly remembers where she is:
But remembers the Nevsky Prospekt now in May,
The lime-trees coming out along the Neva,
The long vista of the Admiralty,
The droshkis waiting in the street,
At her door the carriage with coachman obedient
Of the time of the Romanovs—
St Petersburg in spring and all her vanished loves.

Dick Holdsworth, R.A.F.

Killed, May 1942

There is the house, full of Victorian what-nots,
The indescribable confusion of bric-à-brac,
Framed photographs, footstools, pots of ferns,
The festooned windows that look out upon

123

The happy commerce of the river in May.
The lilacs, purple and white, are now in bloom,
Bend over to watch themselves in grass-green water,
Cherries and apple-blossom out, the blackthorn over.
The house stands up upon its strong supports,
The arches where the little moorhens nest,
Regards with blank indifference now
The dinghies with clamorous sea-scouts rowing
Their vigorous irregular strokes upstream,
The punts with R.A.F. men and their girls,
The soldiers, the young men in canoes
Coasting carefully about the nesting swans,
The lovers that recline upon the river margin,
The airmen with their WAAFS, the ATS and WRENS.

There is a smell of rain in the air,
The scent of sap in the trees, the leaves,
A raindrop hits my cheek,
And Dick's underground.

I seem to see him there in the house,
A small boy home from school, an only boy,
Surrounded by his toys, the engines of seven to eleven,
The cricket-bats and football togs of thirteen,
The sweaters and scarves of the full-blown rowing man.
I see the strong arm of the undergraduate,
The affectionate smile, simplicity of heart.
There is the warm and palpitating life
Full of friendship and busy activity
Projected upon the screen:
Holidays in the Channel Islands or the Hebrides,
The bathers leaping arc-like into moonlit water,
The summer sea scattering its flowers of foam
Around the wrinkled rocks, the lithe young figures
Climbing them, the linked and changing patterns
Like life itself, the writing on the wall.

I look again and see myself upon the screen
Walking happily upon the Downs,

124

Along the Ridgeway to Wayland's Cave,
Or more sedately in the summer garden
Accompanying Sir William on the lawn,
Admiring the border, pausing under the mulberry tree
Followed at heel by Dick's old faithful dog.

So I remember the last gathering there,
The game with the ball, while all stood round in a ring,
The verge of the war for a moment withdrawn
While the ball went faster and more merrily
And came to rest at the feet of Dick's bride to be.
So the war went on, the happy life of that house
Held in suspense, Dick away at his station,
The danger of the air brushing him twice with its wing,
Laying its spell breathless upon those that loved him
Waiting and watching, apprehensive yet unafraid,
Until the third time brought the news that kills:
The strong support removed from the house
That looks blank and bewildered out upon the river,
The young men in the vigour of youth,
The vegetation in all the flourish of May,
The threat of rain and the thought of Dick
underground.

Answer to a Young Poet

Were I to cry, who in that proud hierarchy
Of the illustrious would pity me?

SIDNEY KEYES

The illustrious dead, the great, the famed
Would understand—
None better—
The heart-ache, the grief, the bitterness,
The draught of hyssop and vinegar to the man on the
    Cross,

Cranmer plunging his right hand
That did offend first into the fire,
The man of destiny nursing his cancer
Lonely upon an island in the evening of his years
For ever scanning the horizon for a sail,
Or this one that after the storms
Of Paris and Chartres in that dawn of the intellect
Found quiet in the haven of the Paraclete,
Passion and torment of the flesh
And even grief now over:
These are they who understand,
Reach out a hand from their calm altitude
To lay a finger upon the wound that bleeds
And stay for a moment the heart's solitude.

March Madness

March like a lion goes out
That came in like a lamb.
And I walk under the catkins,
I that am
Mad and alone like Tom o' Bedlam,
Smelling the storm
In the west wind beating up
Out of the cup of Penrice
Easterly into the bay.
The moon has changed today
And with the moon, my mood.
My taste for solitude
Leads me to the cliff;
And if, looking into the water
My world should shatter,
The rocks leap up:
What matter?
I am out in the wind and rain;
Am I sane?
I ask again and again.

Or has the world of men
Some inner sense
That I escape?
Like a seascape
Glimpsed in the sun
And in the rain
Gone again?

The Ash Tree

Song

I look at the moon
And the moon looks at me
Between the slender fingers
Of the ash tree.

I never knew how sad
Sadness could be
Until I saw the moon's fingers
Through the ash tree.

The homing rooks
For the woods are bound,
From an old clothes-line
Drop to the ground.

Do you think my love
Will come to me
When the moon's face looks
Through the ash tree?

The familiar depths
Of misery I plumb,
Though I wait for ever
He will not come.

I never knew
What sadness could be
Until I saw the moon in full
Through the ash tree.

Sunday on the River in June

O to stay the moment of honeyed happiness,
    the bough of hawthorn over the boat,
    the lyrical movement of the solitary poplar,
    emblem of the perfection of the moment,
    June roses, wild briar or eglantine,
    or clump of comfrey at the punt's head:
    the gay canoes dart by under the bridge,
    the coloured prints of the women,
    the flashing bodies of young men bathing—
    the Seine at Argenteuil, a Monet, a Sisley—
    the sun-glitter of the vanished eighties on the
        water.

This is a gentler, more English scene:
    Sunday in June, the nineteen forties,
    the rocking of the boat
        the rhythm of contentment
    the licking of the water
        the oars that dip and swing,
    the gathered figures waiting at the weir,
    in clusters under the silvery willows
        feather-waving in the sun—
    and all the world of men and women
        plumed trees and boats and flowers
        reflected in the moving water,
        a world of shifting insecurity.

O that the water dripping from the blade would cease
        to run,
    the lyrical motion of wind and trees be still—
    so that this moment of time might hold,
    retain the ripe perfection of happiness
    so long desired, so late attained,
    that nothing might come
    to lay an injurious finger upon whom I love.

If only the moment might remain
with all things in suspense, a breath inbreathed
on which my universe depends,
the tongue of time for ever stilled
which carries the boat each minute away
from that still scene, that unimagined happiness.

Absence

The honeysuckle is all gone
The scabious missing from the hedges
There is something.wanting to the summer
That was radiant and glad in your presence.

The ilexes construct their green cavern
Over the white gate on the road to Trenarren
The plumed elms hold up their feathered fans
Against the blue background of the bay.

Your face is wanting to the landscape
That so lately held you in its embrace.

When you were here
The day dawned with more gladness
The headland stood on guard more proudly
The ivies in the wood gleamed brighter
Summer flowers were in the hedges
Foxglove campion honeysuckle vetches.

Now all are gone
Harvest time has come upon the whitened corn:
Still the landscape reflects your countenance
The image of happiness attained.

As I Go Down Trenarren Lane

As I go down Trenarren Lane
   Stonecrop and scabious star the hedges;
A yellow-hammer sings on a bough,
   Rest-harrow, thyme and purple vetches.

'A little bit of bread and no cheese'
   Says the yellow-hammer on the bough;
Birds and flowers, a solitary heart
   The company the place has now.

'Except Ye Become as a Little Child'

Lay upon my tongue a live coal
To give my inner silence
Utterance: Release my soul
Enable me to say
What lurks among the crevices of the heart
All that is so carefully papered over
Lest too great a hurt
Should once more tear my life apart:
Lay bare the passion behind
The so meticulously drawn-out reason
Lest the watched surface of my happiness
Give way and disclose
The waiting depths of melancholy
That lie beneath:
Make me to speak
Such words as will break
The film of cobweb that enshrouds
The truth of the eyes, the warm blood in the veins,
The sensitive responses of the touch,
The sympathy spontaneous, electric, of a child,
At once denied, overlaid
With the cautious reserve

Of the adult afraid:
Make me to break free
Of my other self that is
Become the stronger part of me,
The suspended judgment,
The caution, the irony
That measures words with a tape-measure,
Carefully weighs out the possible,
The permissible, the impermissible,
Until the ice forms along the veins
And clouds the arteries:
Make me to speak words
No longer of wisdom as the world sees,
But words of such audacity
As will shake the roof-tree,
Awake the flight of birds
The bats in the eaves
The autumn sun in the gold leaves,
Put into syllables
What the colours mean
That in the evening
Fall upon a tomb
In a forgotten church,
The memories of a room
Where much unhappiness has been
And a life played out its tragedy:
Make me weak
That I may see with a child's eye
The worlds that round us lie
Folded leaf within leaf:
Break my proud spirit
That I may learn humility
And as a child inherit
The promised kingdom.

Autumn is Here

Autumn is here and the barracking birds,
   The leaves lie thick upon the ground,
The herded ambulances lie
   Under the trees, without a sound:

Motionless in line they rest,
   Hooded and shut they wait their day;
The dark-faced Texan stands on guard;
   The voices of children peal at play.

The golden light hangs in the trees,
   The western air is kind and mild;
A soldier leans on the gate with his girl,
   His laugh as eager as a child.

The sick man walks along the road
   Nor concerns himself too much with these:
He once was avid of life as they,
   Now finds those pleasures mockeries.

Fear in his mind, anguish in his heart,
   With slow considered steps he goes;
Around him the voices of birds and men
   Unsuspecting the truth he knows.

Dream-Poem

In my dream my father said
   'This is a hard bed that I lie on';
I saw him there, the figure of a child,
   Twisting and turning on that bed of iron.

In the house the beds were filled
   By friends and strangers, guests unknown,
Whom I would not displace for him
   So long forgotten, ill, alone.

So many years since he was alive
   Whose house it was where we all lay,
And I had come into possession
   Where once he held unquestioned sway.

I looked upon his case with pity
   Yet could not do that which I would:
There came some obstacle of will
   Between me and my willing mood,

My duty to the child-like figure
   That lay there restless and in pain,
Appealing for very helplessness
   Upon the outstretched counterpane.

Yet still I made no move. Instead
   I woke to the grey light of day,
And realised that harder still,
   And narrower, his bed of clay.

Campdowns

Christmas Eve, and I will bring you to a place
Where the winter heliotropes grow,
A kind of Golgotha or place of skulls:
So many dead men once worked here:
See, here are their workings,
The leaden and ochre stains of refuse
That make the place more desolate,
Speak their own language to the faithful mind.
Once it was a scene of happy activity,
The tramp of men's feet upon stone,
The lifting of ores, the stamps, the rubble screens,
The busy hum of a hive.
Now all is silent under the lead-coloured day:
Only the memories of miners and their songs
Hang in the trees, and after them the gipsies,

The shafts derelict and overgrown
With gorse flowering at Christmas and winter
    heliotrope.
All is at a stand, for ever waiting:
Here scrub and furze-bushes, dead brambles, ivies,
The rank vegetation struggling over the quartz;
There a clump of silver beeches
Like a family group somewhat withdrawn,
The dark pine-woods of Crinnis neighbouring;
At the turn of the road a dead oak many-horned
That would have caught the eye of Constable.
Over the cliffs a bomber of Coastal Command
Returns to base.
A moment later, slowly and laboriously
A train draws its snake-like length out of the wood.
I wait and watch among the winter heliotropes
That blossom in this forgotten place at Christmas time,
Breathing in their heavy musk-like scent,
Aware of the insatisfaction and the pathos of life.

Home-Coming to Cornwall:
December 1942

A landslide on the line, the train diverted
Back up the valley of the red Exe in spate
Rich with Devonshire soil, flooding the green
Meadows, swirling round the wooded bends,
The December quality of light on boles of trees,
Black and shining out of the gathering dark,
The sepia brushwork against the western skies
Filtering the last watercolour light.
(Why should the eyes fill with tears, as if
One should not look upon the like again?
So many eyes have seen that coign of wood,
That curve of river, the pencil screen of trees).
I fall asleep; the train feels slowly round

The unfamiliar northern edge of Dartmoor.
It is night and we are entering Cornwall strangely:
The sense of excitement wakens me, to see
Launceston perched on a shoulder like Liège,
The young moon white above the moving clouds.
The train halts in the valley where monks prayed,
Under the castle-keep the Normans ruled
And Edward the Black Prince visited. We stop
At every wayside halt, a signal-box,
An open waiting shed, a shrub or two,
A friendly voice out of the night, a lamp—
Egloskerry, Tresmeer and Otterham—
And out upon the shaven moonlit moor.
The seawind blows from the Atlantic coast,
A seabird sails over, whitens in the moon;
The little scattered houses crouch for shelter,
A few withies about them, a stunted elm
Or shawl of ash or thorn, a pool that gleams
In the strange wavering light upon the downs
That look towards Rowtor where King Arthur hunted
The red deer, and met at last with Modred:
Where all day long the noise of battle rolled
Among the mountains by the winter sea.
In the mind's eye I see that older poet
Search still for Arthur's grave in this waste land
Where fragments of forgotten peoples dwell.
All is bare and silent: no light shows:
The white sheep crop on the glimmering pastures;
There is the unforgettable smell of the moor,
Of the seawind on a hundred nameless herbs,
On bracken and gorse, on heather and fern and ling.
(The sick man leans upon the window, weeping
He knows not why, at his home-coming
After many weary months of weakness).

In the moment of breathing in my native land
I remember to hate: the thousand indignities,
The little humiliations, the small insults

135

From small people, the hidden enmities,
The slights that hurt the sensibilities
Of the child that, longing for affection, learned
To reward envy with contempt, to speak
The biting word that freezes sympathy,
The instinctive expectation of a blow
To pride or self-respect or decency;
And as a man to mark the averted gaze
Of petty shopkeepers on their paltry pavements;
The meanness of the moneyed middle-class,
The slow passivity of the workers that know
Not their own interest or their enemies.
But, most of all, the vast misunderstanding
That divides me from my people I lament,
The self-willed folly that condemned me long
To opening the eyes of fools, the task
Of a Tregeagle or a Sisyphus;
The million fond stupidities that make
A modern electorate. Alone in the night,
At the window looking over the moonlit land,
Alone with myself I could beat my head against
The walls for rage and impotent defeat.
Quick! Shut the window. Pull down the blind
Over the lovely landscape. Shut out the sight!

December on the Ledra

Here between land and sea
    between the clamour of the rooks
    and the crying of the gulls
    where the curious cows contentedly
    chew the cud rootedly
    stand and stare and one
    makes water quietly
    a silver stream in the afternoon sun

Here where the sea
    lies like a mirrored lake
    or still mill-pond without complexity
    and behind the heave of the hill
    the church-clock chimes a quarter past three
    where the obtuse mole burrows crookedly
    her passage athwart the path
    and the rabbit scuttles timidly
    into the hedge
Here where campion blooms in mid-December
    and the magpie flies uncertainly
    by the cliff's edge
    where ponies crop upon the ledra placidly
    and the voices of children come up from the valley
    where the hayrick rises forbiddingly upon
    the shoulder of the near horizon:
Here could I contented be
    at length to lie and hear
    the crying of the rooks
    the laughing of the gulls
    the lapse and call of the sea
    or possibly may hear
    with equal ear
    no noise at all.

The Bridge

I walk around the winter walks
    With thoughts of Libya in mind,
The Mediterranean sky is blue,
    The golden crocuses are kind.

The willows wave their swaying nets—
    February and the dykes are full—
Yellow aconites star the grass,
    The Sung-green of the willow pool.

The river in spate flows under the bridge;
  Superbly down the stream a swan
With proud and delicate arched neck
  And powerful stroke is swiftly gone.

The snowdrops hang their heads and dance
  In a little wind that comes and goes;
The tower in the west holds up its crown;
  From the evening sky the colour flows.

Time itself runs under the bridge,
  And I remember that you, my swan,
Will all too soon now reach your term,
  Like crocus and snowdrop, be gone, be gone.

Call-Up

The window open to the grove:
  The leafless trees are very still,
The sky is clear with February light,
  The stream runs swiftly from the mill;

Along the paths the people walk,
  Fresh from church they sniff the air,
Considering the crocuses,
  Frilled aconites and snowdrops there.

Within the room a lad takes leave
  Of things familiar as the day,
Puts on his soldier's uniform,
  Packs his kit and goes away.

Across the grove the spring birds sing,
  The water glistens on the weir;
A moment more and all will be
  As if you never had been here.

Your room another occupant
   Will have—some one whom you knew not
Will sit in your chair, work at your desk,
   Read by your kindly fire at night.

Time like an ever-rolling stream
   Bears all its sons away;
The water passes under the bridge,
   The silver light has left the day.

The people now are gone from the grove
   And all alone I make my way,
Thinking my melancholy thoughts,
   The meadows green, the sky now grey.

The snowdrops ring their bells in the wind
   So silently you would not hear,
The crocuses hold up their lamps,
   The drooping willows hardly stir.

Down the alley path I come,
   Halt on the bridge beside the grange,
Look up to see your open window
   Already shut, remote and strange.

Iffley

The shadows on the Norman tower
   Make clearer still the vivid day;
They write their living signature
   On all that stands, and go their way:

Images of Time that moves,
   Touching with tip of careless wing
The subtle fabric of our loves
   Silencing the hearts that sing.

139

The almond-trees are out in flower,
   The water plashes from the weir
A softer music: the year was young
   When you were here, when you were here.

The villas on the river bank
   Look gaily down their verdant slopes;
The quiet anglers cast their line;
   Against the wall the water laps.

Over the meadows the floods are out,
   A silver shield upon the mere
Burns and dazzles the winter eye:
   Islands of green and blue appear,

A fringe of snow-white gulls, a swan
   Sailing the blue and silver flood
That drowns the plain: the placid lake
   Reflects Boars Hill and Bagley Wood.

A distant drone of aeroplanes;
   The barges corrugate the stream,
The aspiring poplars shimmer and sway;
   The click of the gate disturbs my dream—

And I remember when you were here:
   Something has gone from the living day
With the shifting shadows upon the tower,
   Now you're away, now you're away.

The City

'Spartan Control' the notice says:
   I walk up the accustomed hill,
The evening light is on the trees,
   The happy birds are loud and shrill.

A purple haze now bathes the city,
   The palings shadowed on the grass
Define the park; the American guard
   Shows his gun to the girls that pass.

Where are you now? I stand and think
   Of Kentish lanes, where pack on back
You march all day, and at this hour
   Weary return upon your track.

There the orchards are in flower,
   Here the walls are green and gold;
You haul your guns all day in the sun,
   While here of nights the stars are cold.

The evening shades draw darkly down,
   The people pass in their Sunday best;
In the distance Hinksey and Wytham Hill,
   The sinking sun lights up the west.

The poplars build their sombre screen;
   Beneath the bridge, the wilderness;
Evening flames on spire and tower:
   O darling city of our happiness.

Listening to Handel's
Messiah

Comfort ye, my people—
your face speaks out of the orchestra,
your hair entwined among the strings of violins,
the oracular certainties of Handel:
And the glory of the Lord shall be revealed.
Lent and the primroses of childhood
in Pentewan Valley and the fields of Pondhu.
Behold He shall come, saith the Lord of Hosts.

But who may abide the day of His coming?
The pathos of life, tenderness,
propitiation for mankind,
the garlands of women's voices singing *Hosanna,*
the comfort and strength of the men.
O thou that tellest good tidings to Zion:
afternoon sunlight upon upturned faces,
here a young man in uniform,
there a girl's face, hair under a ribbon,
the tides of music running through the veins,
The people that walked in darkness
Have seen a great light.
The church bells of Georgian England
Ring out in the inner world of the ear,
Sing in the heart alone in the throng of people.
For unto us a Child is born—
But not unto us:
through the mist of sunlight music faces faith
I feel your presence.
All the same this is an end:
the Thames at Abingdon,
the river bank at Easter, hawthorn in flower,
white sails on the blue river,
the reeds the wind the sun
a pastoral interlude, all at an end;
or walking the valley of the Windrush,
the cowslip-sweet banks by Minster Lovell,
the ruined manor across the water-meadows,
the clink of harness at the ford,
lingering with the music on the bridge,
while time stood still.
There were shepherds abiding in the field keeping watch over
    their flocks
And lo! the Angel of the Lord came upon them.
The eyes fill with tears for human hopes,
the music swirls round me and I am lost,
lost in the contemplation of your absent heart.
Does no echo reach you

where you tread the lanes of Kent,
rise in the moondawn to steal through the woods,
mount the hills, pack on back, march
till sundown and quiet evening,
bugles and comradeship and sleep?
Why do the nations so furiously rage together?
Yet your golden nature does not complain.
I am left to realise in the music,
in the crowded hall, in others' happiness,
that all the same this is an end.

In the Train to Cambridge

Canals, bridges, back-gardens,
Monday and the washing hanging out on lines,
the black and white maps of the cows,
the grey stubble golden in the morning light:
the train chugs on through the English fields,
a black colt, ears pricked forward,
alert, enquiring at an unfamiliar noise,
the combed and harrowed fields,
moving shadows, the bright sun
upon hands, the open page of a book:
Marsh Gibbon and people asleep in the compartment,
the plume of smoke moving across green slopes,
four plovers rise from a furrow into flight,
a spire pricks the horizon: Steeple Claydon,
a country lane leads into the beckoning distance
and we move on through pastoral Buckinghamshire:
Swanbourne and a touzled wood of oaks,
rooks foraging among the furrows,
sun-glitter on water, the February heat-haze,
catkins bursting, pear-blossom, blackthorn, prunus in
    flower,
the serrated ridge of pine-woods:
a lyric thrush calls the little place alive
where the train stops, nameless, unknown:

Gamlingay and the music of a tractor in the afternoon,
a yew-tree nods its seeding plumes over the country
     platform,
a horse ploughing in the distance the rich black earth
(Is my team ploughing, that I was used to drive
And hear the harness jingle when I was man alive?)
So passes the commerce of the fields,
So passes the cortège of the train,
Bearing these fragile fruits
Of momentary happiness.

Evening in Wartime

The quiet evening, the throats of birds
That sing, and on my lips the words
I would use if you were with me now.
Blackthorn is out upon the bough.

Two aircraft return, where went out three,
Over the wood that leads to the sea.
The road is white and bare as a bone:
I walk along it now alone.

In the green hedge the secret lights
Of innumerable violets;
The haystacks ruffled by the gale;
In the bay a solitary sail.

Dandelion clocks mid the flowers
Stand up erect to tell the hours;
As if there were need of their alert:
Your absence writes it in the heart.

Duporth Lodge

At Duporth Lodge I stand and wait
   For revelation from the skies,
Remembering another night
   Your presence made a Paradise.

The stars shine through a screen of trees,
   The house stands black and sinister,
Rising from dark shrubberies:
   Above the roof, a jewelled star.

A distant searchlight flicks the sky,
   Westward the planet suspended low
Hangs in a haze above the rick;
   There Orion points his bow.

Some animal cries—a cry of fear;
   The chime strikes clear from over the hill;
Beyond the wood, the sound of the sea
   Lapses and sighs. The wind is chill.

At the cross-roads alone I stand and wait:
   Nothing stirs save the night-birds' cries;
The listening earth turns on, and I
   One with the movement of stars and skies.

Bus-ride

The bus goes up the valley road
   With mounds of gorse on either hand
That burn and blaze amid the brake
   And clothe with fire the hills of sand.

Sunlight on a grey stone house,
   The ivies glitter and catch the light;
The sparse and scattered Cornish trees
   Announce Carthew, and now the white

L   145

Claypits on the pock-marked moor:
  We pass the granite cottages,
The gardens with a shrub in flower,
  The rude and honest villages,

Treverbyn, Roche and Stenalees:
  We mark across the open moor,
Sunshine and shadow on the flank,
  The rhinoceros of Helman Tor.

A lane leads to Tremodret farm—
  Name of ill omen for Arthur's kin;
The old toll-house of Lockingate,
  The chess-board fields are brown and green.

White drifts of blackthorn fringe the road
  That winds and swerves among the hills,
The black ploughed earth, Lanivet tower,
  The gulls afloat on inland pools.

How different a countryside
  From where I seem to see you still:
The water meadows of the Stour,
  Constable's ford and Flatford Mill.

The Gribbin:
Palm Sunday, 1943

Above the port a ship's balloon
  Plunges blindly like a fish,
Noses the air a moment, then
  Dives and with a sudden rush

Rides supreme above the bay—
  A silver sphere, superb and still—
Turns a fin and glides away,
  Sinks and dips beneath the hill.

146

Fragile and rosy in evening light,
    Behind, the slender headland lies,
The landmark loved of mariners
    Catches the last glow in the skies.

In the fields the birds are sweet,
    The bay lies blue and quiet now;
The purple acres are all smooth,
    The harrow following the plough.

Beyond the seas, in other fields,
    So many lads are sleeping still:
Your image fills me with unease,
    And yet I recognise your will.

The risen moon looks down serene
    Upon this Easter loveliness;
The silver fish carries his cargo:
    My fragmentary happiness.

Easter Day, 1943

In the apple orchard I hear the bells
    Ring once more for Easter-tide,
The wind sings softly in the pines
    To celebrate the Crucified

Who now this day has conquered death
    And put on new life with the spring;
The splendid seagulls sail the sky,
    While over the hill the church bells ring.

They are the church bells of my youth,
    Hearing them disturbs the heart:
I see again the country lad
    On Easter Day, solemn and smart

In Sunday suit, walk down the lane
    To sing with the others in the choir
'Jesus Christ is risen today',
    The voices rising high and higher.

The church smells sweet of Easter flowers,
    The altar frontal is of white;
There is an air of festival,
    The familiar faces are glad and bright.

Yet where are they now, the people I knew?
    (As I walk the orchard, the petals drop.)
Many have gone their different ways,
    But most of them have fallen on sleep;

And I a man much changed by time,
    Alone with my passion and my pride,
Whose heart the church bells still can touch
    With the tenderness of Easter-tide.

Easter Moon

Over the headland the moon like a ghost,
Rose-flushed and full and threatening,
Rises like a face out of the past:
A reproach: an orb perfect and yellowing
That grows like terror or fear,
Swims clear, rises into the sky,
Looks me full in the face
Across the salt space of the bay.
The leaves and flowers are frightened;
They shiver and twist in the wind
Like souls that are afraid
And look for somewhere to hide in.
The moon looks in at the window:
The man looks at the moon,

Becomes aware of the moon's indifference,
Her sad determined journeying,
The blue of the sea now deepening,
The gold of the moon more metallic, more remote.
O world without passion, without remorse or pity,
I see your meaning:
You prophesy the determined way,
Friendless, unaccompanied, alone.
You fill the world with your cold light,
A bitter wind blows about the earth:
Yet I am not afraid.

Greta Bridge

I walk in a dream beside the Tees,
   The birds sing loud on either hand,
The banks are white and blue with flowers:
   There is happiness in all the land.

Beneath the bridge the ledges of rock
   Are lit by sunlight through the leaves,
And up and down the peat-brown river
   The busy birds pursue their loves.

From Abbey Bridge to Greta Bridge
   I walk along the banks and braes,
Happy as they with the thought of you,
   Content to be with you these glad days.

A water wagtail over the stream
   Dips and starts and dives and soars;
The woods are white with hawthorn sprays,
   From tented leaves the birdsong pours.

With stitchwort, campion, forget-me-not,
    The ways are white and red and blue;
I pause and stooping pick a sprig
    Of wild forget-me-not for you.

My dream is made of light and leaves,
    Of maytime white among the trees,
The plover's call, the thought of you,
    The sounding waters of the Tees.

Summer Evening

At this mid moment of the evening
I miss you most. Quiet descends upon the garden
Where a little rising wind flutters the chestnuts,
Stirs their tresses, lifts their fronds,
Opening what green glooms within,
Inviting, disturbing, holding up the heart
Of him who sits with Froissart open on his knee,
Looking out of the summer window
To hear the brazen tongues of the clocks
Strike nine—the time when you would come
To inhabit the other chair drawn up to the fireside.
Voices are gay in the gardens of Oxford,
Friendly steps crunch the gravel on the path
On the way to a hospitable call.
But not for me those steps, the cries of the girls
In the street. I am a man dedicated
To being alone, for ever waiting, listening,
The sensibilities sharpened by this condition,
The state of being separate from whom I love:
Nourishing my difference,
Never wholly where I am or what I would most gladly
    be.

IV: Poems of War and Peace

In the Train, Going through Berkshire

Evening and the shadows fall
over the level plains of Berkshire;
the chalk hills and the charlock
mingle in the golden haze that lights
hedges and furrows from the west.
Spring is declared
in the ripening forms of the chestnuts
and in the green veils that surround the elms,
in the young corn and the burst of birdsong
where the train halts at a wayside station,
and in our hearts, the hearts of travellers
that travel each to his destination,
the soldier, the airman,
the contented lovers nuzzling each other,
the old man sleeping in his sunny corner,
each one to his private probable fate.

Cueillir des Roses: July 1941

Never have I known till now
Such sense of joy in life,
The days that pass not idly by
But full of purposeful activity
And happy contentment like a bee
That visits in the summer garden,
The drunk and sleepy flowers weighs down,
Passing from one to another all the day
In the hot sun. The violated flowers,
Fluttered by the butterflies,
Raped by the bees, now sway
This way and that under their thrust,

Hang their heads in ecstasy
At their embrace; then, the moment over,
Recover their primal chastity
Until their next lover,
The next ravisher of their beauty,
Seeking their secret liquids,
Passes by.
So I
Pursue the passing moment,
Suck its sweet hidden liquors,
Until the evening comes,
And satisfied, replete
With work and pleasure
Steal happily to bed
And straightway fall asleep,
Nor ever wake to the noises of the night
Nor notice in the half-light
The shuttered flowers that spill
Their scents upon my window-sill
O, that such a happy state
Had greater certainty,
And like the flowers
Did not depend
From day to day,
And with the hours,
On what is passing in the world
        or is to be.

The Man among the Corn

The mingled oats and barley in the field,
The feathery grasses at my feet,
The varied movement of wind in corn,
The night-wind blowing in the trees,
The melancholy ashes that speak of rain,
The church-clock of my childhood
Knocks at my unrepentant heart,

Touches the waiting mood to tears:
A door opens on the furtive latch
To watch the broken solitary man
March up and down the path among the corn.

On the Road to Trenarren

The coloured evening, blue and rose and white,
The clouds drift onward to the sea:
Far out in the bay the M.T.Bs manoeuvre,
The Catalinas of Coastal Command
Homeward come.
There is a sweet scent in the air,
The undergrowth of Penrice Wood,
Earth, roots, fern, woodbine
All combine
To make this nostalgic scent of home.
The barley field looks to the sea,
Cape upon cape in perspective
Peers over the hedge;
Across the bands of colour
The moon raises a white signal.
Over the sequestered house the owls begin.
In the strange light
The shorn sheep are very white;
The yellow ragwort drains colour from the moon.
A sheep's cough alarms the landscape,
The crescent moon hangs still.
My feet find the hardened track under the turf
Trodden by the primitive people my forbears
Going from camp to cliff-camp.
I enter now the sunken lane
Between rampart and rampart,
A soft touch on the spine, light as a feather,
Cold as the hand of a dead man,
And now I come to the Field of the Dead,
Ploughed and sown.

Cornish Landscape

The rich red of evening sun on the harrowed field,
The chittering of birds,
The insistent drone of planes out at sea,
The scolding rooks,
The colder tones of the water:
What is there in a Cornish hedge,
The broken herring-bone pattern of stones,
The gorse, the ragged rick,
The way the little elms are,
Sea-bent, sea-shorn,
That so affects the heart?

Above Polrudden*

The field of clover sloping to the sea,
The white sail of a gull dipping into the blue,
Clouds chasing across the cliffs of Lantivet bay,
The lizard neck of Black Head at Trenarren,
The memory of John Polrudden of Polrudden taken away
By the French in the time of King Harry—
His deserted house standing forlorn
Among a few shorn trees—
The ceaseless sound of planes far out in the Channel,
Of a tractor inland harrowing the ground,
The boom of a bee, the sweet puffs of autumn wind
In the hedge, among brambles and bracken and sloes,
The dazzle of white light on the sandburrows,
The loveliness of autumn, blue sea and dipping birds,
Harrow and plough, sweet wind and voices
Accentuate, not still, the trouble of my heart.

* This place-name is pronounced Polrédd'n, with the accent on the
second syllable.

November Ploughing

The whole bay brimming with the silent sea,
The call of a curlew, the creaking of a plough,
A black and satin plane slides suddenly over
Wheeling to the coast,
The smell of November in the air,
The mould, the dead brambles, the year over,
In the distance the familiar cone
Of Rame Head, so known
To Drake and Hawkins and Frobisher
And all those long-dead seafaring men
Outward bound to the Spanish Main,
Or homeward driving with a merry gale
Of spring or autumn centuries ago.
Yet still the coast they'd know
And find it only strange that other men
Should claim priority in places that were theirs.

The red stain of autumn on the upper slopes,
The noises of afternoon, trees, plane, gulls,
Rising and falling to a subdued murmur,
The vivid red of leaves, of herb robert,
The flower dead, the corrugated rocks,
Skin of rhinoceros or mastodon,
The cleft coves cloven by evening shadow,
The winterblue wind when the sun goes down,
Insinuating in the window-seams,
Makes clear and poignant the lines of the landscape
Like a picture of one's childhood, exposed, irrevocable.

February Evening near
Castle Gotha*

The rooks of Trenarren cawing at home-coming,
A winter robin in the brush,
The finger of doom upon the Gribbin;
Beyond, in the evening mist,
The pyramid of Rame Head,
Drake's headland, on so many voyages
Rounded, going out or coming home;
The horses graze at edge of cliff
Silhouetted against the Channel,
Where those other silhouettes,
The *Scharnhorst* and the *Gneisenau,*
So lately passed.
A seagull cries above the green hollow,
A ribbon of wake stretches across the bay
To Trenarren where I stand:
A black speck appears above the surface—
For a moment I think the head of that drowned lad
Met by chance and become my friend.
The evening light, candid and sad,
Depicts the cormorant on the wing.

* Means in Cornish the 'old camp'.

At the Cross-roads by Duporth

It is the hour of twilight, when the day's work is over:
I stand at the dip in the road, a flittering bat overhead,
A diminutive frog crosses rapidly at my feet,
In my ears the drowsy night cries of the gulls,
The particular sound of the sea splaying up over the
    beach.
Here is the crushed tobacco scent of new-mown hay.
Now I enter the region of honeysuckle,
The smell of the wood, the corn and things growing:

In my mind the thought of Jack at sea,
Harry in India, and Stephen far away
At camp on the Yorkshire moors.
There is the dark entry to Duporth:
The road leads down to the outer wood
Where Christopher played as a child,
Who now plays a more dangerous game in Sicily.
At the cross-roads, the lowered signpost
With wings removed, for this is war-time.
Beneath me, the valley extends to the town
With which I can even be in love
At this hour, the busy tongues stilled in sleep.
The young oaks droop their plumes,
The soft summer rain touches my brow with kindness,
Around me the plumed and decorated emptiness,
The formal framework of my chosen life.

Richmond in Yorkshire

Late light upon the roofs of Richmond,
  The glistening streets at end of day,
The peat-brown river, the Castle walls:
  I see them still though far away.

The clatter of feet on the cobbled square
  Comes to an end as night draws on;
The soldiers cross the fields to the camp
  Two by two, then one by one.

The belated sweets of the northern spring
  Accompany their unheeding step:
The glimmering hawthorn, the buttercups shut—
  The song of planes to soothe their sleep.

Venus hangs over the western hill,
  The road to Hudswell and Catterick;
A light in a cottage, the black-out drawn,
  The trees are dark by Waitwith beck.

And here I say goodbye to you,
    Turn back alone to the darkening town;
Your hurrying figure mounts the hill,
    By the plantations and over the down.

The Castle's Norman magnificence
    Confronts me now across the dale;
The resounding noise of rushing waters;
    Owls hoot in the valley of the Swale.

Your image makes these places live,
    Waitwith Bank and Holly Hill;
Though far away from them and you,
    I see them still, I see them still.

Looking North

I look out upon the leafless trees of the park
Your reflective eyes have often rested on,
Remembering the play that has disturbed my heart,
Compelled my mind and rendered my imagination
Susceptible, full of a nameless fear.
Darkness descends and with it the dusky rain,
The rain drifts like smoke across the grove,
A strange, autumnal light lights up the stone,
Gleams in the north to remind me I am alone.
The air is full of living noises, the sad
Swaying and splaying of the trees together,
Opening and shutting their branches like a fan,
The waters at the meeting of the rivers,
The weir, visible from your window, the rain.
I am driven to take shelter, your room not yours:
Behind the shut door, another occupant,
Voices, tea-time, the gay laugh of a girl.
I lean my head against a pillar of stone,
The scrannel cry of leaves upon the pavement
Your footsteps knew, the cloister that contained your life.

At Iffley: March 7, 1944

The red house, the grey and the white,
The leaning figures of the silver birches
Like Baucis and Philemon,
The music of the weir, the planes, the birds,
The purple catkins of the alders:
This perfect moment of contented afternoon,
Blue skies above the domestic English scene—
Yet what disturbs the heart?
The dimpled, dappled river,
Crimpled by the wind,
Moves swiftly onward to the sea:
It is my life the river bears away
And all the temporal part of me.

Before D-Day

The wind thundering in the vacant air
Whips the black January waters
Where skiffs skim and a prim eight goes by
Reminding me of the year when you were here.
In the distant sky the rumour of planes, vibrant
And strong, the threat to all that we hold dear.
There is the Norman tower among the trees,
The village, lawns, river villas, so many
Disjecta membra of the Victorian peace.
(Dick dead, Christopher wounded and ill.)
Smoke goes up from a cottage that might be
An illustration for *Alice in Wonderland*,
Two little girls astride the shut lock gate.
On the horizon the dreaming spires of Arnold,
A shaft of light on Magdalen, the memory
Of Clough, the scholar on the hills, the Tree.
Now our world is quivering on the brink
Of what's to come, our private universe
In suspense, under threat, and all that I can think
Of now, my fears for you, my fears for you.

These many days I have lived in apprehension
As the climacteric of the war draws on
And the hour comes when fellows are flung,
But flesh and blood, from barge and boat against
The immutable barrier of a defended coast.
The clever offer philosophic words
Of consolation that do not console.
Is it not better, they say, that a young man should
Fall instantaneously with no pain
In the moment of his perfection, before years bring
Disappointment of early hopes, the coarsening
Of fibre, the ineluctable decay
Of eye and hand, strong arm mind and limb,
Or probable mediocrity of fate,
The splendid spring over and nothing come?

These sentiments I find inhuman, quite
Contrary to common men's experience,
With whom joy in life continues, delight
In the affections of the family,
In watching children grow and plants and things
In the garden, who find an easy contentment
Like the fruits and flowers that fulfil their time
And are not destroyed, cut down before their prime.
For others more various fulfilment waits
Of what plans and projects to be carried out,
The ripened harvest of the darling years.
'When I have fears that I may cease to be':
There is no greater agony of mind
To bear, a contingent sentence. And then the loss
To the world of men who should have held their place
In counting-house and office, in fields and pastures
Of the countryside, in northern wolds and dales,
In little scattered farms on western hills,
In folds of the downs where Bredon looks to Wales,
Or the rich mill-houses of East Anglia:
Following there in the footsteps of their fathers,
Strong of arm and thigh, breeding up

Sons and daughters in their turn so that
The generation of the world continue.
All is but loss that they should be gone from us.
There are no philosophic consolations
That can console for the loss of those kind eyes,
The shy and deprecatory smile, modest
As a girl's, the vacant chair drawn up in vain
To the fireside as in days when you were here.

Fear holds my heart, touches my heart
With soft and delicate moth-like touches. I hear
In the mind the marching pendulum of the clock,
Alternating joy and apprehension.
Perhaps I have loved too much, and that invites
Fate upon too great a happiness?
A hundred times a day I touch the wood
Of the Holy Cross for your safety, all that remains
Of prayer in a sombre, unbelieving age.

Redeem the time! if only one might recall
The time, not long, when you came over the cliffs,
Along the path from Crinnis to Charlestown,
The scented pine-woods, needles soft under foot,
The gulls for ever wheeling and crying, the sea,
At the turn of the road the great dead tree.
The war that has divided so many lives
Has kept us apart in the ripening of love.
I have almost become used to your absence
Who should be here to correct my melancholy,
Enjoy the fruits of natural harmony,
Of music and compatible experience,
Concord of taste and temperament.

I shut the shutters upon the heroic song
Of that brave man who nursed his loneliness
In the interior island of deafness and solitude,
Like a blind Milton or blind Maionides,
Bringing forth from the iron rock what sweet,

What living fountains of water, the waters of comfort
To refresh the parched and quivering souls of them
Who have given too great hostages of love
To time and chance, devouring circumstance.
Hark now! in that pure language without words
The heroic, disembodied spirit bids us
Have courage, gay endurance that flowers in faith,
Like a bird singing from a furthermost point of land
Clear and loud in the storm of wind and wave—
Faith in each other and in our threatened love.

Moment of Waiting

This moment of summer afternoon,
of flowers and leaves and voices on the lawn,
the tall chestnuts stand up like stiff brocades,
move and lapse richly in the wind;
a mingle-mangle of bells on the outskirts of the city
explore the familiar chords of the heart.
All is happiness and gaiety.
Lakes of blue sky break through the greenery,
the Judas tree is in full flower,
the colour of blood.
Who would believe it was two years since
that Sunday in June
upon the water, the tunnels of greenery
and birdsong and happiness,
the water lapping the boat,
time running off the blade of the oar?

There was no staying that moment of perfection:
a year ago you were at Catterick,
the cobbled square at Richmond with its crowded
        humanity,
the tramp of soldiers, the sudden quiet
when evening descends and the groups

make their way along the flower-lit lanes
with humorous obscenity back to camp.
Now through the lucid light of leaves and flowers
another vision lours, the future that frightens me.
I cannot bear the moment of waiting.
Where are you now, who should be here
among your companions,
sharing the happiness of the hour,
a familiar voice among the voices on the lawn,
or calling in the darkness up the stairs?
Only a wind stirs the laden branches
punctuating the emptiness of so much
beauty without love.

Spring 1944

The trees pass like puffs of spindrift
  and the flowering, feathered rushes;
  the strings of gliders parallel the train
  two by two upon their course, then turn away
  over the horizon accented by a spire
  like the churches of the Pas de Calais:
  O you, who are ever in my thoughts,
  what to me are the loveliness of the landscape,
  mirrored skies in the level canals,
  the sunglitter dancing like fish upon the water,
  the waiting horses in sunny farmyards,
  the rides through tasselled woodland,
  vistas of hope and gaiety and spring—
  what are they all when every moment
  brings you nearer to danger
  and me to the precipice between
  apprehensive happiness and certain misery?
The white swans stand upon the river bank
  and preen themselves in the sun,
  glad in the moment, while you ride upward

to the crest of your wave.
I hold my heart and fascinated watch
lest the wave topple over,
my swan borne down,
the sun gone out.

Fourth Sunday in Lent, 1944

O you that stand undaunted in danger,
Every day that passes is a prayer for you:
The spring flowers breathe for you,
Dance in the wind that blows from the sea,
The soft, south wind that blows from France:
The sun is on the headland,
The finger of God that points
Safety for mariners,
Safety now I pray for you,
Your spirit present in the white seagulls
That pass like butterflies across the painted bay.

Here is emptiness:
The coloured skies enfold the land,
The murmured music in the trees
Lapses and runs and sighs;
The spring sun prints their screen
Upon the dun, dried furrows:
And all is nothing without you.
I pray I may not have to learn
To live my life again
Without your spirit to sustain:
Give me faith, I pray, faith
Even against death.

Summer Spell: June 1944

The scented gardens of Oxford in summer
Speak of your absence who are now in danger:

The ceaseless procession of planes in the sky
Goes over to the beaches of Normandy.

In Cheney Lane the acacias in flower
Let drop their petals on the honeyed air.

Here in the cathedral aisle of trees
The nostalgic sun makes lattices,

Lets through the flickering memories
Of fragmentary happiness.

So full of planes the crowded air
That phantom flesh can hardly bear:

These are the shadows over our lives
That threaten to sever our eager loves:

On all we do and are and have
A spell laid on us from the grave.

Now is it the Time

The angel stands on guard at the gate,
The angel with the sword, the Angel of War:
No entrance now to that lost Paradise.
Within, the blood-red hawthorn hangs over the lake,
The fallen petals sprinkle the tree of the Rood,
The snowdrifts of white may mounded high
In the lush and lovely green of English meadows.
Now is it high summer,

The nightmare summer of my fears.
Now is it the time of June daisies, buttercups and clover.
See! I have got by the keeper at the gate:
I walk in those walks we once frequented,
The rumour of the world outside prevented,
And we for a moment secure and unafraid,
Time stayed. But only for an hour.
Now the wind rises, rages in the trees—
All the green world shakes and sways—
Makes it to speak with a hundred warning cries,
The tongueless sibilant voices of the lost,
Scatters a thousand petals on the waterways:
And I am here alone, accompanied by a ghost.

The Hour of Sleep

Now that I am home again
What do I notice? Chiefly the moon
That from Duporth hill looks down
Upon my garden of roses and
The surrounding seas of sleeping corn:
Silence and stillness, the silence of sleep.
After the unceasing noise of planes
Going and coming, filling the skies,
The pulse of engines, the beating of the heart,
Not even the beating of birds' wings,
Nor the flowers' alert: they are in deep
Sleep. Only the murmuring cries
Of distant gulls in echoing coves
On the coast. Now the pink foxgloves
Nod sleepily in a little wind.
Over the lip of wall the green waves
Of landscape reach out, fold on fold,
To the headland and the slumbering sea.
Yet I cannot forget that beyond
The silence and stillness, the contentment

168

Of moon, young corn, and nodding flowers,
Battle rages in Normandy.
All the landscape holds its breath:
For many this hour of sleep is the hour of death.

Castle Gotha

I have seen it sleeping
  its winter sleep in the sun
  the clustered trees motionless
  the sheep still as monuments
  the pillared shadows pointing up
  the seaward slope of cliff
And everything so still
  as if time moves not
  and this has always been
  as if one dares not breathe
  for fear of breaking the spell
  that lies on all the place—
And then a plane passes over out to sea
Breaking the absorbed sleep of centuries.
I hear the soft and sibilant licking of the sea
  the cry of farmyard gleanies and the gulls.
And there beyond, my native landscape see
  the mounded burrows of white sand
  the corrugated moor
    tumbling from the land
    downwards to the sea.

Two Summers

Syringa, columbine, delphinium
Light with white and purple-gold and blue
The verdant alley-ways that I walk through
Now that the high midsummer pomps have come.

Dog-rose, honeysuckle, our Lady's lace
Strew with country scents the sunken lane;
But little they alleviate the pain
Of remembering here that sweet surprised embrace.

This was the place. At the familiar gate
That looks over all the bay I turn to see
Between us now the salt estranging sea
In which time drowns. Alone I stand and wait.

The Owl

Silently, softly,
With unhurried, moth-white wings
The visiting owl voyages over the cornfield
At the oncoming of night:
The wings but skim the blades of wheat,
Making no noise. So Death comes
To the small creatures that wait.

In the mirror I catch sight as I pass
Of the white owl-like face
Of the sick man, with great dark eyes
Looking out of the glass.

This is the nocturnal hour
When predatory fears
Put forth their power.

The Conjured Spirit

Sitting in the garden this evening of July,
The secateurs dropped on the grass verge,
The bright blood of carnations spilling over the border,
The church bells come to me in the wind,

And like a drowning man I see my past go by:
The lonely boy, ambitious and proud,
Then the sick man, now the conjured spirit.
A transitory gleam lights up the trees,
The wind blows coolly in the barley,
The ants on the pavement are very busy.
A power-cable runs a gap through the beeches—
If it should break, snap, coil like a snake
About me, there'd straightway be an end.
The wind blows for rain. A chill wind
Blows in my heart, the wind of absence,
Loneliness, this Sunday evening of high summer
That yet is autumnal. The years go by
And you away, living another life,
Becoming someone perhaps whom I know not,
Who knows not me, with affections, persuasions
Of your own, in which I do not count,
The circle formed, the closed circle of experience
Shared, of common danger, of loves and likes,
Life lived together at its highest moment,
The unforgettable hour, the bond of blood,
The sacrament of death: and I outside,
For ever outside of life and love.

In Memory: Adam von Trott

The raging sun-struck sea explodes
In beauty round the rocks.
Who could have known when I knew you first
Of such a fate in store for you,
Laid upon that grave and lovely head?
I look up at the house you knew,
Grey among the stripped autumnal trees;
Down upon the shore
The spring-tide flows up to the purple cliffs.
The spring-tide of your life already over,

171

I meditate upon it here alone,
Unsure what part I had in your strange fate.
The white horses march across the bay,
The targets bob up and down like buoys.
There is Duporth, here the sacrificial grove,
Here on the headland I saw the Ship of Death.
Now you over the sea,
The hangman's noose about your neck,
Sleep soundly in a traitor's grave.

Leaving Cornwall: Autumn 1944

The bent bulrushes and late valerian
Fringe the stagnant waters here by Par.
We pass the marish wastes, the mundic dumps
Of disused copper mines, Fowey Consols
An ochre stain along the clean sky-line.
Now comes Lantyan, the red farm in the bowl,
Nursing its memories of Tristram and Mark,
While I recall the sulphur smear of spring
Primroses on the sheer Lostwithiel slope.
The woods cut down, you hear the owl-hoot of the train
In the hollow valley towards Boconnoc park.
A solitary horse crops on the bare
Shoulder of a hill whence the trees have gone;
In the deep valley bottom, the darkling Fowey.
Along the embankment the quick shadow-show
Of sun shuttles in and out again.
In the carriage I note the medieval faces:
An old woman with a countenance
Out of Breughel or Dürer or Jerome Bosch,
The skin wrinkled, innumerably creased,
With eyes sunken, eyes that have seen too much,
Heavy-lidded, and infinitely tired;
The corporal in the R.A.F. with plain
Blunt face of a peasant in painted window; the sailor

That might have come out of Chaucer, rubicund,
Cheerful—shipman of Dartmouth.

                                        And I have come
Out of Cornwall, out of the kingdom of *cliché*,
Out of the region of misunderstanding, out
Of the dark realm of suspicion and misapprehension,
The nerves held taut as if for a blow, from the eyes
That watch for an opportunity, away
From it all into the broad Devon day,
And I am free. Yet each step that takes me away
I see these evidences that I am bound,
Bone of my bone, flesh of my flesh, eye
Of my eye, one with the land that has denied me:
I am the stone the builders have rejected,
I am the son my people would not have.
Yet the roots of the trees are rooted in my heart,
The little declivities and streams that run,
Run in my veins and in my blood. This earth
I breathe in my nostrils and that gave me birth
Will one day stop my ears and mouth, the stones
With their vivid orange stains are my very bones,
The wires along the loved familiar roads
The fibres of my body, the nerves of my eyes.

My heart a stone, my will locked in a vice,
My face set, though tears besiege the eyes,
I pass over the bridge that divides me from my people:
Now I can breathe in the pure air of Devon—
Sun shines over the landscape and in my heart—
The tension over, the strung will relaxed,
And I become anonymous and free!

The Parting

Tonight as I sit by my fire, solitary in Oxford,
I hear the cry of my people three hundred miles away,
Saying—'Do not turn away from us wholly,
Do not desert us utterly'.
I see the faces in the flames turned to me,
Pathetic, beseeching. I recall the fisherman
Painting his boat in harbour, down by the quay,
Looking up and saying, gently, reproachfully,
'You don't come down to see us much nowadays'.
And I turned away, feeling I had deserted them,
Tears in my throat so that I could not speak
Until I found words of pride
To hide the sensitive place and said
'There is a limit to what one can stand, you know',
And was surprised to see
He understood perfectly and complained
No more, but turned to his work,
Accepting the fact.
                            I never should have thought
I should so feel the parting: perhaps the place—
The difficult fishing-village with the mercurial temper,
Elusive as a seagull, electric as an eel,
Shifting like the tides and currents at the door,
Impossible to grasp, and yet with warmth
Of heart, of interest and vivacity,
Like the gleam of sun on the silver bellies
Of fish upon the quay.
For days those words rang in my mind
Like the knell of a bell-buoy at sea:
'Too late, too late for me': a hurt irreparable
In the inmost recesses of consciousness,
The wound opening inwards,
The spirit too proud to admit an injury,
Incessantly grazed and torn again
By the insensitive, the enemy that hates

174

Difference, quality that escapes submission
To common complacency, impure hypocrisy—
That would annihilate what is uncommon,
Challenging their meanness, their shibboleths
With something electric and alive, a vibrancy
That offers not a new Heaven and a new Earth
But life, more life and light—
To be rejected.
To be rejected by what one loves is not
Pleasant. The conjured spirit returns
Rejection with contempt, defeat with scorn,
Misunderstanding with contumely:
Never raising a finger to put what's wrong
Right. Rewarding envy
With bitterness, the corrosive acid
That eats into the secret places of the heart,
Instructs the instinctive cunning where to hurt
Most, where to return with interest
An eye for an eye, a tooth for a tooth.
To what end?
That the proud spirit may lay up its treasures
In the locked and barred tower of solitariness,
Sterile, aloof, nursing its own resentment;
And that my people, who are flesh of my flesh,
Bone of my bone, whose every impulse is
Felt in the blood and felt along the heart,
May be left without their natural leader
To worship false gods of numb respectability,
Of outward form and inner insincerity,
Tribute to whited sepulchres, the lie in the soul.

For a moment in the firelight three hundred miles away
I saw them in a different mood,
Themselves rejected, despised, contemned—
For a moment would yield, the wound staunch,
Look upon them once more with kindness,
Let the healing waters of forgiveness flow,

175

Turn back the way to natural affection
And mutual friendliness. Or so I thought.
And then the morning came, and then I knew
I would not, but let the tale unfold
To its appointed end.

January Snow

O hear, in the still January air,
The church bells ringing over the snow,
And come and walk with me now
In the places where we used to go.
Down the frost-white street and in at the gate.
In the red-berried crategus a blackbird fidgets,
Pipes across the grove a note of spring,
To which my heart responds that you may come.
(The buds already tip the branches with sweet gum.)
The bellies of the trees are stroked with snow:
Here Addison sedately walked,
An undergraduate prim, precise,
And made his verse with regular stance and beat.
In the meadows, a crow like cassocked parson
Considers with surprise this world of white,
Prods with distaste his gold beak in the snow.
The bushes wear aprons,
The squirrels play hide and seek in the trees.
And here, at Dover pier,
The gay and gallant cavalier
Kept watch and ward over the Cher.
I note the reflections of snow upon stone
Lemon-gold and winter-green, the colour of aconite,
Observe the intricate threads of birds' feet.
(Tread softly: in the grove the fawns lie sleeping.)
And so, back to the red glory of the crategus
All aglow in this white and water world,
Standing sentinel at the bridge till your return.

Spring in the Walks

The daffodils blow in the April walks,
  And blue squills burn their delicate lights,
Even the chestnuts burst their buds:
  But you are away from these delights.

The scented wind, fragrant like musk,
  Blows from the twin-branched balsam-tree,
Lays an enchantment upon the lips,
  Stirs the heart so poignantly:

For this is the season, the year at the spring,
  When first you left these haunted ways;
The bells call for you over the meadows,
  But you have been absent these many days.

An evening wind lifts the dead leaves
  Of last year left upon the bough;
A sudden fear invades my heart—
  O would that you were beside me now!

But you are of those in bond to danger,
  Dedicated, changed, unfree;
On shoulder and breast the badge of duty,
  Sealed to service and loyalty.

The almond tree flowers for you in vain,
  In vain the wind-flowers swing their lights,
Or balsam poplar showers its scents—
  Now you are away from these delights.

President Roosevelt

Here in the Field of the Dead that looks to the sea,
The blue and smouldering western seas in spring,
The hedgerows white as for a bridal day
With blackthorn, stitchwort and wild strawberry,
I remember the man who has gone from the earth.
Here in this remote far tongue of land
Whence our forefathers sailed for America
Grief comes to us out of the new world they found.
The familiar voice, resonant and strong,
That made him a friend at every fireside
Here in this little land, thousands of miles
Away from where he lived and worked and died,
The voice that brought courage out of despair,
Out of defeat gave assurance of victory,
Is stilled at last. He is gathered to his own,
A prince of his people, his place is with the great
Ones of the past: the cool and lofty spirit
Of the First President, founder of the state;
The warm and infinitely human soul
Of Lincoln, the depths of those prophetic eyes,
Those pools that mirrored all man's tragedy.
Tonight he lies with the kings of thought and action,
Removed from all clamorous aspersion,
All questionings done and his account shut up.
The heart that pulsed with human sympathy
Is stopped for ever. Yet in this hour of grief
We celebrate with pride all that man's life
Can achieve, the spirit's victory over the body,
The crippled limbs, the indomitable will,
The gift of gaiety surmounting pain,
The lonely dedication to the end.
A star has fallen from the western sky
That lit our lives and lent us hope to be:
Now all is still, save for the birds that cry
And in the night the sighing of the sea.

Lent, 1946

Lent is the time of waiting, and I wait
Here in the garden, here in the grove
Where the fallow deer leap,
Perform their ritual courses,
Coursing in and out the shadows of the glade.
All things germinate:
The almond-tree begins to flower,
And by the water-side
The tadpole crocuses
Leap out of the ground:
So many drops of sperm
Ejaculated out of the spawn
Wherein the new life stirs;
Here the phallic beauty of the hyacinth,
Erect and still, yet leaning to the sun.
The birds prick the air with song,
The bells yammer from the latticed tower.
Under the soil a million seeds now stir;
In me the seeds of hope begin to spring,
The days of waiting move onward to their end.

All the Birds of Oxfordshire

All the birds of Oxfordshire
Are singing 'You will soon be here'.

Mnemonic noises of the night,
The distant surges of the street,
The water rushing from the weir,
Remind me you will soon be here.

The willow throws her shawl around,
Fringes falling to the ground.
The candles of the crocuses,
The frilled and prinked anemones

179

Light with variegated hues,
Under the darker green of yews,
The woodland path where soon you'll be
Walking once again with me.

Over the bridge, a grinding gear
Sounds like music to the ear
Across the grove, where bells are ringing
And all the birds already singing
Wildly that you will soon be here.

On Richard Wilson's
'Lake of Narni'

The tops of the pines are like a balloon
   Floating in the Italian sky:
An emerald bubble that seems to move
   And yet is held eternally.

To left, the pillared cypresses
   Stand on guard above the stream,
Whose placid surface mirrors a wood
   Where all is dark as in a dream.

The roadway winds around to the right,
   On the bluff a ruined tower;
The lake is bathed in golden light,
   Magic in this surrendered hour.

At the foot of the trees, a peasant troop
   Of gay and coloured figures lie,
Taking their delightful ease
   Under the mellow April sky.

Here in the foreground look at these:
   A contadino leans on his crook,
Takes the hand of his girl in his:
   So they stand and exchange a look

That lasts for ever. O moving light,
    Liquid and living on mountain and stream,
On country boy and girl that stand
    In the green landscape of a dream:

Stillness and innocent and peace:
    So let them stand, so let them be,
So let the loving light suffuse
    The Italian sky eternally.

Corpus Garden

Maytime's come in Corpus garden
As in a green, leaf-shadowed room,
With wallflowers and forget-me-nots,
Auriculas and golden broom.

The young men who've returned from war
Play at bowls in the level sun:
The dull woods, knocking against each other,
Resound. And now the play is done.

A canon's ducks quack over the wall,
Echo their reverend owner's words;
Blood-red peonies light the border,
And all the trees are alive with birds.

A little wind now lifts the leaves
And whispering lets them fall again;
A lyric thrush pours out his song;
Columbines, lupins just begin.

Turning round I see your window
Wide-open, cool and summery;
Beneath the sill wistaria droops,
Hanging like vines of Italy.

The window opens a dead mouth
Into the darkness of a tomb:
How well I knew in former years
Its green and friendly summer gloom.

Maytime's come in Corpus garden—
But you have not survived your war,
Who lie with Shelley and Trelawny
Under a cold indifferent star.

Alfoxden

(To Jack Simmons)

Along the roads of Somerset
   We walk, my friend and I,
To Alfoxden from Nether Stowey
   Beneath the April sky.

The hedges starred with primroses,
   The woods with hollies gleam,
The world wakes out of winter sleep—
   Yet we move in a dream.

Two other friends there are that walk
   Out of an earlier time,
Who often came this way together
   And heard the self-same chime

From all the birds that haunt the coverts
   And all the woodland rides.
Noon strikes across the quiet field
   The shadowed tower bestrides.

By Holford church we leave the roads
   And make into the hills;
And now a sound most musical
   The listening forest fills:

The sound of running water, cool
  As a thousand freshet springs
That run together in a secret glade
  Where all the woodland sings.

And here is the sacred river Alph
  That, in the poem, ran
Down to a sunless sea, through caverns
  Measureless to man.

Now the house breaks on the view
  In the curve of the quiet hills,
The silver beeches of the park,
  A pool of daffodils.

Deep in the brake above the house,
  Under an oak we lie,
All through the dreaming afternoon
  Beneath the blue coned sky.

Silence: no movement and no sound:
  Nor yet a leaf that stirs:
Only the birds that come and go,
  Those singing voyagers.

The sun gleams white upon the front
  Of that enchanted place
Looking upwards to the hills,
  The haunts of ancient peace.

Everything is hushed and still:
  Some magic of the sea
Has fallen on roof and ledge and sill,
  On every twig and tree.

But whose are those figures that emerge
  And cross the printed lawn,
One with slow step and sure, the other
  Shy as a startled fawn?

Though all is still, he hears the woods
    Raging like the sea;
He hears the voices of things growing
    Calling him silently.

He studies the path of the crescent moon,
    Though the sun is high and bright,
And watches the eyes of the fallow deer
    Shine in the white moonlight;

Walks once more in the shadowy groves
    In the cool of the slow day's end,
After long parting and separation
    Meets once more with his friend.

The presence of genius is over all
    And such its inner power
That time stands still beneath its spell:
    Once more it is their hour . . .

The hours go by, and we return
    Along the woodland ways
From Alfoxden to Nether Stowey
    In the afternoon heat-haze.

The singing woods of Alfoxden
    Behind us in the lee,
We leave the hills—the plain ahead—
    And in the west, the sea.

The Choice

O look at all the apple-blossom, the buds of May
That dress with white and glimmering array
The lawns of Spring at this mid-moment of evening;
O look at the lemon-green of lime, the gold of beech, the
    dark yew,

The plumes of poplars that wave and lean together to the
    east:
All the trees in the garden are singing in the silence.
O Life, O World, O Time: if only one might arrest this
    moment—
But time and life move on into a world that knows one
    not.

Look now upon this other side:
The formal magnificence, the Roman world of stone,
The wheeling dome with its volutes and urns,
This learned prison, the walls that shut me in,
This ribbed and shuttered quarry, the coldness of the
    tomb,
This cemetery with its ordered monuments.

Like a madman I go from one side to the other of the room,
Look out upon this scene and now on that,
Avid of life, by dream and fever of mind possessed,
Poised like the frozen eagle for flight into the unknown,
Like him confront the formal West, turned like him to
    stone.

January Fire

The girl is gone:
Along the pavement I watch her walk alone,
Self-possessed and elegant and sad:
No-one to escort her through the street
To her supposititious destination,
That is but a station on the way,
But another beginning
To a journey that has no end:
Having found the promise of another spring
But another deception
In the game that offers no solution,
The play that has no answer to the question,
The dance no end.

Behind the dark and leaning dome
The sky is aflame with January fire:
The universe opens its heart,
The Arctic pathways of the unattainable,
Transitory glory of the untrodden rose
That illuminates the pathos of our state,
The sunset caught in the candid eye
Of the girl now turning the corner of the street:
To whom I have said goodbye.

I look out on the wounded world,
For a moment hesitate
Before drawing the sombre curtains over
The disturbing splendour and the glow
In the west, return to learned order and the gloom
Of the disciplined, deserted room.

The Transparent Room

The wind marches *à grands pas de loup*,
Prowls up and down seeking whom to devour,
Roars in the chimney at the midnight hour.
The clock ticks in the room, while outside
Each hollow arch in the colonnade
Shelters a black and silent catacomb.
In the frozen space that is my empty home
The obscured star now tops a pinnacle,
Is lost again in the cloud-pushing wind;
The swift weathercock flashes a wicked signal,
The buttressed shadows are regular
As cathedral aisle or prophesied prison:
Rush, rush, while there is yet time
To this other side, a happier clime
Where gas-light in the deserted lane
Speaks of the nineties that will not come again,
Of Toulouse-Lautrec and Symons my countryman.

Wavering frost-flowers of shadowy wind
Weave up and down on the window-pane,
The leafless fingers flicker across the lit lamp,
The bare tree erects a feathery plume
Against the Antarctic continent of cloud
Rimmed by the light of the westering moon.
The lamp at the corner where lovers should be
Winks at me across the candid space,
Leers and suffers, signalling something
I cannot translate—here where I wait
For the door to open to the unknown man
Here where the pane taps   the shutters crack
The clock ticks   the wind walks
In the transparency of the unshuttered room.

Lazarus in New College Chapel

This is Lazarus: the head an egg
Laid upon labouring shoulders,
Or like a stone laid upon a cave.
The clear spring light gives life
Making the cold stone breathe and move.
Awake, O awake from the dream of death,
After four days laid in the grave,
The mumbled lips still shut, breath
Withheld, tongue seeking an outlet,
The eyes still sealed in sleep
Resisting awakening, the pain and grief
Of life, the body unfree, still bound
In the wound grave-clothes,
Arms pinioned, arrested in motion,
The body's life stirring in the wrapped
Limbs, now lapped and lipped in light
Passing a bird's wing over the stone erect.
Now a cloud sends Lazarus back to the dead;
And now the returning sun

Of spring, of moving wings and flowers
Shooting from the earth-bound soil,
Of birds calling in the grove,
Calls him to awake and live.

This is Lazarus: this is he
Whom Jesus loved, over whom
He wept when they had laid him in the tomb
On the bitter road out of Bethany.
Now he has heard the word: see
The coffined breast bursting the bonds,
Leaning forward, urgent for life.
Not the life of stone intolerable to be borne
But the life of moving things,
Of growing flowers and birds' wings.
In the stillness of the cave,
In the still chapel of the grave North
He begins to stir and move:
He has heard the Word:
'Lazarus, come forth!'

Spring Landscape, 1952

In the bare gardens of the French Institute
The ranked crocuses are there to greet
The ageing statesman who does not appear:
Another crisis of the franc, we fear,
A fall into the abyss. We walk away,
Enjoy this moment of declining day,
Flutes in the air, and in and out the trees
The blackbirds weave their sleepy harmonies.
Fleets of bicycles push northwards home:
Up the Woodstock Road the workers come
From factory, shop and press. This is the hour
Of domestic happiness, when fancies flower
And hearts begin to shoot their buds of spring.
The men come home from work to wives waiting

In lighted window, tea ready to begin.
Look down the area at this pretty scene:
The handsome fair young man, large as life,
Relaxes in the arms of his little wife
Enfolding him from behind his chair, while he
Lies back helpless contentedly,
As weak as water or a Wykehamist,
Watching their hopeful offspring, is fondly kissed.
The child lies on a chair wriggling its bare
Bottom, embryo animal, in the air,
Drooling with pleasure, intent vacuity.
The youthful parents with complacency
Inanely contemplate what they have made
And, like the Creator, seem to find it good.
Spring's in the air and soon they'll be in bed
Another bounteous offering to shed,
With no libations for the forgotten dead.
Suddenly the wife looks up, to descry
The look in the face of the unknown passer-by,
Starts back with terror, sees the thoughts that rage:
What price this bliss in an atomic age?

Søren Kierkegaard

His life was a perpetual Lutheran Sunday,
Cheerless, loveless, impotent and null,
Tortured alike by doubt and doubting faith,
Lacerated by the sense of sin,
The guilt brought down upon his innocent head
By the father who, driven by a rebellious will,
From a hill in Jutland cursed God and all his works.

Now he sits in the cold autumnal garden
Melancholy with the weight of the curse
Upon him, the sin of the father visited
On him, the cheerful sparrows at his feet

Unseeing, the ducks of the world of Hans Andersen—
A family party on the pond—unheeding,
Nor feels upon the weary leaden shoulders
The soft caress of birch fronds as they wave
To and fro, moving in the autumn wind,
Lightly touch and withdraw—a woman's hair.

This is the latitude of Edinburgh,
The latitude of the tortured conscience,
I remember. In this kingdom he received
The stigmata of genius and pain,
Imprisoned in the primal fear of the flesh,
As now in lead and stone.
                                        I am back again
In the garden—the clock strikes the three quarters—
My footsteps lead me to seek the company
Of the solitary man whose mind researched
Into the innermost recesses of guilt
As the tongue seeks the sore place in the tooth.
Inventor of the formula of *Angst,*
Come and solace me now, you who knew
The strength in the treacherous reserves of doubt,
The courage and contempt to be found in fear,
The consolations of solitariness.
Your eyes that now see nothing once looked out
On human misery and understood
Every inflection of its voice and mood,
Hugged its satisfactions to yourself,
The concave mirror of a fractured world,
Where all is microscopically clear:
The nightmare of a too percipient mind.

Aloft he sits, slightly askew on his chair,
Uneasily to the world, alone and very famous,
The man that died of spiritual pride.

T. E. Lawrence

Whitsun pours out from the churches on to the
    pavement
And in the petals pattering under the rain;
Impoverished ladies in Edwardian hats
Shuffle along in their penurious goloshes.
The naughty choirboys leapfrog out of church.
This is the Betjeman country—
Laburnum, copper-beech and may—
On my way past St Philip and St James
Along the roaring Woodstock Road to quiet Polstead.
The sanctus-bell of St Margaret's rings
For the Elevation unheeded by the former occupants.
But they are all gone away, they are shadows now,
And I wait in vain under the rain,
Under the flowering may, for one or other to appear.
Within, the windows are the same, the outlook
On the acacias opposite, the red chestnut
Over the wall that lit up with summer dawns,
For ever beckoning to the East, grown bigger now.
By the path a rambler rose, peonies and arabis,
A white flowering shrub beside the Gothic porch,
Planted by father, flowers bravely still.

Whitsun morning and no-one appears,
No-one who knows what in former years
Went on there, or what moves the stranger to tears—
The five boys bent on bikes, mad on architecture—
Nor what brought the mother and father
So strangely to rest together here.
A motor-bicycle comes up the road
Too swiftly, disturbs the dream
With sudden approximation to reality.

This is how the boy whose genius brings all alive
Came to his expected end,
By then, choosing death rather for his friend.

'These journeys, you know, don't really end
Till we do.' And again, 'The difficulty
Is to keep oneself untouched in a crowd,
In a populous place find solitude.'
'There is nothing I want to do, and nothing
                                    I am glad to have done.'
'It were well if from the universe
All animal creation had been left out.'

How can he have come to this,
The glad and eager boy, living his life
In the boy's world of fantasy and innocence?
Writing home to mother from the dark womb
Of St Sauveur at Caen, now all ruin and desolation,
The punctuated end of a civilisation.
When did he learn, the boy who found out
That life was an enacted lie,
No faith holds, no bond or love or loyalty,
And laid aside the name to which he had brought
    fame,
Renouncing friends, with whom he had once felt,
Renouncing art, skill of brain and government,
Renouncing life itself,
To breathe out his spirit on a road's green verge.
Some trauma of the soul, some wound
Beneath the skull, some revelation
Of the fact of life that stopped the flow
And shattered the cherished fantasy,
The world of innocence for ever gone.

The Ford

December approaches and the rule of Sagittarius
Under which I was born. Here at the bridge
The night-black mirror of the pool is still,
The old road to London disappears
Under the weir.

A chink of light behind a bedroom blind
Winks up from the surface to remind
Of winter solace and war-time gaiety.
The water talks.
In the walks only the dark limbs of trees
And memories of a different childhood
Haunt the mind:
Night-scent of the downs on the slopes towards
    Carclaze,
Boscoppa stamps repeat their beat
I thought forgotten,
The similar sounds of the railway in the west.
The exhausted city sinks back silent,
All petrol spent.
An improbable plonk of a fish,
Solitary and foiled as I,
Disturbs the lamps on the bridge that gleam
Sunk moons in the depths of the stream.
Come out of the park! Shut the gate
Upon the dark:
Come into the light!

All Souls: February Evening

O bird- and bell-bespoken city
Ring out your chimes to the baffled air
Of February, waiting for Spring
That soon should be there
The ladders wait for the men to move
One, apart, is raised for the Crucified
The stones are erect, the headstones in the corner,
The shroud of tarpaulin, the pullies, the cranes,
All, all is waiting
In the expectant air of February evening
The air itself is soft with expectancy

Shades of the precursors pace the lawn
The worms feed on their bodies
Their images undimmed beyond the corner of the eye
All is still with expectation
The drum of the dome, the listening roofs, the sky,
All awaits the application of love
For life to begin, the world to move.

The Woman with the Flower

In a by-street I saw a woman
  With a flower in her mouth:
A small house in a side-street
  Looking to the south.

She came to a knock at the door,
  Her shoulders in a shawl,
Looked on the first Spring flowers,
  The time when catkins fall.

O snowdrop, crocus, daffodil,
  Sweet in the soft spring rain,
Primrose, squill and hyacinth
  She will not see again:

In the street that looks to the river
  Flowing onward to the south,
I saw an ageing woman
  With a flower in her mouth.

Buckinghamshire

Snow of thorn in the fields
Of cow-parsley and the white
Frill of foam along the hedges
As night comes down and a green light

Punctuates Bicester hill
And day recedes along the edges
Of Buckinghamshire
Where the white-maned horses take fright
Stampede into the twilight
And the sedges of mid-May
Are here caught in the clear
Dark pools that hold
The cold and sinister
Last invitation of the day.

Cliveden

The mingled blue and pink
Of herb-robert and forget-me-not
The cuckoo in the woods of Cliveden
Echoing across the quiet Thames
Amid the Sunday cawing of rooks
And crowing of bantam cocks
Here in these English woods
The river running a hundred feet below
Behold in a decorative balustrade
The Renaissance dream of Italy
The passion, pride and power
Of Borghese, Sforza, Medici,
Sculpted in stone the eagles spread their wings
Gorgon Medusas masks of lions
Lit by the flickering English sun
Filtered through leafy glades
The fountains on the slope now stilled
Florentine figures that once frequented them
Or leaned over the balustrade
Upon a different scene
Olives and oleanders vines and cypresses
Looking down upon the Arno
Of Lorenzo and Giuliano

A history unremembered
Obliterated by the sights and sounds—
Church bells, birds singing, raindrops falling—
Of an English May.

November in Blenheim Park

Woodstock chime comes across the water
To where the massed and mounded beeches
Rise in russet and gold magnificence.
Upon the lake the busy water-birds
Like so many craft hurry to a rendezvous,
Here is an enclosed and ordered universe,
Yet, over the quarried edge, outside
Suggests a normal countryside:
The Roman pomp imposed upon
A pastoral English scene.
Aloft upon his column the Duke
In panoply of arms holds out his wreath
Of victory, surveys his battle-field
In regimented groves of trees.
Around the railing at the foot
The fallen leaves now fuss and fume,
Scratch and pile up against the stone;
The lemon scent of trodden elm
Comes up from the frequented path.
All round, the world of water holds
What whispered springs,
What images of summer skies;
While by the bridge's parapet
A lean familiar shade looks on
The house withdrawn
Upon the painted scene.

For the Funeral of King George VI

Behold therefore, I will gather thee unto thy fathers.

2 Kings, xxii. 20.

The thronged grove is full of the throats of birds
Speaking a language like the wordless words

Of the many muffled bells that mutely toll
Their message out unto the world and tell

The young men walking in their Sunday clothes,
The women that pass upon the public paths,

And out beyond the trees to the city's roofs,
Over the meadows and into the field of graves:

Today a King is buried: the people gathers
To watch his long last journey to his fathers,

Become one more among the memories
Of all that line of royal Edwards and Henries,

And former Georges, joining his dust to theirs.
It seems the earth is sentient and wears

An air of mourning: the solemn trees are bare
To the wind and sun; upon the hushed air

Comes the cough of cannon; the birds that sing,
Sing of renewal and the promised Spring.

Shingle Street

In Memory of Alun Lewis

Over the silver bents, over the pebbles
The swallows dip and wave and dive,
Bathe in blue air,
Communicate in silent ecstasy.
Across the herded common,
Trenched and dyked and brindled,
The cliff of Hollesley tower
Rises rib-shadowed above crested elms.
A puff-ball of golden broom
Glows between sea and common,
The feathered tamarisk over.
Sun glitters on the sea,
A school of silver mackerel.

Here the poet came—
Pointed out by destiny,
The somnambulist certainty of death—
To speak for a moment his grief
To this estranging eastern sea
Welling up over the shingle,
Filling the crevices and meres,
Overflowing the land at length
With tidal apprehension and primeval fears.

Blackpool out of Season

Sand-lavender and gulls and ladies' dogs,
And old men skulking in the Gents,
Along the sea-front out of season.
August for the people, but February for elderly
Couples and comfortable widows from Manchester;
The Fancy Goods Fair is over:
The commercial travellers have departed.
From the Gynn to the Obelisk

Trams clank and jangle to an empty town.
One solitary sweatered athlete
Makes his morning run, unable to forget
Tobruk and Monty and the Desert Rats:
A sprinting memory now engulfed by Suez.
The land contracts upon itself, a people ageing;
Punjaub, Peshawar, Rangoon and Mandalay,
Khartoum and Omdurman, Majuba, Mafeking,
But names on a monument of Victoria,
Looking out on a Lancashire square
That faces the encroaching February sea.

Approaching Cornwall:
Easter, 1948

O country of my humiliation
That yet smiles at me in the pools that pass,
In railway cuttings starred with primroses,
In valleys where vanished viaducts
Have left their bones of ivied stones and made
A desolation in the deepening shade,
Lit by the shuttling windows of the train
Approaching Cornwall in the setting sun.
A presence I already feel like a cloud
Descends on the mind that yet was free
A moment before, that now is possessed,
Moved to unrest with every motion
Into the obtuse, malevolent West.
This is Easter time. The Cornish crowd
Into the compartment, chattering
As ever with platitudinous vacuity.
The train moves over the enchanted gulf,
Trematon mirrored in the evening water,
Mount Edgcumbe drowned in woods of the sea,
Sunlit ridges folded with shadow,
Hills of home where my Passion-tide begins.

Death-Bed

Late September sun fills the room with light
Where my mother is lying,
Ribbons in her hair, hands shrunken on the white
Counterpane: she has gone back to childhood:
She is dying.

Through the open window in this strange house
I see in the afternoon haze St Stephen's church-tower,
Where as a boy I sang and returning late
My mother came down from the village to wait
For me in the summer night.

She is beyond remembering, she is already elsewhere,
The liquid eyes clouded, the speech thickening.
She has been waiting for me to come:
It is the hour of Evening Prayer.

'Lighten our darkness, we beseech Thee, O Lord,
And by thy great mercy defend us
From all perils and dangers of this night,
For the love of Thy only Son,
Our Saviour, Jesus Christ. Amen.'
She does not speak again.

It seems that this was what she was waiting for
To die in peace. Too delicate,
Too proud, to ask. All too late
We come together after years estranged,
And still we do not meet.

It is too late. If only one might recall
The bitter words, the anguished years:
I bury my head on her breast.
Too late, now gentle as a child at rest,
She is no longer here.

Quietly I withdraw from the light-filled room,
Taking my last look at the familiar face,
Already so strange, head fallen to one side:
I leave her in this strangers' house, I
Leave here there to die.

Charlestown Harbour by Moonlight

Dear Hardy, dear spirit, dear ghost,
Here I come, worn out with moil and toil
With cark and care you knew so well,
Down by the water's edge to the little port
Lit by the light of the moon in late September,
To refresh the spirit. Giving myself up to watch
The cruel crawling sea that creeps toward me,
The moonbeam, the moontrack pointing where I
      stand—
Where the quay's neck joins on to the land—
Absorbed by the spectacle of moon and sea.
The blunt dark nose of Napoleonic fort,
Gull Rock, Trenarren and Black Head in échelon;
The lights of Polkerris answer the lights of Trenarren,
The dedicated days of war over at last,
Though the beat of returning bombers at sea
Awakens nostalgia, the rumour of apprehension.
Far out, the Eddystone and the horizon
That beckons ever on and outward
To illimitable seas of boyish adventure.
Turning round I confront the harbour,
The small boats dipping and plunging,
Jibbing and slacking, bobbing and bowing,
That keep perpetual dance
With the pull and motion of the tide;

Coastguard Terrace and the old cottages
Moonwhite moonblue in the ebb light.
Beyond, the hills of home, with that
Inextinguishable reference to the heart,
And over all, the inscrutable comment of the Plough.

Spring Afternoon at Charlestown

Behold the gulled and gorsed rocks
Afternoon honey in keen wind sunlight
Myself on an ultimate stone
A water world about me
All movement and wind and sea
Bobbing seaweed flotsam and spars
Waves heaving and dipping
Making uncertain the Napoleonic land
Little port with deserted fort
Beyond ranked and ranged headlands
Trenarren, Chapel Point, Dodman and the Nare
The Gribbin milk-haze in sea-mist
White peninsular coves along the flank
The erect forefinger standing serene
Over the ebb and flow of tides
Over the bell-rung flowered sea.

Cornish Spell

O white sheep under a purple sky
Do you know who it is goes stealing by?
Or why the sunset fills the sky
With fitful anger—do you know why?

Owls that hoot in the covert woods
Can you guess the secret of his moods
That looks for lurking solitudes
Among the marching multitudes?

Neighbouring whistle of passing train
That crosses the valley and back again
The beggarly parish given to gain
In summer and winter, drought and rain,
Curse twice over, once and again!

Hear the song of the telephone wire
Cold and shrill, high and higher,
Singing aloud in mournful choir:
Children to bed, time to retire.

Look down that doleful avenue
Of beeches that the road goes through,
Do you see anything it leads you to
More dark and sinister than you?

What is this sweet and summer smell
That hangs in hedge and field as well
And speaks of what I cannot tell
But what is dead—a honeyed spell.

At Fowey: For Q

Valerian, privet, escallonia
Look seaward from the Haven
He will come no more home to.
There is the green boat laid up for good.
The melancholy wet lovers look out to sea
On the promenade made for the people
Where the sea-wall garlanded with toad-flax
Gave on to the rocks, the seaweed, the fairway

Out between Readymoney and St Catherine's
And so to sea.
In summer dropping with the tide
Down Channel to untrodden beaches,
Coves alone before people were thought of,
And like Adam created to stand stripped
And plunge in at Silvermine, Porthtowan or Pendower.
Now the boat is laid up for good,
Has come to rest in this seaward garden
Where the windows are all shut, blind faces that look
Across to Polruan and up the creek to Lerryn,
Away to Lansallos and along the coast to Talland
Where his forebears are gathered by the church-walk,
And over the hill, the sea.

Hallane: Sunday, 24th July 1955

Here is the empty packet of Players
Thrown aside in the lane,
Himself thrown aside as easily
With a sudden contemptuous gesture of the sea,
Reaching a longer arm than his
Up the familiar strand, into the rocks
Known and assumed from boyhood here—
To sweep him off into the unknown
Crevices of the bay, borne by the current
Hither and thither, to visit what unfamiliar
Caverns, hear the ghostly singing of mermaids,
Mumbled by fishes, the ears deaf now
To the one word
'Drowned'.

The life of the farm goes on,
The animals demanding to be fed,
The cows milked. Rover barks
As volubly the valley over as before
The young master went away,

Uncomprehending the reason of his absence.
I hear his voice: if I were to say now
The word 'George . . . Where's George?'
The amber eyes would shine with expectancy,
Then cloud in bewilderment, uncertainty
At George's not coming home.
George is gone to sea.

Over Trenarren a seagull mourns
With plangent, more than human cry
For the dead boy, so difficult in life,
With the sullen resentful grace,
The brown fine hair curled like a fern,
The voluptuous ungracious lips
Never without a cigarette;
The golden skin tanned olive green,
The large hand quick at sheep-shearing,
Manoeuvring tractor, harrow or plough,
Or handling a girl.
The fields will miss him: Leslannow and Hallane,
Higher and Lower Trewins, the Brake,
Black Head, Ropehawn and the Vans.

He was the apple of his father's eye,
Always about with him in field or paddock,
Up on the ledra, in the steep farmyard—
They two and Rover—
Until the evening came and girls called:
Then, off in the car I would hear
Softly turn in and up the lane at midnight
Come to a standstill under the shed—
Where the boy's car awaits him still:
While I, apprehensive, unappeasable,
Would turn over to see the moonbeams
Printing their tracks through funereal ilexes
Upon the magic lawn looking downward now
To the quiet sea asleep and still
Lying innocent, incapable of ill.

George Bovey

A pheasant squawks hoarsely in the spinney:
If he were here he'd be after him with a gun,
Or cornering a vixen on the Vans;
He'd recognise the cries of birds that baffle me.
All round are the fields he worked,
The headlands with curves he turned at plough—
Ploughed by another hand this season, now—
In the hedges the flowers he took no notice of,
Foxglove, honeysuckle, campion red and white.
I see him now loitering up the lane,
Hands deep in corduroys, Rover at his heel;
His father in at the gate a moment ago—
The dark eyes searching my eyes unquiet
As if I had some answer to the secret,
Some knowledge that was anodyne for pain—
Spoke of his boy: if he were alive
He'd be married now and down at the farm
At valley's mouth where all is out of hand,
The fields and flowers untended, overgrown.
Spring wears on and tilling time has come:
If he were here he'd be rattling up the road
With tractor or drill, but never a smile
For me who now remember him,
Or coming back after the hard day's work
In full view of Black Head and the bay,
The sea that held no fear for him:
Nothing he did not know about its way
Until that last fearful moment
Transformed things here, left a space not filled
In the valley where the birds brave it out,
Shout across at each other from first light
And the sea-birds suddenly rise
All together and cry aloud in the night.

Late Spring at Trenarren

Over the unawakened land he knew,
Fume and smoke and haze of Spring:
Sheep like monuments or megaliths
Stand out on the sunlit slope above Hallane;
The headland animal-like extends
A tentative paw into the sea:
There is the neck wrinkled and ribbed,
Brontosaurus old or primitive lizard.
The sea-birds are away; even the rooks are silent.
Along the rocks are the crevices he explored,
The forbidding blunt nose of the Vans
Where his first fox he ran to earth.
A continent of cloud above Trenarren
Simulates sunrise, but arctic-cold
As the wind that ferrets the harrowed field.
No birds that sing, no flowers that grow,
Only the hedges snowy with blackthorn:
A bridal wreath above the sleeping sea.

V: American Poems

Spring in the Atlantic

Spring in the air
Yet nowhere
Visible. How can one tell
In the bare spaces of a ship
Washed clean as a bone?
Some look in the faces of people
As they turn
The wind in their hair
Hand to their head
The pale sun from the Atlantic skies
Reflected in white teeth and upturned eyes.

R.M.S. 'Queen Elizabeth'

Looking Away towards Indiana

Here is the poorer quarter of the town, beyond the
    University,
The ragged edge between campus and prairie,
Looking away towards Indiana from Illinois.
Here, at the close of evening, I take refuge from
'Read your *Daily Illini*! You guys got
Your *Illini*? Keep up with your campus news!'
Here patches of marsh mallow, petunia,
Matted convulvulus accompany the step—
The careful, apprehensive, apologetic step,
Exploring forwards like the smoke-blue cat
That disappears in undergrowth beside the track.
The railroad cuts the long evening distances
Across the prairie from Indianapolis to Peoria.
Here, behind the heaped-up gasoline tins,
Rubber tyres, bicycles, discarded junk,
A family sits down to Saturday barbecue,
A teen-age girl at the steaming cauldron.

Upturned chairs in the outer porch
Beckon to the white painted Baptist church.
At the corner a dusky girl,
Uncrowned Cleopatra of the block,
Flaunts slinky haunches, no Ruth
Among the alien corn. Here and everywhere
The sumach has not turned;
Willow weeps above the City's Service,
Milemaster tubeless tyres, Quaker State motor oil;
The chestnuts fallen on the pavement,
The smoke of evening fires rising amid the lots.
Here morning-glory climbs the fence,
While everywhere, in the unfamiliar skies
One hears the disconsolate cries of nameless birds.
Returning, I unexpectedly confront,
Above the Wesley Memorial,
A silver moon that looks on remote,
Indifferent over all.

Sunday Morning in Illinois

This is happiness. At last in the open air
Beyond Lincoln and California Avenues,
Beyond Green Street, Nevada and Idaho,
Here is the picnic pinetum. A patch
Of primitive woodland, untouched by the axe
Of the pioneer a hundred years ago,
American elms, maples, a fringe of pines
That sing to the stranger like the pines of home.
The autumn floor is alive with squirrels,
Large eupeptic robins that from time to time
Ascend the trees, while the busy squirrels
Leap and hurdle the leaves, ripple
Along the path, pause with inquisitive eye
To eye the stranger. 'He's all right,' they seem
To say, assume security and perch

On a fallen log, by last night's barbecue,
To scratch with dainty precision for a flea.
This is Sunday morning: the well-dressed girls—
Hymn-book, prayer-book, Bible in hand—
Emerge from sorority-house, parade to church.
I think of older girls, their predecessors
In the earlier days of the university,
Not long after Lincoln's Presidency,
Days of carpet-baggers and Reconstruction in the
South,
When all was yet to do, and eager young
Professors came back from Germany
To sow the seed of methodology acquired,
Grow into the elderly persons portrayed
On the walls, the light of learning somewhat faded
In kindly eyes, a little jaded by the years
Of teaching, yet contented, undismayed.
Here a patch of pink persicary
And featureless fat-hen speaks to me
Of the cliff-walk from Porthpean to Trenarren
Past Castle Gotha, in brave view of the sea.
Do not move! Oh, do not break
The magic of the moment, the right
Relation to nature at length achieved
Beneath the immense and cloudless sky of Illinois.

Abraham Lincoln at Springfield

The house at the corner of Eighth and Jackson Streets
Now buff-painted, green-shuttered as of old—
The brass plate gives you the name of the occupant
That was: *Abraham Lincoln*. Enter now.
Within, the wine-coloured light of October falls,
Filtered through Victorian curtains looped and fringed,
On figured carpet and mahogany furniture,
Falls on the horse-hair sofa of extra length

To accommodate the long lean figure of a man
Of melancholy aspect, marked by fate
In the sad depths of the eyes, the lines of the face,
The full foreknowledge of man's tragedy
The burden upon him, a willing sacrifice.
Afternoon light spills into the sitting room
All honey and gold, has nothing of crimson in it:
All is placid and calm. Turn but the corner,
And here the family is together once more,
Mary Todd coming downstairs from her room,
To see to things for Robert's coming home,
The sullen difficult son at odds with father.
The still, reflective house wakes from its trance
For an evening-party for the legislator-elect:
Lights in the chandeliers, Mrs Lincoln in silk
And lace fichu receives the visitors,
Friends and neighbours, folks with full arms,
Bringing good wishes for Thanksgiving Day.

Here are the fragments of family life shored up
Against a day of ruin—Thad's little chair,
Favourite companion of the President—
Who died in the White House at the worst of the war,
Leaving the sad heart lonelier still.
See here on a bracket the logman's scrawny hand
That signed the Emancipation of the slaves.
A long shadow falls athwart the room
Obscuring the latticed sun, leaving an outline
Hard to glimpse amid the dancing motes
That register life in all created things:
The shadow is of the dead, that speaks a tongue
More moving to the imagination than what's alive.
Observe the sprawling figure on the floor
Playing with the cat, a fondness he had
Improbably in common with Richelieu,
Some solace for the politic cast of mind.
The day comes to take leave of this loved house.
Loved?—yet always the sense of insatisfaction,

Desire unfulfilled and disenchanted love—
Folks crowding round for an affectionate farewell,
To hear the familiar voice for the last time:
'My Friends, No-one not in my situation
Can appreciate my feeling of sadness at this
Parting. To this place and the kindness of these
People I owe everything. Here
I have lived a quarter of a century,
And have passed from a young to an old man.
Here my children have been born, and one is buried.
I now leave, not knowing when or whether
Ever I may return, with a task before me
Greater than that which rested upon Washington.'*
(He dreams again of the ship with black sails,
Forewarning of what, omen that never fails.)
Too late, at last the son comes to revere
The famous father he had not loved in life,
Himself an old man now in Washington
Would every evening have his carriage driven
To look on the lighted figure, his father's shrine
Where now aloft, the slain god of the Republic
Sits with open welcoming arms to the throng,
The moving escalator of citizens,
Of sailors and airmen, fathers handing their children
Up the high steps where now he belongs to the ages.

*These are the words of his Farewell Speech.

The Dying Centaur

Behold the Dying Centaur, set in this improbable
        glade
Of the Middle West; observe the rude young lovers,
Two by two, arm in arm, body against body,
Lurching up the rides—unwanted visitants
To these haunts of the solitary bachelor:
Nothing less welcome to his defensive home,

The so much cherished privacy,
Than these couples, brash and uninhibited,
Leaning together against the flanks of the Centaur
In whom the departed owner, shy millionaire,
Saw himself, wounded by a similar blow.
Here he constructed his dream by the Sangamon,
The woods where grape-vines hang upon
Hackberry, hickory and oak,
Took the shadows that flickered among leaves
Of sumach, sassafras and maple,
Wove them into the careful, cultivated life,
Withdrawn from eye alike of friend and foe.
No-one to intrude into the solitude
Of regular routine, surrounded by objects
Of beauty and an eclectic taste. Waited upon
By English servants to the number of eight,
Carefully chosen to move noiselessly about
The silent, apprehensive house:
Here he lived in considerable state
For half a century. He would have his meals brought
To him in whatever room he happened to be.
He travelled to assuage the unappeasable thirst,
Bringing back objects of desire he valued more
Than vulgar flesh and blood. But most
He liked to watch the workmen at their work,
Shyly, unobtrusively, himself unseen.
He had no love of riding, with an obscure
Instinct avoided horses, would rather walk
About his woods and walks. I see him now,
A reflective figure alone beside the pond
Reflected with the house he built,
A fabric of water and of light, himself
Now altogether withdrawn into the sea.
Across the waste land of the Middle West
I recognize a kindred spirit intent
On the life of dream and inner ecstasy.
Behind the autumnal spiders' webs
Winking in the reluctant dew, I see

The sad unquiet eyes, for ever uncontent,
The sensitive line of nostril, curve of brow
Averted from the world of commonplace.
The dream achieved, given shape and form,
Now left to be trampled by unheeding heels:
A persimmon splashed at the Three Graces,
A handkerchief hung upon the Chinese garden god,
Here litter, there a fluted sexy laugh
As the excited youth pursues his girl
In and out the glades of the rich
And melancholy celibate, their former occupant.
Only the ritual bronze of the Singer of the Sun
Holds out arms in narcissistic ecstasy—
Until the last futile couple have gone—
Beneath this concave roof of sky,
This grave and empty, threatened dome.

Campus

(*For Allan Nevins*)

Le vierge, le vivace et le bel aujourd'hui
Afternoon sun, October, the coloured crowd
Weaving and unweaving with the light
Across the green wide spaces of the campus,
Under the elms and maples, lime and butter-gold
Men are at work on the red brick mountains—
Insects among the cranes, the distant hammering—
High up against the blue Italian sky,
A scene such as Leonardo might have drawn.
Here on a granite boulder in the grass
Is inscribed '*The Class of '76*'. Where are they now,
The boys who were glad and young in '76?
All dead,
Their dust scattered about a score of states;
Or come to rest in country towns not far
From these former haunts; or over the seven seas.

A gust of maple wind drives the leaves
Athwart the flowing stream of campus girls
In sage and bright green, orange, rust and red,
That pass in these places transient as the leaves.
Where will they be in a few years from now?
Anxious mothers of growing families,
Teachers in village schools out on the prairie,
Looking back upon this Indian summer,
These golden hours unsavoured, unrealized
In the moment of experience,
In the coloured patterns of the dance,
When life lay easy on them and the years
Stretched away before them like the prairie,
Full of promise, inexhaustible, no end in sight,
Under the spaces of the sky, the honeyed leaf-strewn
      light.

Urbana: Before the Snow

Mild south-westerly blows across the field
Awaking reminiscential oceans in the trees,
Wind flutters in loose trousers of young men
In cherry-coloured sweaters, orange, red and green.
The figures weave, unweave, converge,
The trees hold up their spreading crowns
Beneath the mild forgiving sky
In this autumnal pause before winter comes,
The maples now stripped, and driven ghosts
Of leaves scrattle across the pavement.
O, which in this sun-warmed moment
Between the passion of summer and dead winter,
Which are the figures and which the leaves,
The driver and the driven?

Late Evening at East Hampton

Here are the dunes, upon them the last of the sun
Going down beyond Long Island Sound,
A shadow-sedged mere among them,
Mirrored light and sombre shadow—
An Harpignies' *Crépuscule*;
A multitudinous tongued congregation
Of settling dune-birds all around,
The lapse and sigh of the receding tide—
As it might be Cornwall, and Perranporth
Looking towards America, as this place
Looks back across the seas to home.
Here the Shinnecock Indians, first settlers,
Had all their menfolk lost at sea:
The level inlets and the level lands—
One upsurge from the Ocean would sweep
Over all, obliterating fields and farms
And all the careful garnered landmarks.
Turn down Lily Pond road to smell
The scent of resin in the leaning pines,
The aromatic sweetgrass, the shorn
And nibbled turf, sand underfoot.
Follow the rail-fence rambled by roses,
There golden rod stands in rank like soldiers,
Catching the reflected glow from the west.
The dune-birds are quieter now,
A single pipe of a wild canary awake.
The arch of coloured raincloud spans
Amagansett, where the rainbow comes to rest.
Last light burns in windows looking west
Before a sudden hand
Extinguishes the land
And night falls dark
On the loneliness that is America.

Fall in Nebraska 1957

The leaves are falling in Columbus, Nebraska,
Raked together by men with the tired faces
Of professors, full of disappointed hopes:
No longer keen as the cruel winds that blow
Across the prairie's winter emptiness.
Now the land lies honey-drenched in light
That touches the quaking-aspen tops to silver.
The poplars are already stripped of leaves,
The line of the Platte drawn by cottonwoods
And willow-trees. Winter-wheat glows green
Beside the prairie-hay heaped black and dun.
The masts of unshucked corn stand up and fly
Their tattered summer flags far into fall;
Here golden corn-cobs fill the silver bin.
A Lutheran community there closes in
Round church and windmill, the small cemetery
Of St Lawrence lost in the plains' immensity.
Ken's Cabin bids Attend Church—as if
That afforded prophylactic for our ills.
Houses like ships ride anchored on a sea
Or cor, beneath a sky drained of cloudless light.
Evening cattle come down to the dam to drink.
The light is failing now and we are borne,
A schooner with its freight of lights and lives,
Along the road to the west that goes on for ever.

All Souls Day in Wyoming

The saddle-back hills and cattle millionaires
Of Omaha are a November night away:
I awake to find the country white with frost,
Snow-fences already up along the track.

220

We're in Wyoming and, high up, shortly stop
At Laramie of the old Oregon Trail:
Beside the station a dainty yellow coach
Used in Yellowstone in earlier days.
All night we have been slowly climbing up
To this bare plateau, snow mist over uplands,
Nothing in sight but cattle and icy streams,
Nothing but the ghosts of vanished Indians,
A hawk planes over the wastes, and here and there
A house huddles beside the railroad track.
The long slow reptile of the train winds round
A bluff, piñons holding to the living rock.
This is Rock Springs, an arctic settlement
Of miners, seeking gold and drilling oil.
Green River, a platform swept by bitter wind:
I scurry to the warm station-hall and return
With *The Quiet American*. Onward we go
Through driving sleet and vagrant snow that shuts
Out all but the vicinity of railroad sidings,
Disused coaches, metal containers, huts.
Now over the Continental Divide the ground
Is free of snow: haystacks stand in meadows,
Some trees and ragged willows flushed with red;
Overhead, a flight of mallard from the lake.
At Soda Springs, a desolate hard-bitten spot
With stores for Stockmen's Hardware, Groceries,
The bars and dives that nourish their hardened lives.
As day draws in, I see a different scene:
Candles lit in a dark panelled room
Flicker in the pools of mahogany,
Firelight on coved ceiling, a bust of Wren
Looking serene on the familiar gathering;
The glasses are filled with wine, the feast wears on.
This is All Souls' Night. The great Christ Church bell
And many a lesser bell sound through the room.
Perhaps a ghost may come, for it is a ghost's right.
I eat the bread of voluntary exile:
Alone in this wilderness I celebrate.

Leaving New York

Gulls, skyscrapers, funnels, masts,
The wind whipping a rope in the sun
Or fluttering in the black veil of a nun,
Light breaks over New York and among
The cliffs and canyons of the middle town:
A harbour helicopter surveys the scene,
The traffic on the freeway streaming by
Beneath the bow of the proud ship towering high
Above historic Pier Ninety on Fiftieth Street—
Empire State and Grand Central full in eye
Under a billowing, cumulative sky.
The deep hoarse note of the *Queen Elizabeth*
Reverberates about the wharves and docks,
Thrills with pride the silenced passengers
Standing there on the decks, waving good-bye—
Or some with none to whom to wave on shore.
Men fasten the last ropes, descend the rigging,
Swivelling capstans let loose the hawsers,
The ship slides swiftly out into mid-river
Then slowly turns to face the open sea.

Setting Sail in the Fall of 1961

Southampton sways with the great ship turning,
The cranes approach, the derricks dip and bob:
The world swings round on its axis
Into a wilderness of water.
Everything swims into a different focus:
The liners were head-on, now present their sides,
Red and black funnels, lavender-white flanks;
Gatcombe, Romsey, and *Clausentium*
Heave and tug, plough up the waters,
Warp and weave, chug and smoke,
Draw near each other, strain at the hawser,

Till the immense vessel slews round:
The crowded terminal a coloured parterre
Where people stand still with surprise,
Silent and hushed as the ritual of the sea unfolds,
Having said their separate goodbyes,
A few wave handkerchiefs hopeless of identification:
No-one moves, the terminal itself swings into position,
Passengers lined up on an ultimate deck.
O, which is ship and which is terminal,
Which are those on land and those at sea,
All alike under the destiny
Naufragantis saeculi?

In Mid-Atlantic

Bergs of clouds and mountains of surf,
Five seagulls follow the lone ship
In mid-Atlantic, where the rainbows
Haunt the horizon,
A column of colour joining cloud and sea,
Lighting up a fancied landscape toward
Greenland and Labrador;
Or reflected in another sector of sky,
Moses' pillar of fire reigning over
Ahab's world of waters.
Turn to the south, the silver track of sun
That leads to the Azores and fabled
Atlantic islands sought for with longing
By Henry, Prince and Navigator,
Virgin and seer, whose eyes
Sought some certain end not known to men
Under those skies.

Pilgrimage to America

That I all unbelieving should have to be the priest
Saying the last prayers by her bedside
How strange a fate, like everything
In the involuntary mesh in which caught
I had my experience of life,
Unknowing, unknown, all unforewarned,
Yet with strange intimations of the truth
Occasionally glimpsed through the veil
Of make-believe I held for truth:
The face at the window saying farewell
To the child apart that might be his,
The sense of the man whose track I follow
Across the Atlantic, whose image haunts me
On these pilgrimages without purpose
(Or is the purpose also withheld from me,
This the unknown reason why I go?)
Of a man long dead, under his mound now
In Montana, his warfare accomplished,
Leaving never a word, a signal, a gesture,
To one following in his footsteps
To say he ever knew, or was aware.
In myself I recognise some of his traits,
Temerarious like him, like him impatient,
Cursing the fate that is in oneself,
But most of all the temperament of the gambler
Whose ideas were too big for his boots,
Leading him to cross the Atlantic,
To find a wider scope and at length a grave
By the foothills in far-off Montana.

On the Dead President

I will not perturbate
Thy Paradisal state
With praise
Of thy dead days.

FRANCIS THOMPSON

How like the age to lop the tallest flower,
An age that envies difference, quality.
On this malign day the mountains are lovelier still:
The San Gabriel range looks down unknowing
Upon the old fractured Mission of his faith,
Where the fathers lived their spartan lives
Among the Indians, *Cordis Mariae Filii.*
Levavi oculos meos in montes,
 unde venit auxilium mihi.
Today the scene is sadder for its unfeeling beauty,
Unconcerned with the ills of man, unsharing
Our sorrow and grief for loss irreparable.
The cool and golden head that held all clear
Shattered by an irrelevant lunatic shot;
The voice that spoke hope to a discordant world
Suddenly stilled, in the twinkling of an eye,
In the evil glint from an upper window;
The courage that had come through the waters of the
 Pacific,
The plaudits and the abuse of the mob alike,
Stopped by a bullet in a chance Texan street:
Everything in that too fortunate life—
The golden youth so carefully groomed,
So nurtured, so prepared for politics,
The clarity of mind, the boyish grin—
All fated to lead to this unmeaning moment.
This meeting with destiny, this encounter,
From what different paths, of the slayer and the slain.
The map of life, full of promise and smiling hope,
All spread out like a mountain slope

Q   225

With many honeyed folds and tawny flanks,
Suddenly crumpled in a blood-stained car.
To what purpose? To what end?
Nothing that can portend
Any good to the human condition;
Nothing that means anything,
Or speaks anything but misery.
Let him that can, then, pray—for what
Consolation that offers in a faithless time,
When even crime has no gesture of grandeur,
Nothing in it but what is insignificant and mean
To bring disgrace upon the human scene:
Deus auxilium meum et spes mea in Deo est.
Deus, adjutor noster in aeternum.

An Episode in the Korean War

See these three G.I.'s caught in the eye of a camera:
There has been some accident of war, or all too usual
    event.
One of them reads gravely from a book,
A service-book, the service of the dead.
The youngest one, the little fellow, in hysteria
Has thrown himself into the arms of his mate,
Who holds close to him the small head,
Neat fist clenched in grief
For his buddy dead.
The large, long-fingered hands enfold,
Spread-eagle the tensed-up back,
Console the shaken, childish frame.
The noble head looks gravely down,
Inclining gently towards the grieving boy,
Grief graven too in the grown man's look.
The third goes on reading from the book:
Greater love hath no man than this, that
    a man lay down his life for his friends.
The grave in the foreground is unseen.

Popham's Beach

(*For Rick Harwell*)

September sea-mist swathes the long fingers into the
    ocean:
This is the land of Kennebec, Penobscot and
Pemaquid.
Quiet inland waters stand reflective among the reeds.
Follow the road among rocks and early cemeteries,
The lobster-men's cabins, fringed by fall-asters and
    golden rod,
Past the silent bittern camouflaged beside the road.
The Ojibways call him He-looks-at-the-sun,
And so he does, long neck tilted up to eye the man.
Brave by the road a pheasant, old redcoat, stands
    sentinel;
In the creek a heron plunges beak into the sludge.
Red of sumach, gold of yellow birch,
A sparrow-hawk crosses the lemon reeds,
The chipmunks, striped gold, run the roads;
Through the pinebelt, and we are arrived at the sea:
After the woods and rocks the sweet rank scent
Of seaweed piling up the wrack of the past,
A half-moon of sand, islands out to sea,
A world of singing surf in the ears,
The combers breaking upon the sandbars,
As when they built their fort between river and ocean,
And first wintered in the New World of America:
Honest old George Popham, of an unwieldy body
And timorously fearful to offend;
Ralegh Gilbert with all the arrogance of his family,
A loose life, prompt to sensuality,
Humorous, headstrong, of small judgment and
    experience.
The preacher was most to be commended
Both for his pains in his place and his honest
    endeavours.

Here along edge of the sea we tread in their tracks.
The store-house burned over their heads,
The agèd President died in the bitter winter,
While they worked upon the pinnace *Virginia*,
And all elected to return home in the spring.

In Central Park

The bones of original America show through the grass.
Autumn is in the acacias turning, the planetrees
　　sloughing their skin, and in the hips and haws.
September warmth has brought out the exiles, the
　　hopeless of heart stretched along the benches.
A sick bird looks up for pity, where pity is improbable.
Fat blondes jabber in German, ease off their shoes,
　　ankles swollen over.
Here in this place where Columbus confronts
　　Shakespeare,
And FitzGreene Halleck—a poet of whom one does
　　not hear—
Confronts nobody, looks up in portentous inspiration,
One of the people for whom this show is meant
Has put a cigarette box in the hand of the bard.
　　　　Who cares?
The pigeons ruffle and preen in muddy pools;
An unpopular grackle forages for himself with plaintive
　　cries.
A Chinese negro passes, strange pride of race in such a
　　face.
Nurses push dribbling children in fringed
　　perambulators
Along the paths, these asphalt glades
Where a tamed Diana still affects to hunt the woods,
Arrested in stone,
Like this civilisation without a soul,
　　　　In search of one.

The Six o'Clock from Grand Central

Six o'clock, Grand Central, Track Thirty Four,
The Twentieth Century Limited awaits
Tired business executives after a rugged day
From R.C.A., Rockefeller Center, 666 Fifth Avenue,
And many another office-building in Manhattan.
With weary step and slow they descend the ramp,
Step into room, roomette, allotted space
In coaches that already open up
Vistas of a now submissive continent,
The Mystic, Merrimack and Mistanee.
The train moves slowly through the suburbs of the city
And out along the winking verge of the Hudson,
Lists like a ship around the curve of the river,
The jade-lighted bridges that span the void,
Up the incline to Harmon, Albany, Syracuse,
On through a night punctuated with lights
To Toledo, Elkhart, Englewood, Chicago.

Independence Square

The half moon of late November
Looks down on Independence Square.
The slums are cleared, the gardens rise,
The fountains play to the unheeding people
More intent on the Army and Navy Game.
Myrmidons of Army and Navy parade
The streets in groups, or with their girls.
The trees are yet young, younger than they:
Crategus and maple, cherry and crouched juniper,
Leafless sumach, bunched berries at end of bough;
The lampstands are erect, and shaded lights
Squat like toadstools upon the matted ivy.
Buses coagulate upon the streets
To Chestnut and Spruce, Walnut Street and Vine.

229

Have a Pepsi! Save at Fidelity!
New Size, Your Size, '61 Chevy.
The neon lights blink, blot out the moon:
Independence is diminished, lost
Amid the monoliths of modern America.

The Golden God

Autumn flies in all the flags
And in the melancholy sound of many waters.
Juniper fringes the vacant space where soon
The variegated figures will dance their ballet,
Cut their capers on the frozen parquet
Under the high and leering moon.
Now on a September Sunday afternoon
The clouds billow above the monoliths of stone,
Sun comes and goes on the glass menageries
And on the golden water-god arrested in mid-motion,
Curtained by falling spray in the act of blessing
His parterres of restricted ocean.
The polyglot crowds pass and repass,
Express surprise and pleasure in their rapid tongues,
Extrapolation of an older continent.
The innocent, spectacled sailors of the new
Look for objects for their affections,
For some affiliation to their land,
For security
After the sea,
For the tomb
Of the sought womb.

Pavements

The pathos of people on the pavements
Hoping to attract amorous attention:
Each woman views herself in the window,
This one in violet to emphasize the eyes,
That one in mink suggests that she is rich.
Another, with green scarf bound around the brow,
Tiptoes crazily along on stiletto heels.
One with head carefully arranged as bird's nest,
The next, a negress, has removed the natural curl
To give a sinister Chinese effect;
Above a plain face, hair coiled like a snake
Ready to strike at the unnoticing passer-by.
In every eye insatisfaction, longing to attain
Something for ever unattainable,
Always around the corner of the possible,
Always on the alert for something to turn up,
When, if it does, it but staves off despair
Briefly, for a moment, without even the aid
Of illusion any more, vacuity returns,
The avid stare in a thousand eyes
Reflected in windows with the wintry skies.

Married Couple

They have nothing to say to each other,
Having said it all a hundred times before.
Now they sit face to face in the hotel dining-room,
He slightly askew, apologetic, a quiet bore,
Spectacled, lean hands spread in deprecating
Gesture, as a hundred times before.
She sits, tiny, coiled, an electric spring,
Clad all in black, false pearls at fat neck,
Very well made up, girl's hair parted in the middle
Falling short on the nape, still nut-brown,

Middle age revealed only in the creased skin,
Short of sight, the perceptible second chin,
The restless eyes blinking crossly at her spouse,
Small feet out of her shoes dancing with disdain.
The placid breadwinner settles to his steak;
She fidgets with the crabmeat on her plate,
The dietetic grapefruit, slimming fare.
They have nothing to say.
Then the baby-face leans forward, stabs the air
With slim forefinger, wrinkled hands betray
Middle age, eyes cross with lassitude,
Sparkling with contempt, the brilliants on her ring
Mocking the gold and quiet band
On his hand, badge of his servitude.

The Species

The natural instinct of the male for the female
Is something universal, hardly comprehensible.
The fat Jew taximan on the way to Idlewild
Notices the nondescript nurse at the corner of the
        block.
'You like them dark?'
'Yeah, I prefer them dark—more aggressive.'
The cab half-slews. 'Want a taxi, miss?'
A smile is exchanged. At the airport
The tall New Englander in navy blue,
Unsmiling Puritan appearance, automatically
Appraises the barely decipherable girl going by.
I have known in an ancient common-room
A young stallion snort at female voices in the quad.
What is it to be shut out from this play of life?
One observes, with Henry James, the human
        aquarium:
All the fish going round, sad jaws working,
Eyes bulging in ever-unsatisfied stare,

Enclosed within their element, scale on scale,
          Quite unaware
That the female of the species is more deadly than the
     male.

Last Things

Look thy last on all things lovely
Every hour
                                        WALTER DE LA MARE

Certainly look thy last on all things every hour,
For who knows what, at any minute, may turn up?
Behold the city spread below you, block on block,
Inspiring spectacle from the plane that last week
Plunged into Boston harbour with large loss of life.
Or there's the train that, crossing the viaduct,
Inexplicably leaps the parapet.
The Atlantic liner while still only off New York
Is holed in collision and founders in a fog.
The car, swiftly swerving to avoid a dog,
Eliminates a loftier life than his.
Fear the stranger in the hotel bedroom who
Threatens to throw himself from the window
But, thinking better of it, performs the act on you.
What if the surly, sullen negro should
Feel himself insulted and turn round
Upon the admirer of such strength and grace,
Smash his face, deliver a blow
From which there is no recovery?
Or the *matelot* in the *bas-fonds* of Marseilles,
The matador of the *Ponce de Leon* in Madrid?
Such meditations still trouble the midnight
And the noon's respose. No remedy but to
Look thy last on all things every hour.

Riches

The riches of my later life offset
Many frustrations and resentments earlier:
Long illness, straightened circumstance,
Hardly a day outside the parish bounds,
Walking the road wherever I went,
Proud, humiliated, but yet unbent,
No scope, nor variety, rooted in depth
And narrow intensity. Now I am content
Within a hotel bedroom in a foreign land,
My familiar possessions on either hand,
The old clothes-brush known since childhood,
My faithful slippers accompanying me
Into unfamiliar, unknown territory,
Mettatuxet, Winnepesaukee, Narragansett Bay,
Where the solar geese in V-formation
Fly into the sunset and south for Louisiana.
My window looks out not on *The Boston Evening
    Transcript*
But on *The Providence Journal, The Evening Bulletin,*
On *Downtown's Most Centrally Located Parking Station.*
The honeyed light of late Indian summer
Spills through the lattices of the American blind,
The Venetian blind of childhood at Tregonissey—
How remote in time and mood rather than memory,
For I remain still faithful to continuity,
The garnered heaps of grain stored in my granary,
Richly glowing to feed on with thanksgiving,
Plunge my hand in the golden dust,
Stirring up motes in the sun
As in those harvests far away,
To console in days to come and not dismay.

Muskingum

Away from the Presbyterian platitudes of the college
Here is a place where the chipmunks forage
Gold-striped in the grass, sit up to eye
The suspect stranger.

Mid-morning, yet the Hallow-e'en moon
Leers high over the girls' gaunt dormitory,
Where they dream their innocent dreams to be
Mothers of the nation.

Sycamores, maples, willows, dogwood—
A blue jay scolds the quiet neighbourhood;
The monogamous swans in conjugal amity
Patrol the lake.

Blue asters fringe the stream below the Fall
Tapestry of verdure, russet and gold.
A sanctus bell breaks the silence to recall
The ages of faith.

Penetrate the Hollows, where the leaves
Have lived their lives and now detach themselves
Softly from the trees, with papery sound
Fall to the ground.

The fallen giant of primeval forest gives
The illusion of Châteaubriand's Ohio:
At the end of the sunlit glade Atala
Perhaps may appear.

Over the rustic bridge the pretty girls pass,
Rackets in hand. The leaves strew the grass
Even as they will be strewn in their season:
Since all things pass.

Under the Pillared Portico

Driven by the mad professor in the beaver hat
Into the campus superfluously late at night,
Up the snow-covered, ice-bound hill
Suddenly, swiftly swerving round the bend
I catch sight of a lighted scene to chill
The heart, a blow between the unwilling eyes:
Under the arclight of the pillared portico
A rite enacted on the open stage,
Oblivious of time and light and passers-by.
There in the eye of the world for all to see,
Uncaring, mute, in silent ecstasy,
Two lovers in passionate stillness: he
Tall and columnar, slender as the pillar
Erect before the sacrificial act,
Gold-crowned as the god; while she
Held in his arms in one unconscious world
With him. 'Each hath one and is one'
Might be their motto, if they had heard of Donne,
'John Donne, Undone'—by love undone;
Nor any more aware than he
What time will do to turn the trance to prison,
Reveal no world to discover
In one or other lover.
Such are the thoughts that rage
In that age of unwanted revelation
While the car wheels round
And with it the darkened city.

Saturday Afternoon in Madison, Wisconsin

The Saturday afternoon dog barks his head off
On the deserted porch. Improbably
A cockerel crows in the grounds of the campus.
Mount the slope amid the animals

Sculpted in ice, monuments in the snow:
Tortoise extended, squirrel with tail in air,
Couchant cat after a bird, a sad old man
With the hollow eyes of Montezuma
Or Ozymandias, king of kings.
The pretty sculptresses have departed
Home for the week-end to Winnebago,
Windsor or Fair Oaks, Monona or Waunakee.
Love overflows the expectant city
In this suspended moment hung in the air,
Awaiting spring in the rose-tipped elms,
In the powdered flush on the virgin lake.
Enter the hall, tiptoe along the corridors
Where the water-fountains make music
To themselves, no-one to hear.
Look in at the deserted class-rooms:
Here is one I occupy for a fragment of time
And then pass by, not even a memory
To students themselves become ghosts,
Who come and go
Like motes uncounted in the sun:
Even we,
Even so.

Evening Walk in the Middle West

Go down Dayton Street and up Hamilton Avenue
To Jefferson Square, where a few
Lights linger in the Capitol, though
The legislators have departed.
A mob of English sparrows cling
To the inclement ledges of Woldenberg's.
Have a coke with your pizza, chicken, shrimp,
Your spaghetti, spareribs, sandwiches.
Across the dormitory houses the banners hang:
Season in the Sun—Judy.
It's elementary—Watson.

Presenting Polly. Now it's Bonnie.
The earnest chaste young faces pass by
Numb with innocence and naiveté.
The Lenten devotees spill out of the Catholic Church
That elbows St Columba's Presbyterian Church
That nudges the First Methodist Church,
Mother of all the Methodist churches in Madison.
Across the street the pompous portico
Of the First Church of Christ Scientist proclaims:
Our Faith is in God, Our Hope is in immortality,
Our Love is toward all mankind.
A civilisation built on bromide,
Kindness, colourlessness, triviality—
And underneath, the violence and the reality.

The Tree

The chestnut tree at the corner of Gorham Street
Holds up its candelabra to the unheeding crowd.
The young women sway their skirts for the men,
The men in jeans display their curves to the girls,
In this draughty Mid-Western capital
Where the Capitol's gilt image of Liberty
Nods to Old Glory on high at the University.
The sad and splendid tree is humiliated between
Leon's Beauty Salon and Bendheim's Underwear,
Looks across at the immense and luminous
SHELL sign for ever gyrating on axis:
'Shell's On Top', 'Cars *Love* Shell':
The usual squalid city spectacle.
Aloft, aloof and very lonely
Amid neon lights and night-signs
The solitary tree recalls
Improbable memories of Tractarian Oxford,
Of Newman and Manning and the heresy
Of unregenerate baptism.
Here in this land of the living dead,

This spiritual waste:
No dynasties beneath the grass,
Only the wraiths of vanished Indians,
Winnebagoes or Menominees,
Fishing in their filth and squalor
Beside their four remembered lakes.

The Arboretum

(*For Madeleine Doran*)

She showed me Canada violets, white
With yellow centres, the petals blue
On the underside; delicate lavender waterleaf
In small blue clusters; wild woodland phlox
At foot of trees eloquent in the glades;
Everywhere underfoot ground-ivy or mint,
Blue with diminutive skullcaps along the stalk.
Here is a clearing in the burr-oak copse
Made for crab-apple, blossom blown over now,
But cherry's still white along the bough:
An amphitheatre in this far Forest of Arden
Made for *As You Like It* or the *Dream*.
Here by the stream we pause where migrant birds
Splash and make play on their way north in spring.
Down into the wood we plunge, and stay
To hear woodthrush and meadowlark answer his mate,
The catbird delighting the others to imitate.
Here underfoot is a long Indian mound
That in its shape counterfeits animal or bird.
No sound between us is uttered, no word.
Suddenly a blob of crested crimson is there:
The cardinal seeking food for his mate in the nest.
In the marsh below each redwinged blackbird,
A doctor of divinity in scarlet and black,
Clings to his separate pulpit, the bulrush swaying.
Across the lake tall cottonwoods are waving,

The shimmering popples turn silver in the wind.
We descend through what has become primeval
Forest in the mind, bridal-wreath in spray,
To the spring where, flung beneath a tree,
Two lovers unheeding are hot in bird-play,
She, beneath, pretending to resist,
He with all his length on top of her.
Alert, unnoticing, we make our way
To the water's edge. If this were England now
There would be church-bells in the late afternoon,
Ringing to church across the still lagoon.

Farewell to Wisconsin

Through the open door at end of corridor
Abraham Lincoln presides from his chair
Over the view down Bascom hill, up State Street
To the Capitol, now nudged by outsize buildings.
To the left, the lake at length unfrozen runs blue,
The lawns are trenched and hoed and weeded
Yet furnish their quota still of waste paper and milk
    containers.
In the path a cadet holds hands with his girl.
Behind, the carpeted bluff marked with stone
In memory of some bluff Norwegian
Professor or Dean, looks over the furrowed plain
Of the lake marching east under the wind,
And at last it is spring.
Spring in the air, wine-like, beneficent,
Spring in the light, lemon and gold on bark of trees,
In the hoary heads of trees bursting into bloom
Under blue sky and puff-ball cloud
Sailing away and away across the Middle West.
This winter of my content is over,
Winter of escape, isolation, withdrawal,
Marooned like the figures in sculpted ice
On this alien slope in sun and snow:

A warmer winter world in which to inhabit
Than that become too familiar, too well known,
Where I have learned the art to spurn,
To which, reluctant, I return.

Arrival at L.A.

Oleander, palm, hibiscus, yucca,
Sepulveda Boulevard, the Security First National
    Bank,
To tell us we have arrived at Los Angeles.
Ahead the Verdugo hills, reminiscent of Tuscany,
Terra-cotta coloured and serrated ridge
Of old earthquake country.
Here begin eucalyptus, peppers, camphor trees,
The cuttings carpeted with purple lantana.
Now Inglewood Park cemetery, where lies
The dust of a small child of my blood and bone,
A child wise and sad beyond his years,
Who once looked long into my eyes,
Was frightened by what he saw,
Something beyond tears.
The airport-bus billows along Florence Avenue,
Past Realtors, Refrigerators, Records, Eat with Joe,
Every solicitation of eye and ear and taste.
Not a breath in the air. Sweat pours down behind the
    ears.
The scarecrow palms gesticulate
Above the desolation of houses. We journey
In gathering dusk towards still sun-tipped peaks.

San Juan Capistrano

(for Marcellus Steadman)

Twelve years have passed since I was here,
Filled with what alarms and toils, and one great grief.
Today, as before, the peppers planted by the friars
Wave their tresses over the adobe walls
That skirt the Camino Real, running its snake-like
    length
Two thousand miles from Mexico to Monterey.
The flag flies at half-mast for the dead President.
The November wind up the valley from the sea
Stirs in the trees, in the feathers of white doves
That croon about the walks, remembers the friars.
Nothing is further from the mind of the populace
Feeding the pigeons, photographing each other,
Bird on arm or head, bird-eye, bird-mind.
The blood-red blooms of hibiscus, golden
Bird-of-Paradise, flame-vine are out in flower.
Soft crooning fills the Californian afternoon.
Scarlet poinsettias, thirsty, drink the sun.
Within, the paraphernalia of the Faith,
Treasured possessions of the expatriate fathers,
Early vestments of the first Mexican missions,
A retablo from Barcelona, have come to rest
Here far from home. The scent of incense
Recalls one to the church: within is home.
Two Mexican couples, descendants of the faithful,
Swarthy youths with their bright-eyed,blue-silk girls,
Genuflect to the manner born. The hours pass.
Outside, the ancient mossy fountain is profiled
Against low, green hills, the splash of water falls
On into pale evening and into the placid nights
Filled with what nostalgia, with what passions
Suppressed, the regrets of men marooned for life
Between impassible mountains and trackless sea.
Here are the rosaries sculpted by the Indians,

A few shards of porcelain from far Majorca.
A carillon rings the hour to quivering arums,
The toyon berries are rich and ruddy as blood.
An English sparrow approaches, eyes the stranger,
Seems out of place under these exotic skies.
Here is the calaboose where refractory Indians
Were punished and confined behind the bars.
But where are the irons? Where the whips and thongs?
Something has changed in my life,
Turning all to iron, alike behind bars,
Something is wanting, expressible
In the one unspoken word.

San Marino

Bougainvillea spreads an exotic welcome
To the homekeeping traveller surprised
To find himself here: the library lost
In a garden of palms and Californian oaks
Along the geological fault that runs
From Santa Barbara south to San Diego.
From former rancho an English estate he flung
Around him like a cloak, with careful gesture
Manoeuvring the trees into their proper place,
Erecting a Victorian villa on its terrace,
Pivoted on the mountains, criss-crossed by alleys
Punctuated by marble goddesses, Juno
And Ceres blessing the fruits, while Mercury
Speeds with caduceus along the glades.
The palms strip their skin in the crackling heat,
The humming-birds, vibrant with delight,
Feed on the crimson of naked flowering coral.
Timid scholars take the place of the last tycoon,
Eat their frugal lunch beside the ponds
Where bluegills spawn beneath the lotuses;
Jays play bo-peep in the erythias,
Or flutter in the dry fringes of papyrus.

243

Here is cactus land, with jacaranda
And joshua-trees and flame of ocotillo:
Plants stand erect like columns in a temple,
Are tethered snakes upon the desert paths,
Or green flesh takes on the texture of jade,
An improbable flower upon tip of tongue;
The delicate fingers of the deodars,
The Spanish grace of olive-trees like dancers
Holding themselves ready for the dance,
Crêpe-myrtle thick as English hawthorn
In May, in which the treefrogs chirp all night.
The mounting foliage of magnolia
And avocado towering above the dust,
The heavy-sweet scent of the orange-trees
Comes and goes with the pulse of the fragrant heat,
Date-palms strew their yellow globes on the grass,
While persimmons glow like golden moons amid
The verdure of a Renaissance tapestry.
—O, all ye plants and fruits and seeds of the earth,
Praise ye the multi-millionaire who called
All this to life and now lies quiet enough
In the marble mausoleum, rising chaste,
Austere amid the aromatic groves
Between the San Gabriel mountains and the sea.

Et in Arcadia ego

Carob, locust and magnolia,
Eucalyptus and every kind of gum
Fringe the avenues to the Arboretum,
The people's paradise, fallen now from its high
Estate, when it was Lucky Baldwin's ranch.
When it was Lucky Baldwin's, one never knew
Whether the race-horses or the women
Stepped higher or proved the faster.
The Master regarded both with equal favour.
Here are the stables for thirty horses,

The barouche, dirty now, whence Lola Montez
One day dismounted to greet her familiar
Friends from the *demi-monde*.
Here is the portico which Lucky himself
Would come out upon of an evening
After a good dinner, gardenia or carnation
In cheerful buttonhole, no more deceived
By sycophants, the insolence of wealth,
Than by an upward turn of the wheel of fortune,
Knowing, like Apemantus observing Timon,
The downward would as certainly follow.

Now the more domesticated ducks
Paddle around the muddied pond,
More content, more philosophical,
Than their squandering precursors:
Whose ducks' descendants have survived
Bankruptcy, divorce, desertion,
Tremblements de terre and all that's human,
Fatuous and mean. They cast
An understanding eye upon the scene,
Tolerant of all that passes, occasionally
Bat an eyelid in the sun; nor complain
Through the long hot California afternoons.

A Dream in Lincoln, Nebraska

Sleeping uneasily in Lincoln, Nebraska,
Five thousand miles away, I find myself once more
At the clanging gate we used as choirboys
Into the churchyard, fifty and more years ago.
(O the anguish to be sixty and not sixteen again,
O the irreversibility of time!)
There by the vestry door stood the old vicar,
Recognizable as rarely in dream: in faded black,
Flat pancake hat, scrawny neck and Adam's apple,
More a scarecrow than ever, dear dotty Dr Lea.

I was apprehensive, afraid he might not know me,
He must be so very old now, I thought,
At least a hundred I calculated dreaming,
For he was a man of sixty when I was a boy.
He appeared more skeleton than man,
With a couple of wardens, like warders, to hold him
      up;
Something indecipherable between us in the path,
A mound, perhaps a coffin. As I approached—
The familiar scene from all those years ago,
The path, the vestry door, the darkling church,
The grinning gargoyles looking down, the vicar
Himself one—I said: 'Do you remember me?
I was a choirboy here. I used to sing.'

Fourth Sunday in Lent in Central Park

The idiot people swing in the sun: baboons
In the human zoo. Young men spit as they pass,
The dogs lift up their legs and gaily piss.
The primeval rocks are draped with monkey children;
The paths echo with all the tongues under the sun.
Leaves scrattle, squirrels scuttle, bohunks
Rifle the garbage bins; perambulators are propelled,
An old man hugs his unquiet heart.
The bare shadows of the natural world are better
Than all this scum. Balls are caught and thrown,
Returned or purposefully pursued. Dust is blown
Into the eyes and mouth, into the mind and heart.
Dead branches lie, a crimson kite in blue sky
Flutters over the scuffling field.
The bust of Giuseppe Mazzini looks calmly on:
Why is he here?—except to make clear
This is the melting-pot of Europe. A revolutionary
In portentous cape swings bogusly by.

Bicycles circulate. A second-rate orator
Perorates from his pedestal; a Negro speaks
Better sense to his young hopeful: 'Jes you keep
Yer mouth cloased an' you woan't git in noa trouble.'

Here lake water laps, but no church bells chime over
      the water,
No peal rings out to evensong. A sick woman clings
To a bench in the sun, eyes closed, blue veins stand
      out.
The people hold radios, their bibles, in their hands;
The unbelieving churches rear spires on the edge
Of the Park, where the cliffs of the secular world
Predominate. Here among the rocks the old lags
And poufs congregate. You couldn't come here in the
      dark.
Shall we descend into the Zoo? No need so to do.
A woman, dressed in dogskin, fondles her dog;
Hard to tell which is woman and which dog:
A yellow-trousered man carries his cat.
Bolívar and San Martín prance on their horses,
Liberating in vain to the unheeding populace:
The coloured crowd is happier on the rink.
Curious to think of skyscrapers, a planetary fringe,
Rolled round in space. The ducks have no idea.

The Music of Humanity

'The still sad music of humanity':
Terrible voices tear the air coming up
From pornographic Seventh Avenue,
Awake me in the early hours in the glare
Of neon lights through the squalid slats—
A woman's voice shrieking dementedly,
As it might be Janis Joplin or Bessie Smith,
In altercation with her man, obsessive, hysterical:

The man's voice pleading, then growing angry
With her unreason, going home from some lewd dive.
Drink, drugs, money, sex,
The universal burden of it all.
The screaming voice carries on with their footfall
Echoing down the street, to what terminus?
One night on the pavement of Fifty-Fifth I saw
A well-dressed man administer a blow
Resoundingly across the face of his woman.
She took it unflinching, made no moan.
What was that about? Some female lie,
Some malice from a poison-tongue?
What kind of life is theirs? Drink, drugs, money, sex,
The music of humanity. That voice, that blow,
Echo in my ear and fill the night with fear.

The Strange American

The sight of heterosexual happiness
Distastes: see them straphanging in the bus,
Two fools seized by a sudden impulse to smother
Each other with kisses, leaning over the other,
Exhibitionists in the public eye
With less decorum than animals in a zoo.
They as suddenly desist at the look
Of the observer writing in his book
With the mesmerized fixation of a snake.
The enthusiastic lover looks loftily down,
Asks the stranger to open the window pane
So that his love may breathe a little air.
The man refuses, sits stonily there;
At a second request, 'Try another,' he says.
Taken aback that the man should refuse
A demand made as if conferring a favour,
'A strange American,' he murmurs, the colour
Rising as he returns to his adoring girl.

248

Finding a seat at last, she adjusts a curl,
Lays a hand superfluously on his knee,
Baring her cage of teeth at him, while he
Bristles his masculine moustache at her.
The moving hand writes on without a stir
Or sign that it has circumscribed the scene.
All is resumed as if nothing there had been.
There appears, from the corner of an envious eye,
Two heads transfigured against the western sky.

Portrait of a German Woman

Monumental, *unsterblich*, bloody German *Frau*,
Out of whom came the robots who ruined the world,
Hard, unsmiling face, with eyes unseeing,
Turned in upon yourself, rapt
In contemplation of what deadly dream,
What ecstasy of blood and iron, breeding
Sons for *Deutschland, Deutschland über Alles*.
Inconsiderate of ill, under your enormous hat,
Like the Kaiserin's in the Tiergarten
Now shattered in a thousand pieces:
Behind you I see Krupp, Thyssen and Stinnes,
The malign *Macht* that wrecked our century.
Woman with a stance like a Buddha, but evil,
Abstracted from the beauty of the world,
The crimson flowers beside you unheeding:
Yet conscious perhaps of the fate laid on you,
Priestess carrying your unspeakable burden,
Woman of iron, with hands upon your womb,
Woman of the sorrowful face, and of the wrath to
    come.

Before Cortés

Underneath man's innate cruelty
There is his apprehension of beauty
No less strong, inspiring every art
In every form, wood, jewel, stone.
See here the spirit's succession in time,
From Olmec to Maya and Toltec to Aztec.
Observe the mania for ritual, the feeling for
    proportion,
The holy madness, feeding the blood of humans
To the fire lest the sun should fail to go round.
Here learn the closeness of man to animal:
Man carries a jaguar-cub, struggles with snake,
Celebrates the cult of serpent and jaguar,
For both come out of the caves, the underworld.
Here is the headdress of coyote or plumed serpent,
The priest in flayed human skin for the rites,
The bones of blood-brother ritually burned,
The borne bowl of pulque foaming to the brim,
Sprinkling incense in one hand, knife in the other,
Terebinth and turpentine, resin and cinnamon.
The jewels are ceremonially crushed and thrown
Into the cenote of sacrifice to Quetzalcóatl,
Lord of the Morning, or Xolotl, Evening Star.
The hierophants, in ecstasy, the drugged *danzantes*,
Make their demented moan to two-toned drum,
Tear their flesh with sting-ray spines and thorns,
Blood flowing from human hearts impaled
Upon sharp obsidian knives, the captives
Mutilated before slain in obscene ceremony,
The frightened eyes of the victims, accepting
Their fate, for they too believe.
From the severed neck of the victim, blood flows
In five streams rendered in jade, chalcedony.
A terrible beauty is born and reborn
From mad beliefs, made permanent in stone,

All in due order according to the calendar.
These glyphs recount man's madness, record
The appalling distances we have come,
Yet still unslaked beneath the outer skin,
Render the essential cruelty
Under the common humanity.

Middleton Place, Charleston

Gone is the rhetoric of Sumner or Calhoun
That led but to Fort Sumter or Fredericksburg
And ended all at Appomattox—
Gone with the wind that ruffles trees in the park
Named for Francis Marion, patriot of the Revolution,
Who is now no more than a name either.
Who now remembers Moultrie, or Beauregard
Of the dashing looks and cavalry charges,
Or Henry and Arthur Middleton, of Congress
And the Declaration of Independence?
They are better remembered for their garden,
The pleached alleys they planted, the Chinese
Azaleas acclimatised, gingko, mimosa,
Varnish- and spice-trees brought home to Charleston,
The magnolia walk along grass-green water,
The turf terraces that edge shapely ponds,
Native oak, crêpe-myrtle, cherry-laurel,
The spired and pyramidal camellias.
There was the house framed in its formal landscape
Designed by the master and his English gardener.
All was entire before Sherman passed this way,
Left his mark in the burned and ruined flanker,
Spoiling the symmetry that still looks out
Over the acres of lawns and empty rice plantations,
That once sustained the house and the family
Now gathered within the sombre granite vault,
Watched by the darkies sweeping up the leaves,

251

While spring birds sing their funeral lament.
Still the winged house confronts open river with its
    wharves
And harbour, gateway to the ocean sea.

Old Baldy

Here in the foreground, funereal cypress and palm,
There in the background, the eternal snows:
Old Baldy rears his crest
Above the emerald lights of Arcadia,
Glittering and sparkling in the winter air.
The San Gabriel mountains extend their flanks
Lavender and grape-purple, fold upon fold,
Upheaved from the plain centuries before
The Fathers came to name them for the Faith.
Mount San Antonio to them, white and withdrawn,
Takes on a richer hue from the lost sun
Gone down in the wastes of the Pacific,
Is now no more than a wraith withheld
In its own silences, where the winking plane
Makes an insolent comment upon our uncertain day,
Carefully picks its way around the mountain-mass,
Could easily shatter its frail cargo,
Could crack a nut against the mountain side,
Now only a hooded presence, keeping its vigil—
Suspending its unspoken sentence
On the cities of the plain and their ephemeral life—
Into the oncoming night of no return.

The Forest Ranger

Sim Jarvi, the tall forest ranger,
Slim and sun-crowned Finn, died here.
By birth an Oregonian, all his life
He gave to the service of forest and mountain:

252

Here at Sierra Alta remember him.
He knew the secret lair of mountain lion
And where lurked the black bear: killer
And prey were alike to him, both in his care.
The lion roaring after his prey doth seek
His meat from God. To him each had his place
In the harmony of nature, less red
In tooth and claw than the great killer: man.
His clear blue eye would scan the mountain face,
Detect outlined against blue rim of sky
The big-horned sheep or shy mule-deer.
Racoons would come to him to be fed. Even
The rattler crossing his path had no hurt of him.
He knew all the trails like the veins on his hand,
All the secrets of that upheaved land lay
Open to him: the lateral fronds of white fir,
The silver bark of canyon oak, even
The sharp thorns of buckrush were his friends.
He loved the rough striations of the rocks,
Black and white like a giant panda, grey
Or burnt umber and ochre, sepia and rose.
Taking a few wafers and raisins, a flask
Of water to quench his thirst, he would quest all day
Under the sun, in and out the cool shade
Of sugar pines, or the stiff Jeffery firs,
The petrified skeletons of trees
Laid waste by lightning or by forest fire.
On such a July day, the noonday sun
Bringing out the resonous scents,
The aromatic odours of manzanita
And yucca—our Lord's candle—he lay down to die,
Alone in the loved high altitudes:
No one around, only a cicada singing,
In the silent solitudes no breath nor sound.
At night a little wind arose to play
With the fronds of his hair and cool his brow there
Where he lay—of your charity remember him—
Under the glittering Californian stars.

The Road to Claremont

Follow along Foothill out into the waste lands
Keeping the mountains in view in the intervals
Of gasoline stations, trailer camps, dead orange
    groves—
Relics of an earlier culture—with split walnut trees,
Lopped palms looped with electic lights.
Homes! Homes! Homes! Churchill Highlands. College
    Heights.
Camper and Trailer Real Estate on Citrus Avenue.
Et one Brute?—Lay's Potato Crisps.
Gulf. Gulf. Texaco. 76 Minute Man Service.
Dramatic! Distinctive! Daring!—New Chevrolet.
Dallas?—Get Delta's Downy Bird. For Sale
This valuable frontage. *Beautify Our Highways!*
The mountains look down on the desolation,
Torn eucalyptus and stripped palm with disdain.
A frail hibiscus puts forth a flower with no moral.
Subdivision. DEVELOPMENT. PROGRESS.
The fallen leaves scrattle on the pavement,
A mountain breeze blows the toyon berries about,
Arbutus fruits batter their blood on the kerb.
Why pay retail for a car loan? *Attend the church of your*
    choice.
Come winter, come Miami. Happy motoring to all!
Gulf. Gulf. Texaco. 76 Minute Man Service.
No Scotch improves the flavor of water like Teacher's.
Get the best of both in better balanced homes.
City of Glendora, Pride of the Foothills. Don't fence
    me out!
We Rent Tools, Trucks, Trailers. *Beautify*
Our Highways! Throwawayable New Plastic Bottle.
Throw it away into the dying orange grove,
Or by the roadside where the scarlet poinsettias
Light up the smog. At the Christmas corner lot
A monster purple dog arrests attention,
Demeaning the amphitheatre of mountains

Relegated to a backcloth for civilization.
Kitchen Sink on the Blink? Call a P.I.P.E.
Plumber. Robustelli Cars: No Credit Needed:
Bankruptcy O.K. Loosen your seat-belt:
Travel American Lines to New York. Auto Tops,
Cut-rate gasoline. Certified Mortgages. Used Cars.
Hibiscus punctuates the devastation;
Roses and oleander, manzanita and sagebrush
Struggle and expire amid Mobile Homes,
    Add-a-Room,
The House that Jack Built, Income Unit,
Homes on your Lot, Homes—if that's the word for
    it—
Choice Mobile Homes. Mount Baldy, Drive-in
    Theatre, Dancing Nitely.
Attend the church of your choice. A citrus grove offers
To be subdivided for shopping centre. Adorable Pets—
Animals Beauty Parlor. Grooming. Poodles clipping.
Don't forget your Zee Napkins. *Beautify Our Highways!*
Concerning this 486 commercial acres contact
Etiwanda Realty. Shady Acres. Trailer Lodge.
Paradise Hills: Exclusive Sites. Homes! Homes!
    Homes!
Subdivision. DEVELOPMENT. PROGRESS.
Housing Lots. Shopping Lots. Mortuary Lots.
Be fruitful and multiply, copulate and die.
Serenity is Nearby at Rosehills Cemetery.

Christmas in California

There is the mass of mountains under the moon,
There are the lights of Arcadia, green and gold;
Here the palms and olives, Monterey pines:
How different a landscape as I grow old
From the simple and innocent slopes I knew as a
    child,
Up the furze-parks to the downs of Carclaze,

255

Past the claypits and clear pools by the road,
The scent of heather and thyme where the sheep
 graze:
Carn Grey on the skyline looming over the bay,
The same moon suffusing the coast with its glow
For a boy homeward-bound those years ago,
The moorland scent in nostrils as he mounted the hill
In the sharp air towards Christmas, thinking he still
Saw the star above Bethlehem, the faithful shepherds
Keeping their flocks on a similar night,
The Magi make their pilgrimage all in a row,
As if all the mystery of the Orient were there
Over the rim of the headland bathed in light,
The bay filled to the brim with gold, and not far
The Wise Men, Gaspar, Melchior, Balthasar.

Waiting for the Storm

Frightened but fatalistic I follow the rain,
The threatened cloudburst over the mountains,
The ominous sunset into which we go,
Horror in the heart, dying a hundred deaths,
In plane or car swerving on freeway,
Always pondering what end the clouds portend—
The palms await their death-sentence,
The cacti extend their crucified arms—
Apprehensive of any unexpected approach,
Every symbol of reproach on my course,
Caught in blizzard, alarmed at each moment
Of heading off the obliterated road,
The danger that stalks one down the hills:
Life, as a friend found, a track through jungle,
On either hand the panthers waiting to pounce.
The landscape still, now preternaturally dark,
Birds of paradise hold up inquiring heads
Scenting the storm, or rather, the wrath to come,

Though, for the moment, the coast is clear.
How long, O Lord, how long?
We die before we learn to live, just
When we are learning to live it is all over.

Experiment

This is the way it will be when I am dead
Lying outstretched full length upon a bed
No superfluous symbol of faith at my head
Yet arms folded across my breast as if
Making a cross unrecognized in life
Duly arranged by a servant: no wife
To grieve or rejoice or anyone else of my kin
Alone with myself at the last as I have lived
Little but contempt for kith and human kind
Alone upon a bed in a strange land
Far from former home and earlier friends
Sped on before me to a common bourne
Leaving the world poorer that it was
Easier to leave than I had ever thought:
Bare arms folded upon the white sheet
No chalice beside me to indicate the priest
No crozier or pastoral staff to show
The shepherd I might have been, symbols of
Childhood dream—dream or dedication
I know not which—now it is all one
As if my vagrant life had never been:
Here lies one whose inner face unseen
Was turned away from light and faith and hope
By some secret wound or ever he was born;
Cover his face, close his eyes for him—
Unregenerate, unafraid—
Upon a world he never made.

Foetus

I coil up in bed, a foetus in the womb,
Or primitive burial in a tomb.
The bitter light of Fifty-Fifth Street
Filters through slats on the white sheet
Into the sick room lit with flowers,
Where I lie and count the hours
Until I am home again by the sea,
And all that is then left of me
May be consigned to mother-earth:
A likelier, shapelier rebirth
Than this crouched figure in the womb
Seeking a premature, alien tomb.

Sunday Afternoon in Hartford, Conn.

Sitting in the sober light
Of this New England house on Sunday afternoon,
Blinds half-drawn to exclude the sun
Of the Indian summer, while an English sparrow
Scrattles along the chaste birch boughs
Soon to be stripped by winter snows,
I think of you, dear Tom, dear T.S.E.,
With sudden unexpected poignancy,
Of whom I had not thought so feelingly
Since that day along the Los Angeles Crest Highway
I heard of your death, and wept to be
So far away from home, fancied I could hear
The sound of church bells ringing for you
At East Coker, in the silence of the mountains,
And felt their aching void, ridge beyond ridge.

Now here's a bridge to you, your own New England:
The strangeness of a foreign land falls away,
And I feel more at home for the thought of you,

258

In this familiar Longfellow house upon the avenue,
Where your aunt, Miss Helen Slingsby, might have
        lived—
The outlook from the porch across grass verge
To juniper and sumach behind white palings,
To the park where gingko, maple and bog-oak
Jostle marsh-cypress, white pine and many a conifer,
I look upon your book, and read your life,
Look once more into your eye, limpid and sad.
Note the old expression at once severe and gay,
Diffidence and kindness in your anxious smile.

Elizabeth Park

Along Prospect Avenue, the cars speed by
Like sizzling water, by Faith Center
And the Seventh Day Adventist Church
('I'm sorry, but we don't approve of tea.')
Dogs bark domestically
By redberried dogwood and yellow sycamore,
Where squirrels chatter and jays call;
So past redbrick condominium into the park.

Here in Elizabeth Park, where the maples turn,
October sun, I look down the slope
To Hartford, Insurance capital of the U.S.A.:
Grandly the towers rise of the Travellers,
The Aetna, and the Hartford Fire Insurance
        Company,
Hardly distinguishable from St Joseph's Cathedral
Of an earlier form of faith.
The young men exercise their bodies—
All they have to offer—with a ball,
The infantile cult of youth.
A grey-haired, middle-aged man
Sprints vacuously round and round the park

In widening circles, a pebble in a pond—
While I, for all the sun and flaming foliage,
Feel not at home, for ever outside:
An alien wherever I may be.

Chick Austin

Seventeen years since you vanished from the scene
You set, where we are all gathered in your absence:
'The paste-board palace', the Philistines called
Your creation; others 'the stage set'—which it was:
The background to your works and days,
Where you played your pranks, acted out
The drama of your life, 'Hamlet' to your self—
—Reflecting mirror, rather than to stupid others:
The narcissist in love with himself, for whose
Faithless charm the others fell but not understood.
From an older, more tolerant, understanding world
You brought back notions to this Puritan reef,
Conventional, conformist, Congregational,
Of Everetts, Hales and Goodwins, among whom you
        married—
The pro-cathedral in Paris, honeymoon over the Alps,
Harefoot over the moon, Palladio, Vicenza;
The villa on the Brenta lived again in you.
The formal avenue leads to the Venetian front,
Within, the steep curved staircase, breakneck
Like your headlong life, the descent into the drawing
        room
Pannini-panelled, gilt Italian furniture,
Guercino, Ricci, Battoni, the baroque you loved,
The rococo fantasy you lived,
Free as air and as mercurial.
'A museum is where the director is amused:'
The avuncular guardians much disapproved.
Having received your *congé*, taking off
For Sarasota and the gay Gulf, a world away

From Puritan New England of your birth,
Accumulating images of freedom as you went,
Leaving at last houses to the number of seven.
Still finding no haven for your life of dream
And ardour, pursuing the mirage of love
In vain—until at last, stricken still young,
When you came to die you came home to Helen,
Waiting for you in this creation of your mind—
Where I, who never knew you, Chick, remember you:
The dead man more alive to me in all this gathering
Of the phantom living—brought back
To be buried at Windham with your forefathers
A bowshot from the church where you were a boy.

Mississippi Wind

The wind blows puffs of cotton along the verge,
The cotton pickers are in the fields, or baling;
Kudzu vines run up the roadside trees,
Tremble in the wind like stage greenery.
Here I am in the querulous, glittering South,
The land of copperheads and red-necks,
Where darkies couple under the magnolias.
A stiff wind invigorates after the foetid summer,
Tosses the manes of black walnut and pecan,
Scatters the unripe fruit upon the floor;
While blue jays cry across the countryside,
The blue dome cloudless over all.
This is October: the undersides of leaves
Turn silver in the sun, the pyracanthus
Gleams gold across the level lawn, where birds
Are blown and flutter in the improbable wind.
A negro passes on the path, but does not speak,
Maintains dignity and silence, for this is the South.
This is Mississippi, where they live
Their inner life of inscrutable reserve,
A people apart, the progeny of Ham.

261

The Stranger at Gettysburg

Here is Seminary Ridge where they stood
Those first July days of 1863:
Below the Ridge the Lutheran Seminary
With round cupola from which the generals,
First Union, then Confederate, surveyed the scene.
They used the dormitory as a hospital.
Now it's early spring, and the mocking bird
Calls chuck-chuck-chuck, sweet-sweet.
Within, the clear sun of Pennsylvania
Comes silvered through chapel windows:
Ein feste Burg ist unser Gott.

Powhattan Artillery and Dance's Battalion
Reached the field at evening to turn their batteries
On Cemetery Hill: the great cannonade
Before Longstreet's assault on the Ridge.
Pickett's Division of Longstreet's Corps,
Marching from Chambersburg, arrived after sunset;
Stuart's Cavalry from Hanover engaged Hampton's
In the summer evening at Hunterstown.
In Shultz Woods guns blazed among rocks and oaks;
Troops concentrating at the end of June,
Converging upon this murderous moment of time.

In the early morning, soldiers bivouacked,
Smoke of breakfast rising among trees;
Lee, thoughtful and calm on 'Traveller':
'If ours were not so bloody a business,
What a wonderful spectacle!'
Ein feste Burg . . .

Line of battle formed on either side the pike,
The McMillan house, high on the ridge, saw all.
Thomas's brigade of Georgia Infantry
Moved across the pike into McMillan Woods.

Crows fly these peopled solitudes,
Glisten funereal black under the sun.
Meade appeared on Cemetery sky-line,
Where now dead cannon balls gleam and shine.
Ein feste Burg ist unser Gott.

To the west, then in setting sun—
The slopes of South Mountain, now shorn and bare;
Squirrels frolic among the falling shadows.
Here stood North Carolina under command,
Brockenborough, Heth and Pettigrew,
Her regiments in action all through
Those days—one Confederate soldier
In four who fell was a North Carolinian.
All these are English names. A sentinel bird
Is surprised at the stranger in tears
At these men's memorial.

The opposing ridge is a graveyard of monuments—
Two carrion crows fight the battle over again
Across the intervening space. Still
The North Carolina colour-bearer thrusts
His flag forward against a burst of copse;
Still the bugler-boy sounds the assault
For Virginia—looks across to where
The Pennsylvania Centre holds fast.

Oak leaves of winter scatter like paper
Where then the foliage was full on the trees.
Stillness, sun and quiet where so many died.
Big Round Top and Little Round Top
Close the view in the morning haze.
Suddenly a jay rends the silence
With the scream of a wounded man.
The breeze brings balm as there was none
In those hot days of '63, under the sun.

Here the Georgia Infantry broke the Union line
At the Angle—attacked in flank, the Federals
Fought their way out with heavy loss.
A pheasant squawks a comment upon
The Army of Northern Virginia
    against the Army of the Potomac.

From Little Round Top one sees the mountains,
The whole Confederate position screened by woods:
Longstreet's Corps drove back the Union line
Entrenched from Devil's Den to Peach Orchard.
Here Massachusetts held firm amid the boulders,
Where Father William Corby, chaplain of brigade,
Bearded, in long coat, stole over shoulders,
Gave absolution to all men on the field,
Killing each other.
New York Engineers bivouacked by
Hummelbaugh House, bullet holes in the barn,
Where hyacinths now bloom,
The catkins coming out on Culp's Hill;
In the creek the early peepers
Keep up their perpetual whirr.
From Jeb Steuart's monument
A nut-hatch drops, eyes the stranger
Meditating the mingled glory
And idiocy of men.

A broad-shouldered veteran of the late war
Surveys the field with practised eye.
Behind where Maine Infantry stood
Sharp-shooters came round out of the wood.
Young saplings stand erect and straight.
A deer crops here where New York Cavalry
Were halted, eyes the stranger, puts up
A white scut of tail, vanishes into cover.
From Meade's Headquarters Old Glory flies over
Alike the blue and the grey.

Today, a robin chatters among silent guns.
At the crossroads to Hagerstown
The retreat took place, behind breast works
Thrown up along the road to Waynesborough;
And Lee withdrew.

Drifts of dead oak leaves dried in the channels,
The trees begin again to put forth leaf.
A flicker of crimson-headed woodpecker
Crosses the path of the Stranger:
Silence and sun and sadness in the air,
Spring and a hint of Resurrection,
No more.

VI: Poems Mainly Cornish

Passing by the Coast of Cornwall

After long exile and many leagues of water
Suddenly, framed in the port-hole, I see
A pictured lighthouse rise erect,
Nothing around it but the sea.
Then, hurrying on deck, I detect
Reefs and rocks and fragmentary isles,
Recognise it for the Bishop and know the land.
The coast of Cornwall comes into view
Very virginal and white in first sunlight;
Summer is over all the green pastures:
My heart beating against the ship's rail
Knows it for home.
See, the tower of St Buryan church stands up,
The eastern face washed by morning sun;
Not far away I figure the Nine Maidens
Who, dancing on Sunday, were turned to stone.
There are the cliffs, the familiar places
Recognisable, recognised only by me
As the ship goes by and passengers crane to see
Land. 'What land is it?'—a foreigner turns to me
To ask. 'What land, indeed?'
Shall I deny him, as I was denied?
Pride refuses to utter the word:
'This is the coast of Cornwall.'
A bitter coast for those that know it well,
Full of the salt of the sea applied
To green wounds unstaunched, unhealed,
In spite of long silence and abstention.
See, I recognise the green field
By Ludgvan church tower, and Gulval;
Low down on the line is the Mount,
No guarded vision that looks towards Bayona's hold
But lying homely and snug at the end of the bay.
Mousehole, Newlyn, Penzance, Marazion:
There are the white houses along the shore

Caught in the sun. There are the towers
Of the churches. It needs only the scent of flowers
To be wafted, the bells to ring out
For the sea-folk to rise from their caves,
Approach once more the sunlit shore
Where a faithless mortal
Left lonely for ever
The kings of the sea.
The great ship leans to the land, then turns away;
My heart leans with the ship, then turns away.

The Little Land

(*For Marthe Bibesco*)

There is a taste upon the tongue
    if only I could recapture it
Of smouldering summer seas
    running in upon the coast
Or perhaps the sibilance of leaves
    frilled by the breeze from valley's mouth
In the mind such mixture of *wohlgemuth*
    images around the corner of the eye
Of the ferry-boat arriving at the quay
    nosing her way into Percuil
Riverside St Mawes festive and gay
    with tousled summer visitors
Or visiting our toy cathedral town
    from the petunias of Treseder's in Cathedral Lane
    to Pellymounter's musty bookshop in Pydar Street.
How to savour the hours upon the palate
    the honeyed hours of the little land
    with their accumulated memories?
Here is the white gate to Trewithen
    so often passed by with my friend

Now open to me, the hidden pleasances,
    the shadowy park and all within
Panelled rooms of old Sir Christopher
    portraits of Hawkins and Zachary Mudge
    a kingdom of camellias beyond.
The garnered riches of my later life
    are everywhere I turn on every hand.
Here beneath the balcony of the Fowey Hotel
    Q. walks once more in the seaward garden
A more distant memory still
    I see myself a schoolboy
Panting up Polruan hill in the hot afternoon
    to Lanteglos Polperro Looe
One Sunday trudging down the lane to Lansallos
    the tower dark against the sunset sky
The bells suddenly burst out ringing
    sweet and clear to evensong
Or looking down from the cliff upon
    the cornered cove at Talland
Blue sea lapsing idly in
    over seaweed and white sand
Presided over by the campanile built
    upon the living rock looking out to sea
Or high on his inland perch
    the hermit of Roche
Beckons from his roofless beacon
    over the moor to Hensbarrow
North Goonbarrow, Lower Ninestones,
    the corrugated ridge of Helman Tor
Dark in the distance lies
    enchanted Luxulyan
Of long boyhood walks up the Valley
    and round by the church
Where ivied traceries on cool
    moorstone-mullioned windows
    slaked the thirst of summer and youth
Raging in the mind matted
    with wild convolvulus

Red Admirals feeding on pink
    clumps of hempagrimony
Early lemon shoots of bracken
    and tang of camomile
Filling every crevice of the heart
    with remembered honey stored
To feed on with thanksgiving
    in dark days to come.

The Road to Roche

Here is the hard-bitten country of my birth.
In a dank corner between monkey-puzzle and sawpit
Lived, drunken Dick Spargo: how he made a living
I've often wondered—occasional cattle-dealing
And his wife's bit of property, I suppose.
Fridays he'd come rolling home from market,
His breeches as tight, and every variety
Of knobbly stick or cane or switch to brandish,
Long moustaches dripping booze at ends.
A grammar-schoolboy I mocked him with *Spargens*
Humida mella soporiferumque papaver.
On an island-site of its own, grim and gaunt
Like a flat-iron, the house of a double murder.
I knew the murderer: a stranger to the village,
Choirman and St John's ambulance-man,
Sharp-nosed, evasive, sexy and saturnine.
The cottage gardens among granite crevices
Are not less bright with aubrietia and saxifrage.
At the end of the garden-path the Vivians lived
To themselves behind their escallonia hedge:
A family of men, dark and voluptuous,
Who owned and worked their quarry in the moor,
Could ring the jumpers in more senses than one,
Like ringing the changes on a peal of bells,
Grandsire major or minor Stedman triple,
Experts in campanology and girls.

Here is Bethesda Chapel where Mamie and Frank
Sang their way into each other's favour
And further, clinching the matter up Look-out lane,
Amid flowering hawthorn and prickly furze,
Where all the girls got pregnant in the spring.
Careful! the car slews round the half-moon curve
To Carclaze timber-yard where father worked,
The jingling teams came home from Crinnis woods
With props for the pits; and still along the banks
Lie the long decapitated trunks—
One hears the cries of crashing and fallen trees.
See, here from the bourgeois verandah of butcher
    Trays
Breaks into view the sudden beauty of the bay,
Profile of Black Head, the shorn pines of Trenarren
Echo the pines of the Pincio, and shortly the Gribbin
Pushes a long lizard paw into the sea.
Higher and higher, mount the last heave of hill
To where the china-clay country begins:
The pyramids rise pure in colour and line,
On the other hand, the chasms torn in the earth
Vertiginously deep and frightening.
By the wayside pool my old great-uncle George
Would halt his horse to rest after the pull,
Himself fill lungs with wine-like air from the moor,
And lift up voice in clear, quavering tenor,
With 'What is your One-o? One of Them
Is all alone and ever will remain so.'
(The parish is dedicated to the Trinity.)
The road runs downward now through china-clay
Villages with ancient rebarbative names:
Scredda, Rescorla, Hallaze and Stenalees,
A hog's spine of hill mounding the western sky,
Carluddon, Carloggas and Resugga Green,
Penwithick Stents and Treverbyn vean, a tree
Or two in a hollow by the cemetery.
The view to the right across prehistoric moors,
Full of crosses, quoits and standing stones,

Circles and monoliths and dead men's bones,
To Luxulyan tower suddenly lit by the sun.
Now for the indignity of nondescript
And very Methodist Carnsmerry: blow, Bugle, blow
Over the bitter cross-roads where through the Thirties
I often spoke to a handful of lounging men
Of the approaching war, the wrath to come.
Some of them are dead. Here lives still one
Of the faithful, stalwart son now at college.
Enter the last lap, a shallow valley
Of settling-pools, clay-dries and small farms,
Tall chimneys punctuate the tilted slope
To where at the top of the immense, frowning Rock
Of the medieval hermit looms and threatens,
Broken arch of chapel an eyehole at summit,
The eye of a needle the rich may not enter.
Here he kept vigil among the mad winds
Racing across the moor, swirling among rocks
Like up-ended sarcophagi awaiting the doom.
Here walled up, a local Stylites,
He lived on his winnard's perch, kept in food
By the flock in return for his offering of prayer,
Fulfilling the function of psychologist to the folk,
Shaping their fantasies into satisfying form.
And so by the church-tower where Wesley preached,
Though his disciple Sam Furley would never follow,
Take scrip and staff and no thought for the morrow.
Down the descent by cobwalled Rock Inn
To the sombre garden where my ancient friend awaits
    me,
Eyes blue as periwinkle in the border,
A rich and warm expressive Cornish voice,
With the crackle in it like foot on autumn leaves,
Smile like the early April sun coming out
Among windswept daffodils, their heads blown,
Spilled cups of gold upon clumps of heather
In this rockbound moorland fastness hemmed about
By all the temerarious flowers of spring.

Passion Sunday in Charlestown Church

The rain beats down remorselessly
From beech and chestnut on the graves;
My young cousin lies beside the porch.
The parish is all gathered in the church,
The minute bell clangs, last footsteps hurry,
The Mass about to begin.
The holy priest in blood-red chasuble
Brings in the elements, a lighted candle
Goes before; the handsome, dark-haired thurifer
Erect, a slimmer Felix Randal,
Comes down to cense the faithful.
He bows, the parish returns his salutation,
Even the one stray sheep (shall there not be joy in
      heaven
Over one sinner that repenteth,
More than over ninety and nine just persons?)
He has returned, unrepentant, not to pray,
But to watch, observe, mumble with his lips,
Go through the familiar childhood ritual,
Tears hardly held back from the eyes—
Hoping it might be so—while the chants rise:
    Kyrie Eleison,
    Christe Eleison,
    Kyrie Eleison.
Rain patters on the roof,
The wind rushes in the gutters,
Attention wanders, till the Creed:
And was incarnate by the Holy Ghost,
And was made man.
The parish falls on knees, then shuffles up again.
This is the Victorian church my father and mother
Were married in that Lenten day so long ago:
The simple courage, the confidence in life
The son has never found, yet had beginning

In this place. Now come back,
A public man, scarred with injuries,
Seared by sad experience, without illusion
Or any hope, dedicated to despair.
What hope in these tender trumperies
That move the heart, but not the hardened mind?
The moment comes, thurifer and acolytes
Around the priest, aloft the lights,
The church all silent for the Consecration.
Tears burn behind the unbelieving eyes,
Knowing too well no miracle is here
But dear mnemonic mummery.
A hush falls, the sanctus bell clangs out over
My cousin's grave, eager and gallant youth,
Along the road he used to come to church,
Over the roofs and down to the harbour
Where Jim was drowned when I was a child—
They brought him home upon a poor man's cart.
At the Communion, one old sinner I used to know
In her more prosperous days returns to pew,
The haggard eyes not more suffused with tears
Than the known face that greets her after years
Looking up with a chaste and sad surprise.
The lights are out, the incense quenched,
The slim and stalwart thurifer
Back in his place in choir.
The moment of suspended time
Hung between now and eternity is over,
Tenderness floods into the ulcered heart
As the parish files out through the lych-gate
My parents entered some seventy years ago,
And scatters along the unrecoverable road.

Shoes

My shoes in the corner of the room,
Pair by pair in different attitudes:
In one I see myself going upstairs,
The right foot feeling for the lip,
The left already firmly planted on the step;
Two others lying apart, small boats
Tipped on their sides opposite each other,
Listlessly apart, as when sitting
Feet thrust out from comfortable arm-chair;
Another pair, heel to heel, slightly askew,
Others in order, prim and waiting two by two.
In all of them I see the stance of my mother,
At once affirmative and questioning,
Reluctant yet not afraid
To set out on her pilgrimage,
Now long arrived, the journey over.

Contingent Beauty

I do not wish to die—
There is such contingent beauty in life:
The open window on summer mornings
Looking on gardens and green things growing,
The shadowy cups of roses flowering to themselves
—Images of time and eternity—
Silence in the garden and felt along the walls.
The room is suddenly filled with sun,
Like a sacrament one can never be
Sufficiently thankful for. Door ajar,
The eye reaches across from one
Open window to another, eye to eye,
And then the healing spaces of the sky.
How can one think of life as evil,
The world as made by blackguard or brute

When so much beauty lies on every hand
Waiting only to reach out and touch the fruit,
The sensitive soul to wait upon
Moments of apprehension,
Of satisfaction inexpressible,
Penetration of the whole being
In the early morning silence and the sun
Before the day begins to stir?

The Faithful Unbeliever

I stand on the steps of St Peter's, Eaton Square,
Sparrows chirping under the tall colonnade,
The flowering cherry all in surpliced white,
Daffodils and bluebells this late reluctant May:
Rain and sun and wind, the scent of flowers,
The mingled beauty and sadness of the spring.
Two boy-friends eat their office-lunch on the steps.
Within, here is the sanctuary where he served.
The verger says, 'He left before I came.
Several members of the congregation remember him.
He died this year, didn't he?'
This is where he served his first curacy,
A frisky young cleric straight from college,
Tall and boyish, full of pranks and fun.
Here's the pulpit where he preached his sermons
Beneath the hanging Master whom he served.
A secret stillness holds within this place,
Punctuated, not disturbed, by the traffic without.
Here's the font where he baptized, the scene
Of play-acting that was not all play-acting.
Spring flowers light up the sanctuary
With their gold. A flickering morning light
Passes over the altar where he often knelt,
Not at ease with himself, with difficulty
Attempting to follow in his Master's footsteps,

Not often achieving it, yet not wholly out.
Victorian mosaic and gilt, brass eagle and screen,
The angels look down upon the human scene:
Sunday by Sunday the choirboys and servers,
The rich dowagers of the Square, the streets around,
The School journey to his native Newquay,
The boys' Swimming Gala at St George's Baths,
The multifarious errands of the parish,
The life of good works, not unscathed by sin.
'He that is without sin among you, let him first cast a
     stone.'
O, Anthony, how could it have come to this?
The fruitful life, the unsteady course, still
Yielding good, ended by its own will,
After what anguish of mind, what suffering,
Snuffed out like the sunlight flickering
On the altar, passing and repassing
This uncertain spring, perhaps a sign
Of recognition to one lingering in the church—
Darkness in the sanctuary as he withdraws—
The faithful unbeliever, remembering.

On the Sea Front at Hornsea:
My Fifty-fifth Birthday

Fifty-four years have now flown over me:
I celebrate my birthday by the northern sea
At Hornsea, Marine View and Esplanade,
Houses and Properties for sale by Arthur Toby,
Pitch and Putt at 6d. per Round.
The summer beauties of both sexes have
Departed, leaving the seafront to the sun and me.
Nothing but the pitch and putt of the sea,
Nothing in view of Flamborough Head and Spurn
In the light sea-haze of early December.
Nothing but the faint indecipherable smell

Of lemon or thyme lost amid the tattered ragwort.
The strangulated cries of water-birds
Float over from Hornsea Mere. Nothing but
A puff of December breeze in my hair,
The imprint of the sun upon the page as I write.
The Ladies' Luncheon awaits the greying man,
The *commis voyageur* of culture,
In the Floral Hall. I have come through
The rich black loam of Holderness
Turned over, gleaming fishbacks in the sun.
The red-faced, sharp-nosed farmers drive
Occasionally by in black Rolls-Royces.
The immense fields gently undulate,
Waves of the sea from which they came,
The haystacks like cathedrals on the horizon.
Leaning over the seaward balustrade,
Amid thyme and ragwort, a sprig of rosemary:
The thought—'I have not twenty years to live'.

St Anne's-on-the-Sea

In the late afternoon of my life I lie and doze
In the residents' lounge of the hotel at Lytham St
    Anne's,
The candid sun full on my February face
White and drawn with long winter's overwork.
Behind me the silvery chime of a Victorian clock
Tinkles the afternoon tea-time hour away.
No-one about: no-one walks on the sands:
The sea-side resort is deserted, the turreted stands
Of the pier silent and empty as a cathedral.
The quietude of the sea-birds can be heard,
Made more still by one dreamy liquid whirr.
In tunnelled euonymus and veronica
A little cat plays a solitary game
Of hide and seek by herself, animal emblem
In the solipsistic human universe.

The sea's melancholy withdrawing roar
I hear far out from the paved, cemented shore,
Where an old rheumatic couple cripple along
To take their daily ration of regular air.
Above the remote and corrugated sands
A convoy of oyster-catchers rise and fly
Decoratively along the edge of sea and sky:
A water-colour of Girtin or David Cox.
Nearer, the architecture of the Edwardian age,
Minarets and domes, endearing lampstands,
Along North Promenade and South, the Blackpool
     Road,
St Ives' hotel, Glendower and the Esplanade.
Slowly the sun goes down behind the bank
Of low nimbus cloud over the grey waters.
The tide is on the turn and inward comes
Darkness and the ice-cold winter sea.

February Day in the Iffley Road

O February day of consequence and cloud,
High wind blowing ladies' hats off in the street,
Where television's calligraphy scrawls
Insignificance along the squalid roofs.
The copper hydrangeas rust in corners;
Here Mr Wells does High Class Boot Repairs,
Or did in the early nineteen hundreds,
When the gas-lamp focussed the assignations
Of the street. Now all is in a state of disrepair,
Blinds, windows, gates fly open with the wind;
The Capuchin Greyfriars climb their greasy stair
To their lighthouse view of the world, over
Chester Street and Daubeny Street and where
Bedford Street bends round to fill-dyke marshes
Swept by the wind and across to woods of Wytham,
Where bluebells and cuckoo-pint grew
Before time was, when all the world was young.

In Place of Love

In place of love
One purchases deception by the hour
Wide-eyed and well aware—
After all, the assumption is not complimentary—
Waiting in hotel-bedrooms for a knock on the door,
Or at street-corners for a look from the eye,
Adventures on pavements that serve but to disabuse,
Ingenuously disingenuous, innocent
Yet full of intent,
By no means taken in:
Amused not at the other, but at oneself,
Inviting the laugh upon oneself,
Though not precisely welcoming it,
The familiar outcome,
The exchange of mutual insincerities,
Each knowing how to take the other's compliments,
The facile tongues, the easy flatteries—
Nothing moved, save another small corrosion of the
    heart,
Another indecipherable film of scar-tissue
Across the wounded place, whence comes no love,
Accepting all, not in place of love,
But chiefly for the sake of the poem.

The White Cat of Trenarren

He was a mighty hunter in his youth
At Polmear all day on the mound, on the pounce
For anything moving, rabbit or bird or mouse—
My cat and I grow old together.

After a day's hunting he'd come into the house
Delicate ears stuck all with fleas.
At Trenarren I've heard him sigh with pleasure
After a summer's day in the long-grown leas—
My cat and I grow old together.

When I was a child I played all day,
With only a little cat for companion,
At solitary games of my own invention
Under the table or up in the green bay—
 My cat and I grow old together.

When I was a boy I wandered the roads
Up to the downs by gaunt Carn Grey,
Wrapt in a dream at end of day,
All round me the moor, below me the bay—
 My cat and I grow old together.

Now we are too often apart, yet
Turning out of Central Park into the Plaza,
Or walking Michigan Avenue against the lake-wind,
I see a little white shade in the shrubbery
Of far-off Trenarren, never far from my mind—
 My cat and I grow old together.

When I come home from too much travelling,
Cautiously he comes out of his lair to my call,
Receives me at first with a shy reproach
At long absence to him incomprehensible—
 My cat and I grow old together.

Incapable of much or long resentment,
He scratches at my door to be let out
In early morning in the ash moonlight,
Or red dawn breaking through Mother Bond's
 spinney—
 My cat and I grow old together.

No more frisking as of old,
Or chasing his shadow over the lawn,
But a dignified old person, tickling
His nose against twig or flower in the border,
Until evening falls and bed-time's in order,
Unable to keep eyes open any longer

He waits for me to carry him upstairs
To nestle all night snug at foot of bed—
My cat and I grow old together.

Careful of his licked and polished appearance,
Ears like shell-whorls pink and transparent,
White plume waving proudly over the paths,
Against a background of sea and blue hydrangeas—
My cat and I grow old together.

West Country Folksong: Child's Verses for Winter

Devon was white,
But Cornwall was green:
Uncommonest sight
That ever was seen.

When Cornwall was copper
Devon was gold:
On moorland and hilltop,
Pasture and fold.

When Devon was purple
Cornwall was brown,
With harvesting bracken
On ledra and down.

When Cornwall was grey
With sea-mist and spume,
Devon was greenest
With apples in bloom.

Devon was shrouded
With snow on each thing,
But Cornwall was verdant
With promise of spring.

Trinity Sunday

Stoneyard, boneyard, haunt of the loved shadows,
Bells ring out over the deserted meadows,
And it is Trinity Sunday—Becket's favoured feast,
Martyr and madman—parish feast of my childhood:
Upright stands the scaffolding, upright the dome,
Home of dead friends, and long my home.

Flag ripples from flagpole in the June breeze,
Wagtail searches the lawn: no trees
In this gaunt wilderness of stone,
Corniced, Corinthian-columned and swagged
With flowers and wreaths of stone all flagged:
Birdsong in the silence when the bells have ceased,
First Sunday in June, unforgotten Trinity feast.

Portrait of a Scholar

When I hear the sighing sound of Magdalen
Chime, I think of Bruce and the mystery
Of time, some thought of the fifteenth century
He inhabited all his working life;
Of Boarstall Grange surrounded by its moat
We looked down upon from Elsfield and Stow Wood
Where we walked, and I listened to the flood
Of information about Bastard Feudalism,
The facts behind medieval chivalry,
The predatory finances of Sir John Fastolf,
The truth about Courtly Love, clean contrary
To C. S. Lewis's legend and *parti pris*.
Or paying a call on Chaucer's granddaughter, Alice,
Duchess of Suffolk, in her chapel in Ewelme church,
Above the meadows where the cresses grow,
The chalk-stream of ragwort and rare mimulus.
Or again we are walking up the Cherwell Valley

To Tackley church, to see a familiar friend
Dead five hundred years: I watch Bruce bend
Over the cold marble monument
To print a kiss upon the icy brow—
I forget of whom that sleeps in the tomb,
Some member of the Lancastrian house with collar of
    esses
Whom Bruce knew like any contemporary.
And now they share alike time's mystery.

Dover Pier

Who is this shadow beside me in the walks
Always present though he never talks,
At least I never hear him but with inner ear,
Never see, yet he is nearer than if here,
More near and dear for passing beyond the known
Into the unknown where I cannot follow till I die?
He shadows me down Addison's Walk to Dover Pier
Whose name he told me once when we were here.
The strangeness of it!—to sense his presence
Yet cannot conjure him in the flesh to my side,
Ask him questions, see his smile, hear his replies.
Yet he suggests to my open mind he knows
My grief, accepts it as sincere,
Waits for me on the other side of the weir.
The water passes under the bridge as when he was
    here
And crushed the leaves of autumn underfoot—
No footfall now—we exchanged the news of summer,
Confronted the prospects of winter,
Commented with malice on the passers-by
Vanishing down the leaf-strewn avenues
As when he—here or not here now—was here.

Mayday Surprise

'Egocentric, eccentric, he will name a cat
Peter'—thus Auden: myself
Stares out at me from the printed page.
And yet once more I have missed May morning,
Not even heard the bells of Magdalen,
Merely the merry voices of morris-dancers
Returning in Queen's Lane.
O Mayday, come yet once again
For me that I may once in a lifetime
Arise with the dawn, go down the High
To the Bridge, the waters of time moving by
While we await the signal from on high.
But by what unconscious telepathy
Should Wystan have sent this Mayday
Message, traced the fact about my cat and me,
Faced me with myself this May morning
In unexpected printed charactery?

A Forgotten Soldier

Gay and casual and discontinuous,
Taking life and women as they come—
Who is that waiting at the gate for the nurse-girl
When you told me you were going on leave?
Faithless and feather-headed as a bird,
Tethered by no sense of obligation,
Changeable like the weather or the sea:
Here is the source of your unconscious charm,
Young pouf from the London streets,
To whom your old bachelor friend would give
Money, without ever making a demand on you—
You could not understand it, so you said.
Sex or love or gratitude: nothing of these
Meant anything to you, earning your bread

From hand to mouth, from one to another day by day:
Hanging round the Park for a pick-up,
Scrounging a pittance for a meal,
In return for your unregarded body
You set little value on. Then the Army
Caught up with you, taking away
Any care or thought for what may come.
Where are you now?
I doubt if you survived those years ago,
Fighting in the Desert, in Sicily, or at Anzio,
Fulfilling in your fate your last words to me:
'That is a thing I could never understand,
Why anybody should break their heart about me.'

Grantham

The soaring spire of Grantham
Is graven in my heart
From ways we went together
Before we drew apart.

All of eastern England
Spreads out on either side:
The tender green of pastures,
The meadows grave and wide.

Here a drift of primroses,
There a fruit-tree white:
All in the April evening,
The soft and shadowed light.

At top of the rise a church,
A flag flies from the tower;
The village crouches round about,
Awaiting the Easter hour.

On the slope the sheep are feeding,
A pheasant crops among,
In the dip the pale green willows
Trail misty veils along.

In a cutting silver birches
Catch a gleam of sun
That falls on folds and gables
Just before day is done.

All this we loved together,
But now the years have flown:
Absence and separation
Upon us both have grown.

The country we used to visit
Vanishes from the train
With love, with life, the ways
We shall not walk again.

Strange Encounter

In the sharp November air of Armistice day
I make my way through the churchyard, not to pray
But remember the generations that trod this path
Through the centuries before—to push open the door
And find myself alone in the silence of the church.
Thus early in the morning, no one there.
Moved, and yet unmoved to prayer,
I turn and find I am alone with a corpse.
The silence is listening, comes alive: who is there?
Who is it there under the folded pall,
Heavy with silence, as if aware
Of the stranger here, afraid of his own footfall
For fear it awake the dead. The stillness has ears:
The silence finds tongue in the candles flickering

At head and foot, as all through the night.
And now it is morning, no one to care
But the stranger, strangely moved in the half-light,
All unbelieving, goes through the motion of prayer
For one all alone: 'As you are now, whoever you are,
So shall I be, nor the time long ere I am as you.'
So saying, I draw away from the bay,
Afraid to remain close to whoever is there,
Perambulate the church still and grey in the chill
Morning air, moving further away from the bier,
In the shadows the flickering tongues of flame
Still following me, to where the Rood looks down
In pity and charity on him alike and me.

But why none of his family to watch and pray,
Why no one to wake the body its last day
On earth but the stranger, perhaps led this way
All unexpected and unknown to him or me?
Beneath the Rood I learn the dead man was a priest
Brought here for his last night to be spent
Beside the font where he ministered:
Perhaps it is meant I am to wake him,
Was sent to receive his benediction unknowing.
In the silence I thought I heard him sigh,
'And all is well, and all shall be very well.' And I
Ceased to fear to be in the company of the dead,
Of the priest awaiting his requiem, such as may be
        said,
I hope, though unbelieving, nevertheless for me.
All around me the sweetness and the silence
Dedicated to the dead, softly I withdraw,
Leaving him there alone with the Rood
To the absolution of solitude.

Looking up to the Chilterns

The downs today are silver-green and thistle-grey,
The water meadows punctuated by coloured cattle,
The breast of hill marked by prehistoric barrow
Tufted by a tree, the islanded waste
A mass of purple loose-strife and pink willow-herb.
O dark green waters and hills draped with trees,
Arms extended in blessing upon the land,
The scarlet poppies lighting up the corn,
Grey towers in clustered villages
Nestling in the crevices of the hills,
Chalk streams running down from the Chilterns,
Summer at its height in cedars and fringed willows,
Towering chestnuts and delicate spired poplars:
O all ye green things upon the earth,
    bless ye the Lord;
O all ye works of the Lord,
    bless ye the Lord.

Near Boconnoc

In spite of being given to words
I never have been able to express
Fully the sense of life at heart,
Find the right words for the mystery.
But then, who can?
All poets' words are but a charactery,
Notes traced on the margins of experience.
I stand at a gateway in silence
At the ecstasy of swallows over a field of wheat,
White-bellied, black-glittering, darting and diving,
Wheeling and skimming, a tumult of wings,
With the wind rippling in waves
Across a landscape all silver and green:
And underneath the mounded barrows and the graves.

Trewarne

Lapped in the leaf-filtered sun
Lies the grey house of Trewarne,
Looking down the valley to the mill
That clacks no more busily to the morn.

All is silent in the summer sun,
Fragile leaves on printed walls;
Within the flowered and waiting forecourt,
No foot that falls.

Tread softly: do not arouse the ghosts,
Nor wake the house from its long sleep.
Once, in the time of the Civil Wars,
It was wide awake, and down the slope
The sons of the house, confronting the day,
Buckled their armour and rode away.

A shadow clouds the upper windows
Where child-bed and death-bed alike had place:
In the haunted noontide, when all stands still—
The illusory withdrawal of a face.

What face looks out upon the selfsame scene,
Unchanged between Civil War and now?
The house is empty: behind mullion and lintel
No footfall, no murmur, how
Can there be eyes to watch
For the lifting of the latch?

Enter not: peer in through the panes
At bare hall and beckoning corridor:
Only the motes and dancing sunbeams
Scurry along the floor.

The house is withdrawn within its world
Of memory, nor cares who pass
And, looking within, see only themselves,
Transitory phantoms in mirrored glass.

Ardevora Veor

At turn of tide, clear sky,
Seventh September morn,
A boy goes sculling by
Down river from Ruan Lanihorne.

The secret flats of the Fal
Reveal unnumbered birds
Mirrored in quiet waters:
A world still beyond words.

Behind a screen of elms
A deserted house is there,
Haunted by its echo—
Ardevora, Ardevora veor.*

A herring-bone hedge of stone,
A lodge at the entrance gate,
An orchard of unpicked apples:
For whom, or what, does it wait?

Evidences of former love
And care on every side,
The anchorage, the quay:
No one comes now at the turning of the tide.

A planted berberis sheds
Its berries on the ground;
From the windlass and the well
No movement ever, and no sound.

The pretty panes are broken,
Blackberries ripen on the wall:
Peer in through the windows,
Whence no one looks out at all.

* i.e. Cornish for 'the great water'.

No one looks out any longer
Across the creek to the farm;
From candle-lit doorway to attic
No signal of joy or alarm.

Nor any motion of footfall
Beneath ceiling or rafter by day;
All laughter, all merriment over,
The ghosts have their way.

A house alone with its shadows,
The floors strewn with sharp glass,
What may have happened here
At Ardevora, Ardevora veor,
What estrangement come to pass?

Only an echo replies
Into the listening morn
As the solitary sculler
Moves silently down river
With the tide from Ruan Lanihorne.

Trenarren Winter

Smoke rises from cottage chimneys,
The crooked valley comes alive;
Wet roofs among Cornish elms
Shelter the winter hive.

On the way to the headland
The road the cattle pass,
Water in the cart-track
Gleams a ribbon of glass.

And I recall old Ben the bull
Swinging down the lane,
Returning with the herd:
They will not come this way again.

Nor George, the farmer's son,
Who went to sea at Hallane,
While Rover watched the beach
Night and day for a sign:

Who, as a boy, would range the fields,
Dog at heel, gun in hand,
Unconscious of grace and beauty,
Young master of the land.

And master of the girls,
Who have forgotten sooner than I,
Who see him still against the bay
Under a summer sky:

Like the bright day of sun and gale
Scarred in the memory,
The treacherous turn of tide
That swept him out to sea.

New Year in Cornwall

Billowing grey-blue sky,
The umbrella pines of Rome,
The grieving seagull cry,
To remind me I am home.

Along the line of ledra,
The winter smudge of browse:
Turn back up the valley
To the lighted house.

A late rook calls a curfew
Over the winter scene;
In the bank a hollow
Where honey-bees have been.

Now over the magic valley
Through the trees' leafless screen
Rises the silver moon,
Ravished but serene;

While over the shoulder of hill
Strikes on the listening ear,
From the navel of the parish,
The last peal of the year.

Summer Siesta

Waking in mid-afternoon of hot summer
Sun and sea patterns printed on the blind,
I hear myself saying, still half in sleep,
'I used to love Rover.' Dear dog dead
I used to hear the valley over, welcoming
The young master, shepherding the cattle home
Up the lane from the headland in the afternoon.
It struck me strangely to remember Rover
Suddenly, years after, dear visitor
Unannounced, his place long taken
By a young successor.
Why was I so disturbed to remember him?
Defenceless, vulnerable in half-sleeping state,
The will suspended that keeps fears away,
Controls the secret anguish of the mind—
Was it his watching the beach night and day
For the vanished master of the ivory skin and ferny
     hair?
No. It was the unexpected reminder
Of the relentless onward roll of life
Like the unalterable tide across the bay,
The irreversibility of time.
We were younger then when we came here:
The valley was full of youth: the master was alive,

His brother with the sloe-black eyes a boy
About with the cattle in boots too big for him,
Now away on questionable courses,
Never comes home. The farmer and his wife
Are a couple growing old, nothing to do
Who were so active all day long,
Sowing, harrowing, haymaking, harvesting.
No longer the cows come here to be milked,
No Rover to accompany them, in at the gate
With the milk in the fresh of the morning.
One has the sense of everything slowing down.
Youth has gone from the valley;
Only Rover has his sullen successor,
No work to do. I, growing older,
Keep a more solitary vigil
Out over valley, farm and bay,
Remembering their former occupants—
As they perhaps remembered theirs—
Suddenly aroused from summer siesta,
Pierced to the heart with the sense
Of the mysterious continuity of life.

The Beeches at Trenarren

'Let us walk up the road and see the beeches.'
The harmless phrase disturbs the suspended mind—
The road, the lane echoing with the feet
Of so many dead, of my own dead youth,
The eagerness, the ecstasy, the fire,
Sharpness of sensation, on edge with desire.
At Trevissick turn where the road forks
The old folks began to make a carriage-drive:
There the beeches grow, flattened by sea-wind
Like the umbrella pines of the Pincio.
Here, looking out over blue bay, headlands
Brown or green, after-harvest stubble-gold—

The harvesters are all gone into the earth:
Castle Gotha stands witness to the generations
Time out of mind, the ruined rampart,
The home of the silent vanished races
Discoloured earth, a little ash.
How to express the inexpressible
Sense of life, drifting cloud and air,
Of presences in the lane no longer there—
Myself among them—good old Davy,
Stout of heart and strong of arm, nobody
Could manage a roof-ladder like him;
George and Rover dead, Ray gone away,
Debonair and gay, driving his tractor
In the morning uphill to the upper fields,
Or down the lane tired at end of day.
No longer. All has passed into the cave of time,
Silted up like the sands in the bay,
Treasured and numbered, running through the hands
Of the sentinel on these cliffs, keeping his watch,
Overcome with the mystery
Of leaf and lane and tree,
The blue between beeches,
Of sun on sea,
And time and memory.

Distant Surf

'Go round to the front door, and you'll hear
The church bells ringing,' she says.
I obey the call, go up the worn and secret steps
Hollowed out by the generations
To listen up at the back among the beeches.
No longer sharp of hearing, as when a boy
I heard them resonant and loud in the alleys
Of the town, or borne on the west wind
Up to the village, on to the china-clay uplands.

Cupping ear in hand, at last I hear
A faint and distant surf of music on the breeze,
The changes no longer distinct and clear.
But I am pleased amid the melancholy
Wreck of my life—golden glow on the headland,
The rare north light of late summer
Reflected in the north-west, over the upper field
And on the underbranches of the beech-trees,
Upon the big black gate that gives upon
An illusory paradise, so desirable once,
A lonely land, no reverberation of love.
I have lost the distant surf, once so confident,
I have lost my way, navigating towards the end
Without compass or star, without faith or any hope.
Coming indoors, 'Summer is at an end,' I say,
'It is already autumn, it might be September.'
Yet, closing the door upon the world, I am consoled
To think that the church-bells I remember
From childhood can still be heard over the parish,
Out to the uttermost confines,
The headland catching the last light of the sun,
To mingle their distant surf
    with the surf of the darkening sea.

December 4th, 1969

The train ploughs slowly through the frosted fields,
And I am sixty-six today. 'The infirmities
Of sixty-six are coming on me,' wrote Samuel Drew,
My cobbler-townsman, antiquary and theologian.
No theologian I: a disillusioned humanist.
The cooling towers of a generating station
Dwarf the Thames Valley I knew as a boy
Coming first to Oxford. Looped wires and stalking
        pylons
March now across meadow and pasture,

299

Up chalk hills to Chilterns and the Downs
Of old Tom Hughes and the Scouring of the White
    Horse
Above lanterned medieval Uffington.
The filigree of trees stripped of leaves at last
I observe, though no winter blast
As yet to register defeat, withering
Of the faculties, winter of the soul, ice on the heart.
Only subdued grey melancholy
Over the russet and sepia landscape,
Upon which the winter sun rises
With low and level kindness of farewell,
A rarer radiance for being touched with frost.

In Fine

Things have been made easy for others,
But never for me.
Why should this be?—
That is the question.
Too uncompromising?
Too anxious to achieve?
All my life I have tried too hard,
And now that at the latter end
It might be thought
I had the ball at my feet,
I refuse to pick it up:
Instead I take
A malicious delight
In denying them,
And make
No further effort.

November Sunrise

Russet and rusty and gold,
The trees look wintry and old—
Though it is early November,
A month away from December.

Below the window I see
A contrast in greenery:
Puffs of perennial leaves
In mounded and rounded sheaves.

To me within the room
Reaches the muffled hum,
The mysterious harmony
Of the further, outer sea.

Or is it the inner caves
The quiet water laves,
Making a secret sound,
A music underground?

The eastern sky, ice-blue,
Now flushes a rosy hue,
And dawn announces the day
Over the sleeping bay.

Between me and the sea
A screen of filigree:
Dark and skeletal trees
Erect a formal frieze:

Through which an orange sun,
Curtains of night withdrawn,
Rises over the bay
Triumphant—and it is day.

Winter at Trenarren

Winter howls at the window,
    The trees are all distressed;
In the east an angry sunrise,
    Clouds pile up in the west.

Summer, alas, is over
    With all its gallant days:
Moorland and headland and meadow
    With bright sun ablaze.

Clouds gather over the landscape,
    The wind howls like a wolf;
Draw the curtains closer,
    The rafters shake in the roof.

Light the silver candles,
    Poke the glowing fire,
Where the fallen timber
    Makes the flames leap higher.

Bring my books about me,
    Take them down from the wall,
Stack them all around me,
    Buttressed against a fall.

Make my chair a refuge
    From the winter's rage,
And all the room a fortress,
    Firelit, from old age.

The Ancient House

The night is full of noises, false alarms—
O preserve me from its harms—
A summer wasp awakes from winter sleep,
Drowsily explores the hanging at my head;
Bed creaks, door bangs at the far back,
A dull thud among rafters of the roof.
The ancient house, demure and coy by day,
Lovely and withdrawn, reserving her secret,
By night comes alive, to live once more
Her life of the past, respond to footfalls
Of former habitants, answer their muffled calls
For consolation and relief, in suffering,
The awakening of those born and those who died.
This secret life of stifled noises
Like scuttlings of mouse or bat or rat
Warns me of my end in turn
Among all those.
Perhaps the footfall I hear upon the stair
Is my predestined murderer:
Already there.

Winter Splendour

Bands of orange and blue
One sees the black trees through—
Now gold amid the dun
Lit by the risen sun.

And brighter lemon below
Burns an improbable glow—
O saisons! O châteaux!

Season of delight—
Winter, when lawns are white:

303

A filigree of trees,
What brushwork dark, Chinese,
More delicate than these?
Moon and attendant star,
Venus or Jupiter,
Keep watch the white house over
Against what ghosts may hover,
Unearthly light distil
Over sea and hill:

Reign supreme in the sky,
While here at last I lie
Watching the fire's red eye.

Outside, the radiant night
A silver splendour of light—
O world beyond all thought,
O universe unsought,
Before my fire goes out.

Native Sky

For David Treffry

St Mabyn church-tower tops the world,
In the south the woods of Pencarrow,
Clouds dapple the valley to St Kew;
In the field, tractor and harrow.

The farmboy whistles as he goes
Making his tracks across;
A white gull follows his dark shadow;
We sit by the wayside cross.

From the granite steps five churches appear:
St Endellion peeps a pinnacle.
St Eval punctuates the west,
St Minver spires the hill.

Stockinged cattle crop the stubble;
Above, the barrow's edge;
Afternoon sun on the face of St Kew,
A pheasant calls in the hedge.

A signpost points to St Endellion,
Chapel Amble, Wadebridge;
The gulls rise soundless from the loam,
Toadflax glints on the ledge.

The sleeping farms lie all around,
And never shall you and I
Meet this magic moment again
Under our native sky.

End of Day

The sun sets behind Helman Tor
As I journey on my way—
Bradock church, Boconnoc woods—
Home from the delights of day:

Castle Drogo on its height,
With half of Dartmoor all around,
Mortonhampstead, the Dart at Postbridge,
A distant view of Plymouth Sound.

Across the Tamar are the places
Chiefly beloved: Couch's[1] Mill,
Lerryn, Lansallos, St Winnow church,
Restormel keep upon its hill.

These I have known since I was a child—
Sunrise and sunset, they keep me still
Company: Boconnoc and Lerryn,
The river Fowey and Couch's Mill.

[1] Pronounced Cooch; the word means red.

These are the names upon my heart
As I journey on my way,
And sun sets behind Helman Tor,
Homeward at the end of day.

Helman Tor

For Robin Davidson

A buzzard circles Helman Tor:
The prehistoric monster lours—
Saurian or pterodactyl—
Through an eternity of hours

Over its own intrinsic moor.
The mottled cattle crop below,
The stunted thorns creep up the flanks
And sharp their crippled shadows show,

Over the hill the pinnacles
Of Lanlivery church stick animal ears
Into the sky—as at any time
Since down the valley the Cavaliers,

From Stratton Hill to Bradock Down,
Crashed their way to final defeat.
Boulders upheave like elephant rumps,
Grey and wrinkled, out of the peat.

Beyond, the tiny patterned fields,
While overhead the buzzard planes;
Kingdoms are lost and empires fall,
States decay. But this remains.

Easter at St Enodoc

For Anne Mathias

O Mably and Treverton and Guy,
Here at St Enodoc they lie
Together beneath the twisted spire,
Across from Stepper and Pentire:

There runs the blue crystalline sea
Beyond the open estuary,
Where breaks the line of surf and spray
On the Doom Bar of Padstow Bay.

Tamarisk shrouds the church around:
There's the quarry whence came the stone,
Many a headstone on its mound
Lit at night by the light from Trevone.

Here a seaman cast on shore,
Far from the home his footsteps trod,
Nameless, alone, in time of war:
'Unknown to us, but known to God.'

Easter has garnished the graves with flowers
Placed by many a friendly hand;
Tumulus clouds and late March showers
Threaten across the shadowed land.

Up the lane the poet lives,
Flowering currant at his door:
Inspiration receives, and gives,
From hill and valley, stream and shore.

Within the church the candles are lit,
Flicker upon the upturned faces,
Where the assembled parish sit
In their accustomed pews and places.

Spring flowers brighten sill and pew,
Put about by the faithful few;
From the west a transient gleam
Upon the figures rapt in dream:

The western window says, bright and clear,
'He is risen. He is not here.'
Scent of grass and Easter sun,
Service is over and day is done.

Demelza

A mile long lane to Demelza,
    Half a mile to Great Bryn:
At the end of it shall I find the old folk
    In the lonely farm they were in?

The vast hearth open to the sky,
    A wisp of smoke thin and grey,
An ingle-nook you sit inside,
    Look up and see the blue of day.

The midday meal is being cooked
    In the middle of the afternoon,
In a fine muddle of flour and flurry,
    Hands in the dough without a spoon;

Potato peelings and bits and pieces
    Litter table and floor and chair,
Roof and rafters hung with oddments;
    The door opens, and suddenly there

Stand widowed farmer, and son
    A natural, courteous and kind:
This their ancestral place beneath
    The ancient camp, time out of mind.

These are the last of the family—
    What will become of it and them,
Failing and faltering to their end?
    No one to succeed, nothing to stem

The slow and steady onset of time
    In this queer sequestered place,
Surrounded by fallen walls and ghosts:
    The end of their familiar race,

Who built their own chapel by the road,
    Tended by the faithful band,
Now down to these last, of all the ghosts
    On whom John Wesley laid his hand.

The Monoliths

High up on St Breock Downs
Stand those very ancient stones
Of ominous, forbidding shape,
Erect amid recumbent sheep.

Slightly leaning to each other,
Braving every wind and weather
They loom, sulking and solitary,
On prehistoric cemetery;

Between, the breast-heave of a mound
Dominating miles around.
On close-cropped grass and nibbled pasture
They keep their ceremonious posture.

One confronts the rising sun,
The other the west, when day is done.
A farmer, from a wooded dell
Mysterious as Marinel,

Emerges in this lonely place,
Copper-coloured, louring face,
Attendant on the spirits here,
Fancies he sees a human leer

Across the taller standing stone
When day lifts at winter dawn,
And fires are lit on Midsummer night,
Setting the beacon all alight.

For then the centuries fall away
In the glare of night turned into day,
Recall the sacrificial rites
That filled with horror the lurid nights.

The bonfires burning were fires of bones
Burnt at the foot of the standing stones;
The people lacerate with rods
Their manic selves. These were their gods.

St Clement's

A gap in the hedge, a grey church tower
  Backed by the blue of a river—
St Clement's lies on a tongue of land
  Where the Fal flows on for ever.

The grey tower stands in a sea of blue,
  Honeyed light of noon
On lichened face and buttressed grace;
  In the sky a wisp of moon.

Two white cottages for sale
  The pretty place discloses,
Climbed all over by clematis;
  In the garden, roses.

The church gate opens upon the graves,
    Berberis, ivy and moss;
The gravel path leads down to the porch,
    Below stands Ignioc's Cross.

We push the door and enter the aisle—
    Coloured lights of glass—
Read the monuments on the wall;
    Shadows pass and re-pass.

But whose tall shade comes down the path
    From Penmount high on its hill?
The friend of my youth, whose parish this was:
    The place remembers him still.

Summer Work

There's a touch of autumn in the trees today,
A fringe of gold in the serrated leaves
Of Trenarren beeches along the upper path.
All summer long the groups and families
Have drifted by the hedge in twos and threes
To picnic and copulate at Ropehawn, Hallane,
In coves and caves out on the headland,
While I, stripped to the waist, cope with weeds,
Thistles, docks, couch-grass, uncut hedges,
In August heat of the valley open to the sea.
Overgrown orchard unpruned, dropping fruit
For unhived honey-bees and wasps to eat:
The drones of the people have no will to work.
Hook or scythe in hand I watch them pass,
Contempt in my eyes that meet their gaze:
For consolation when I turn my back
Cloudless blue over V-shaped valley,
Fountains of fuchsias, dripping crimson rain
Over the lane, where old Ben the bull

311

Used to come swinging home. No longer now.
A sudden scent of aromatic pine
Comes from the spinney, and over all
The summer gale from smouldering sea
Makes a hive-like murmur from the bay
Brimming with phosphorescent ecstasy
Out to the horizon: the valley filled with a voice
Wordless, the language of dreams and sleep,
Undertow, undertone, a burden of content.

Kenwyn Bells

O Kenwyn bells! the sound that dwells
　　Long after in the ear,
Coming down the vale of Allen,
　　Silvery and clear:

When on the hill-top of Penmount
　　We were still together,
On summer Sundays of the past
　　The chimes ran down the river;

By Killagordon and Ventongimps,
　　And outwards to Polwhele,
Past Clement's Cross and Penair Turn
　　On to Little Penheale.

Beside the tower the bishops kept
　　Their vigil at their ease—
Lis Escop in its hillside garden,
　　Ensconced among the trees.

Time has dispersed us all who then
　　Had not yet left our home,
And he who lent it mirth and life
　　Lies in his grave in Rome.

Bodmin Moor

I used to go this way to Oxford
    Past Penstroda and Trethorne,
On such a day at end of summer,
    A grey and clouded September morn.

The moorland ponies crop the turf,
    The sheep are strewn across the moor,
Grey and immobile as rocks
    From prehistoric ocean floor.

The signposts point to Blisland, Temple,
    St Neot, Cardinham farther away,
Through Bolventor and by Dozmary:
    Bursts of gorse light up the way.

Sunflowers in a cottage garden
    Turn their dials to the south;
A clapper bridge crosses the river
    Where herons rise from the undergrowth.

Perched on the shoulder of Rowtor
    St Michael's chapel guards the height:
A rainbow fills the threatening sky
    With fragile momentary light.

Sudden showers cross the moorland,
    Sunshine, blue sky and mingled rain:
April weather—but this is autumn,
    And not for me comes spring again.

Oxford beckoned at end of journey
    With youth and friends much to my mind:
The rain beats down, the moor is dark
    With advancing clouds, and life's behind.

Yarcombe Hill

On Yarcombe Hill the birds sing shrill
    While Geoffrey and I toil on our way;
The road winds steeply down to the bridge.
    And all is glad on a summer's day.

We look across the heave of the hill
    Where Sheafhayne manor secret lies:
Ransomed by Drake with Spanish gold
    Captured beneath Pacific skies;

Lived in still by the family's
    Descendant, a young Guards' officer,
Returned from the war to continue the line,
    Francis Drake's last, ultimate heir.

On Yarcombe Hill the wind blows cold
    Across the valley from Sheafhayne;
Down the path and in at the porch
    Alone I shelter from autumn rain.

The wind blusters around the church,
    The half-hour bursts upon the chime;
Within, I pace the aisle and mark
    The monuments of former time.

Near the altar I note the tablet
    To the young soldier's memory—
Already inscribed ten years ago:
    'He liveth in eternity.'

All around the saints stand still,
    St James with staff and scallop-shell,
St Peter with his key, St John,
    The Virgin in her tabernacle.

On Yarcombe Hill the snow lies thick
        Upon the silent winter slopes,
All down to where the River Yarty
        Dark under frozen surface sleeps.

Turning to go, behind me the gate
        Clangs above my muffled tread,
Awakes me, Geoffrey, from my dream:
        I cannot remember you are dead.

Marytavy

Marytavy, Marytavy,
        Blinking in the August sun,
We draw up at the churchyard gate
        After a Sunday morning run,

Up the valley from Tavistock,
        Skirting the edges of the Moor—
No one for church at Petertavy,
        Silent the bells and locked the door.

On we go around the gorge
        Over the narrow bridge we slow:
A couple of fishermen at the weir—
        This summer's drought the water's low.

And all around is spiritual drouth,
        Nonconformity in Devon
Dried up, the Methodist chapel shut:
        No one to go that way to Heaven.

And what shall we find at Marytavy?
        Apprehensively we search
Up the path and in at the porch—
        To find the parish all in church.

315

Six candles flare upon the altar,
    There all dressed in ferial green,
Out from the vestry pops the priest,
    Biretta and chasuble brightly seen;

Shuffling behind his acolytes two,
    Spectacles on the tip of his nose.
Under the roodscreen, into the chancel
    And up the altar steps he goes.

All three genuflect together,
    He takes the incense-boat in hand,
Gives the altar a thorough censing,
    While very reverently we stand;

And all the parish sings the Mass
    In plainchant to the manner born,
The *Gloria* first: it's all as if
    The Reformation had never been.

Here on the western slopes of Dartmoor
    The incense mingles with morning air:
Lost in thought, I lose my place,
    Look up, and see the priest is there,

Coming down the aisle, with flick of wrist
    Besprinkles the folk with holy water;
Unaccustomed, to my surprise,
    I suddenly receive a spatter.

Unexpectedly sanctified,
    Rather abashed, we beat a retreat;
The Mass goes on, but all around
    At Marytavy the air is sweet.

The Road to Ken

Turning down the road to Ken,
What should I discover then?
An unknown road, a secret lane:
Shall I ever come this way again?

Above the path a rose-red tower,
On the face of the church-clock the hour:
The gilt hands tell a quarter-to-ten
To the good people of the parish of Ken.

All on a still September morn
When from the fields the harvest's shorn,
A rose-red tower in a churchyard green
Roots in the inner mind the scene,

Gives something to remember when
I'm far from Devon and the fields of Ken.

Up in the clouds, approaching Maine,
The scene comes back in mind again:
The harvest home, the carts in shed,
The church-tower rooted in the dead.

A world away, and I wonder when
I'll see again the lane to Ken?

The Bewitched Woman

The bewitched woman—she was beautiful once:
What can have happened that she got like this?
Wandering around the great house like one lost,
Living all alone, the furniture piled up,
A maze of paths through which to thread one's way,
Brown paper on the floor, no carpet laid,

No curtains or hangings to keep out the sun,
Nor east wind funnelling up the valley.
Behold the swept gravel, the blue hydrangeas—
You'd not believe the devastation within:
Packing-cases unopened after years,
Every piece of tissue paper treasured
To harbour the unswept dust. Nobody comes
To pay a visit, or clean, or cook a meal:
'When I'm on my own, I don't bother.'
She's always on her own, wandering
From precious object to object, laying a hand
On things into which her life has drained and lost
All meaning and coherence. Each thing becomes
An end in itself: an oriental jade-tree,
A lacquer tray, a piece of amethyst;
Or hoarding the locks of ancestral hair,
Flaxen, gold, auburn, chestnut, grey,
Of haughty Pitts and querulous Grenvilles,
The pistols of a homicidal peer,
Who died in a duel—herself as mad as they.
How to account for it? Married to a man
Tepid and impotent, for money and rank,
Love already given to a shooting tough—
See on the chimney-piece his photograph,
All tweeds and knickerbockers of the twenties,
Broad-shouldered, broad-bottomed, affable
And male: he would have fathered a family
Drowned now in the depths of her angry eyes.
The bland and circumspect Queen Anne façade
Gives no hint of the disordered dream within,
The chaos of a ruined mind, the heart
Frozen and empty, the red and roughened hands
That once were fine, enamelled and beringed,
For ever flickering over the stored Sèvres,
Branches of crystal, bowls of golden agate
That, afternoons, hold the honeyed light.
Dust accumulates upon the Hepplewhite
And Sheraton; upon the ormolu table

A cake consumed by spiders—it might be
Miss Haversham's bridal cake preserved for tea.

The hours wear on in this house fallen asleep,
No difference made between night and morn,
The shutters never shut, blinds undrawn,
A sad enchantment spun about it all.
What will be the end of it? I see
Some chance marauder stealthily mount the stair,
Shuffling along the crowded corridor—
And the shed blood upon the cracked mirror.
Or perhaps a quieter end may supervene
In the tumbled bed that never has been made,
A havering light peer in upon the scene
Through cobwebbed windows of the moonlit front
Looking down the valley to lovely Lerryn,
The bridge, the boats that beckon to the open sea.

Boconnoc

I am moved by the thought of beautiful Boconnoc
In all the tenderness of spring:
Golden glades of daffodils beneath the beeches,
Antlered heads of stags well down in bracken,
The aspiring obelisk, the church and King Charles
Sleeping in his coach: all the memories of 1644.
Yet it's not that that possesses me,
But the southward slope where that sad couple
Are now together. I am haunted by the insatisfaction
Of their lives: the grand Abbey wedding,
The beauty of Dropmore and Boconnoc,
Surrounded by tenantry, obsequious
To those out-of-date grandees. Leftovers
From Victorian days: the eccentric state,
Though with hardly a servant to mitigate

Their *tête-à-tête*, which they would punctuate
With improbable journeys to Peru or up the Nile.
Nothing to say to each other through decades.
No children. No family life. Nothing to enjoy
Save the surrounding silence of park,
Rides of rhododendrons, cliff of rock-garden
Variegated with every kind of erica in bloom,
Sweet-scented azalea and broom.
From the church above I looked down on him
Below, moving slowly along the terrace
To the Chinese garden seats, for a breath of air,
Having spent half a sad lifetime there.
Now she comes to join him, remote lady
With the hot and angry eyes,
Never having known what it was to live;
Keeping tryst with the dusty treasures,
Bric-à-brac, bibelots, piles of Sèvres,
Disjecta membra of the Grenvilles and the Pitts,
The busts of the forbears: no thought for successors.

I am obsessed by the mystery of people's lives,
The mingled unhappiness and beauty,
The coldness and courtesy, the ritual and duty
Where there is no love.
Only the memories when days were full
Of observances and routine, attendants,
Butlers and footmen, maids, keepers,
Shooting parties over the coverts:
All dwindling down to a lonely couple,
Beds unmade, stale food untasted—
The wide domain unchanged around them,
The blank windows of the long gallery
Looking down the valley of the Lerryn,
Spreading oaks and beeches,
Plash of unregarding fountain,
The circumference of park around
That sheltered slope, the grave
Open to the sun.

The Devil from Linkinhorne

The ordinary aspects of daily life prove to be of no great fictional interest.
FLANNERY O'CONNOR

The Devil was born in Linkinhorne, they say:
I knew him in the village as a boy: he lived next door.
He came to St Austell as a navvy on the line.
He didn't drink, everything with him was sex.
A wonderful way he had with animals,
Birds and snakes, fitches and ferrets and women:
Reptiles, dogs and bitches would alike respond.
I've seen him take a maggot out of a sick
Ferret's neck not daring to bite the hand
That held the writhing whip of steel by the throat,
And cure the beast. He had a magic thumb.
Out of his pocket with no trouble he'd take
A coiling adder and make it comfortable,
Himself bite off the tender tail of a mongrel.
'I worship the ground he treads on,' said one hot
    woman,
Panting uphill from Holmbush to Tregonissey:
All the women but Jane, who could not hold him—
His wife, who had no imagination for him.

She had been warned about him, but too late:
A piece of lard enabled him to enter—
She found herself pregnant, poor simple fool—
People in those days knew not what to do.
Her godly parents shocked, her pious father
Sat up in bed at night to read the Bible
By a candle to the assembled family
With all the lengthened -èds of Holy Writ,
Spectacles on nose. What good did it do?

Lena Grose at Weighbridge, his fancy woman,
He'd spend the weekends there in bed with her,
Leaving his children in the village to starve,

Not a penny in the house for Jane,
Honest and afraid of him, shining and clean.
What was there about him? The magnetic look
In the eyes, cold and cruel, with no kindness—
Quite young he was a cynic about people,
Knew himself, and thought no better of others.
There was the ivory skin, the pure pallor,
Refinement of line upon sensuous features,
A profile could have gone upon a coin,
The well-cut lips with their upturn of scorn.

Innocent then, I never noticed the curve
In the leathern breeches, masculine and taut.
One day there he bared his chest of hair
Curly and golden, to affront and shock
The priggish boy, showed him a wooden phallus
He had carved, red-tipped and lipped as a rose,
For his erotic purposes.
                    What a gift
He had for growing roses, grafting stolen
Shoots upon wild briar; for making a garden—
With hidden garden-seat for fumbling girls,
The sleepers thieved, brought home by night from the
        line.
What a talent for bush-beating and liming birds:
The court was full of the song of captured
And caged finches, and there'd be a canary or two—
Seeds for them, if no food for the family.
He usually carried a net in his pocket,
Nor failed to mark the run of rabbit or hare—
There'd be a feed next door when we were asleep,
The feathers of plucked pheasant to tell the tale;
While old Cornelius, the crone with witch's chin,
From behind her blind would look balefully on,
Curse and ill-wish him as she did all men,
Having been early deserted with children
By her man—lost somewhere now in America.

He'd steal anything he could lay hand on—
My mother's scrubbing brush left in a bush
By the door, although she was feeding his young:
What did he care? He knew that for all her air
Of being superior she was only a woman,
Flung a four-letter word in her face: she flinched,
Hung back—'You know very well what it means.'
She did: she shrunk away like one whipped.
He had respect for neither God nor woman.
For him they were all Eve, he their snake.
When war came, he was a malingerer,
They never knew where to find a fly-by-night.
Then, run to earth, he hung his chest and legs
Heavy with coppers and keys to induce symptoms
Of varicose veins and swallowed pieces of soap
To fabricate foam at the mouth, affect the heart,
When called up for military service.
Rejected, he was sent to make munitions
In Limehouse. The life of the East End in wartime,
Neglect of himself, perhaps the prostitutes,
Killed him, who was a natural pagan,
A denizen of country woods and fields.

Still a young man only in his thirties,
A shadow of himself, he came home to die
With his little son, his victim, who took his disease:
Both of them tended faithfully to the last
In the stricken court—no birdsong or roses now—
By mute and patient, uncomprehending Jane.

Winter is Here

My life is folding up, leaf by leaf:
First one petal, then another is shed.
I can no longer walk around the garden,
Let alone take tool as once I could,

Hoe and fork on shoulders, shears under arm,
Sally down the stony path to paddock,
For a day's work on border, plot and bed,
The skies of Trenarren wheeling overhead.
Nor take the scythe and rake to tennis-court,
An overgrown wilderness when I
Come home from Oxford in July. No more
Climb up into the rafters of the roof
And out upon the leads, to view the valley,
Green slopes descending to the sparkling sea.
An old man on a stick hobbles round
Terrace and level lawn outside the house:
No more those day-long tramps across the moor,
Up the white and glistening granite roads
To Trethurgy—the otter's hamlet—and Luxulyan,
On through ferny brakes to Lanlivery,
The church-tower rising suddenly on the right,
And down into Lostwithiel, my head full
Of Richard, King of the Romans, the Black Prince,
And all their train sweeping up by the river
To the grey walls of Restormel on its hill.
Or in later years to visit my old friends
At lordly Lanhydrock—myself now old as they
Remaining in the cool and shadowy house,
While we walked up the sloping lawns to see
The magnolias hold their torches to the sun,
Rare rhododendrons and scented azaleas.
No longer scramble down the rocks to the beach
Ar Hallane, past Will Treleaven's flower-fields,
The red and showering fuchsias, the strawberry beds,
To slip into ice-cold water beneath the stream.
The summers are gone, spring and even autumn:
The sere winter of life is here, is here.

To Oxford

Through early Sunday sleep of Biscovèy,
Not disturbing the sleep of my grandparents
Nearby in the churchyard, from whose seed I stem:
I pass the church at St Blazey, lights at the altar,
The celibate priest saying his early Mass.
Lovely Luxulyan Valley of my youth
Opens its mouth to the waterfall, leads up
To the claypits, my poor father's industry.
A rook in the road, black-coated clergyman,
Rises and flaps into the fields of Penknight
Of my ancient neighbours, the Kendalls of Pelyn.
Clematis climbs the wall at No Man's Land;
Irises flag a garden, bluebells in the hedges
And dandelion clocks, the flowers over.
Lostwithiel, the Duchy stannary town
In its hollow, is still asleep. No smoke rises,
But azaleas and rhodos fume upon the walls;
Loveliest of trees, the cherry now explodes
In suburban pink along the bough. Princely
Boconnoc of the Pitts and Fortescues
Spreads its woods upon the skyline towards Looe.
The turning to Lanhydrock takes me in thought
To the grey mansion, nested among trees,
The last of the family sitting out their days
In their redoubt between church and barbican;
The avenue planted in the Commonwealth time
By that stern Puritan, the Lord Robartes,
So past Catchfrench, of kind George Brimmacombe,
Lived there complete with boy-friend and a wife.
Now the high moors—Caradon, Kit Hill—open
Out towards Dartmoor: I prepare to cross the Tamar.
All on a May morning memories throng:
Charles long dead, Richard and Bruce dead,
Geoffrey now dead, my early dearest friends—
I take the road to Oxford now alone.

Oxford Station

See that man standing on the platform
Hat in hand, west wind in his hair,
Back to the passengers waiting for the train,
A look of some disdain for the nondescripts,
Ruffling squalid newspapers, chewing,
Chattering and shacking up with each other,
Acne'd girls and pimpled, graceless youths:
All the *tohu-bohu* of Eastern Europe,
And odds and ends from Asia, Africa.
Impatiently he awaits the signal
When a cat cautiously crosses the track:
He is alarmed for an animal
Self-contained and lithe, beautiful and free.
An engine approaches, across the breast-plate
OMOO—he recognises the signal
From a fellow-spirit, Melville,
Restless and ranging, like himself
Unrecognised by the herd, solitary
And free.

Trowbridge

Sending a book to California
I notice upon the fly-leaf these few words:
'To John, from Mother'—sometime in the twenties.
The book, old Farnell of Exeter's
An Oxonian Looks Back, proud book-plate
Of the young owner, of *Coll: Exon: Oxon.*
There's the high gable of the Sainte Chapelle
The Victorians imitated in their day,
A college room facing away down Ship Street.
Here he lived his quiet life in the twenties,
A sober exhibitioner, a barber's son,
Yellow corn-coloured hair, long of leg,
Like Edward Longshanks with one drooping eyelid—

A curious effect of collusion it gave.
How proud Mother must have been of her lanky son,
Who had won an exhibition to come to Oxford.

This look into the past in a faded book
Opened a gate in the wall, the years now dead
When spring thrilled along the nerves and veins:
In summer those shadowy watered streets,
The Turl, the Broad and Brasenose Lane,
The life so hurriedly lived, so much enjoyed,
And now all over, folded and put away.
The later schoolmaster, talented with boys,
Rumpling their hair, producing them in plays,
The affectation of professional theatre-chat,
With mumbled, half-articulated speech;
The summer conferences organised at Stratford,
Cosy rooms reserved at the Swans' Nest
Looking on the river, Hugh Clopton's bridge.
He had more fun than I with likely friends,
A gleam of expectation in tolerant eyes
Blue as his distant Wiltshire downs and skies.

Today I came through Trowbridge on my way
To Oxford, and wondered where was the barber's
    shop
Vanished these many years and where lived the boy
Who walked across fields to Hilperton and Melksham,
The church-bells of Wiltshire in his ears.
Over the town hung the smell of brewing hops,
Young folk scurrying here and there, as if
He might be one, a life now over and done.
Prunus and cherry white along the bough,
Cushions of arabis adhering to the wall,
Aubrietia blue and bursts of forsythia
In little terraced gardens—I wonder where
They lived, the barber's family now extinct,
Mother's son not one for marrying,
And only I to remember him passing by.

The Revenant

The door opens to the familiar key,
And once more I am within the rooms
Formerly my own, no longer mine.
I am a stranger. Yet so much of life
Passed within these walls, so much
Happiness in work, looking up to see
Gold and black caverns in the copper beech,
The rose-flush of dawn upon the Camera,
Moonlight upon the dome sifted with snow.
So much, too, of anguish and waiting—
Waiting for whom, or what? I will not say.
My feet echo along the empty corridor,
Here are the bookshelves that held my books,
The gaping windows that leave too much
     exposed—
The familiar ghost, the unwanted *revenant*.
The floorboards quicken to my faithful feet,
Send back an unacquainted sound.
Nothing has changed. Yet all has changed:
Some spirit has flown, gone out of things,
Leaving untouched only a glimpse of the garden
From my bedroom of inner memories,
Of illness and intermittent happiness.
Autumn is evident in the garden beds,
Rain on Michaelmas daisies, the lemon-gold
Of leaves and bedraggled flowers.
And it is All Souls' Day, when we pray
For those who were here before us and felt
Perhaps as I do today. A bell tolls
Its melancholy note: Remember them,
The souls of the faithful departed
Who once lived here and had their being
Even as I. The door clangs behind me—
I could tell its sound a hundred miles away;
My feet recall the tread of the stone stairs:

I could find my way blindfold
Who now go down for the last time
And out of the door, for ever, away.

Summoned by Bells

Two ghosts stood talking in the Turl—
'And are we dead?' said one to the other:
'So many of those we knew and loved,
Were young with, are.' 'Perhaps we are, brother.'

At that the bells rang out, over the roofs
And down the street, into the heart
To remind them their friends were not forgot,
Their lives caught up in the tongues

They knew when they were alive and heard them
Just as we, meeting in the street years after,
Were speaking of their endearing ways,
Carefree youth and happy laughter;

How one, though given to malice, was concerned,
When his friend was ill, lest he should die;
How another he loved could not respond,
Yet treasured his letters now too late.

'Too late, too late': these were the words the changes
     rang
Like fate, all down the scale, and in and out
As those two survivors stood and talked
On the worn pavement, where they had walked

When they were young: recalling their friends,
Their years summoned up so vividly
That which were the dead and which alive
They hardly knew in that moment of mystery.

The Road to Stratford

How well I know the loved, familiar road
Across the Cotswolds, over the divide
At Great Rollright, the standing stones he knew—
The folklore king and queen holding their court—
And down into the rich Vale of the Red Horse.
I think of him spurring his tired jade,
Measuring the miles away from his friend.
Here the English names lie like a garland
On signpost and turning—Tredington and Shipton,
Ilmington, Idlicote, Alderminster,
Clifford Chambers with its memory
Of friend and poet, fellow countryman,
Now but a name on a stone monument.

Today, at Welcombe, a blue Umbrian sky
Over green lawns; the valley leads the eye
By willow-drooping lake to white fields
Drifted with daisies; the further distance gold
With buttercups, kingcups and his favourite cowslips.
This is the moment of forget-me-nots and flags,
Of thrushes echoing in the coverts, shouting
From tree to tree, woodpigeons, cuckoo-notes
Thrown across the valley, a chime of birds.
Bees visit and knotted snakes emerge
From winter sleep. A Spring breeze filters
Through the beech-fronds, bends over the long grasses
And daffodil leaves bereft of flowers. Puff-balls
Of white may stand in the hedges, a heavy
Chestnut candelabrum hangs over the lake.

Here and there in the glades the lovers walk—
A tall, fair officer out of the R.A.F.,
Strong-shouldered, lithe, short-sleeved shirt,
Complete with spectacled nondescript on arm
(Sweet lovers love the spring). All afternoon,
Amid the scents and sounds of flowers and insects,
I hear the wistful music of Falstaff's dream.

Now on Whit Sunday, at Shottery, after the war
The twisting lanes and gardens are all tulips
Red and white, bluebells and yellow arabis,
Clumps of lavender in front of Quyny's cottage.
The slope down from Hathaways' is alive
With the movement of blown trees in shadow: their
   yardland
An orchard now, beehives screened by poplars.
A Whitsun crowd, brought out like insects
By the sun: young men in shorts, on bicycles,
Taking photographs; solitaries, children, dogs;
A mouth-organ plays a sad little tune; American
On bike, back from the Pacific war.
Suddenly a bell rings to church
Across gardens ringing with birdsong.

Beyond Long Compton, Brailes Hill stands up
Above the butter-yellow fields of May.
Alighting from the bus a young soldier
Plants his wallflower wife, like a Madonna
With baby, on suitcase in the village street;
The corner decorated with blue irises,
Lilacs blowing their heads about in the breeze,
Dark blue and purple aubrietia, white candytuft,
The thirsty cups of tulips drink in the sun.
And high above heave of hill—the divide,
In blue of sky a pale ha'penny moon
Looks down upon the road he came and went.

Winter in Stratford Church

The winter wind rattles in roof and rafter,
Yet all the townsfolk are in church—needs must.
The morning's milk came frozen home in pail.
A flurry of snow dusts the churchyard path
By the charnel house where he saw his little boy:

'I am afraid, and yet I'll venture it.'
The choir where canons of the College prayed
Is empty now, boarded up, derelict.
Hear the rain and wind beat dark December,
Loosen the leads, worry the quarried panes
Where once glowed saints in all their coloured glory,
Brasses ripped up, slave to mortal rage.
Late-comers arrive, shuffle along to pew,
Huddle together to keep warm in their own steam
That mingles with smoke of brazier at the back,
Spiralling up into the tower by the font,
Where he and all the family were christened.
Now they are gathered up in front, below
The pulpit where coughing drowns the parson's saw.

Suddenly a word is dropped into that well
Of the imagination, the listening ear:
'Therefore hath he mercy on whom he will
Have mercy, and whom he will he hardeneth.'
The ears that take everything that people say,
Automatically register absurdities,
Shut out the noises of the congregation,
While thoughts stir behind the secret forehead.
'On my frailties why are frailer spies,
Which in their wills think bad what I think good?
No: I am that I am.'
                    The homely wife

Sits unstirred, unobtruding, beside him,
Noticing nothing, no disturbance of mind—
Or how much does she know or guess, who keeps
Silence, never uttering a word?
Remorse of conscience for what cannot now be helped
Enters the crevices, thoughts cohere
While eyes wander around the white-washed walls
That yet not obliterate the Risen Lord
In judgment, the Doom looking on the scene,
The good and bad in everyone, the true

And seeming, the ineradicable fault
In nature. Words from around the Figure
Now but a shadowy outline on the Cross:
'Why, all the souls that were, were forfeit once
And he that might the vantage best have took
Found out the remedy. How would you be
If He, which is the top of Judgment, should
But judge you as you are. O, think on that!'

Stoke Edith

This way the Lady Emily came to church,
'For sixty-seven years a constant worshipper
And generous benefactor to the poor:'
Now a name on a tablet in November sun
Among the ordered Georgian pews—the one
For the family deserted, up by the altar
Where they are gathered in, the line ended.
One has the sense the place is not attended
As when the Lady Emily lived on in state,
A widow in her weeds for half a century.
See the grateful poor from the cottages
At church on Sundays—their pale faces press
Against the yew hedge that's still in shape,
Though overgrown with ivy, laced with elder.
A little frost in the carriage-way—one might
Still think the print of horses' hooves; at night
She would command the carriage for so short a drive.

Here is no mystery to penetrate,
No superfluous spiritual illumination,
As at Burnt Norton or Little Gidding, only
The loss of money, failure of a family—
As if that is not mysterious enough,
That one generation should be able to create
And build, and then the vital spark give out,
Flicker feebly for a while, then go quite out.

Leaving this hole in the sky where a great house was
With its eager life, the footmen pursuing the maids,
The stables full of hunters and carriage-horses,
Saddles and harness bright as battering sandal;
Portly butler at the front door where I stand
In vacant space; the oval that was lawn
Still there untrimmed, awaiting the carriages
For Sunday church or a neighbourly visit.
In the stable wing a trapped bird beats itself
Against the glass. The garden is waiting there,
Overgrown with old man's beard and spindle,
Shadowed by cedars looming darkly down
On the ruin and devastation, where all was order,
The paths prim and swept, the lawns razored;
The hounds and hunters gathered for a meet,
The family assembled for welcome or farewell.
I am the only visitor, a man
Dedicated to remembering such things,
To recovering the irrecoverable,
Gathering the fragments to shore up our ruin,
Nourish the shadows no one cares to think of,
Cherish the ghosts to give them a little warmth,
A local habitation and a name.

The Squire of Felbrigg

Gather these fragments from my friend's life,
Rounded and finished, returned to the soil
He loved, woodlands and fields of Norfolk,
The belt of trees the forbears planted
Between Felbrigg and the sea.
Here the boy at Harrow hears
The wild duck winging over the house at Beeston,
Smells the fresh air from the sea, yet flower-
Scented from the garden. Here's his bird
That sang through months of illness and winter
To cheer him. Here is his golden retriever,

Ruby, with the master in the woods all day,
The peopled trees he loved, squirrel, finch, thrush—
Though more for themselves, for their upthrust
To the skies, the spareness of silver beech,
The strength of ribbed oak, the wonder and worship
Of woods, spread with bluebells in spring,
In autumn carpeted with fern.
Summers in Le Fayet and Chamonix,
Lucky boy, already familiar with antique shops,
Mezzotints and lacquer trays,
Knew the blue of Tibetan poppies.
Your brother dead, you became my friend:
Now dead in turn, my junior in years,
I find these fragments of your early life
I did not know,
Piece together the portrait of what you were
Near fifty years ago.

In Memoriam:
Elizabeth Harcourt

Behold the brecklands of Norfolk
        this November morning:
Intermittent sun lights up
        a Cotman church-tower like a cup,
Catches the bellies of wood-pigeons in flight
        across ploughland and pale park.
The early sun gleams on the dark
        ivied trees of Old Crome,
Russets the plumage of beech and oak
        over the undulating pastures.
Pheasants strut in the stubble, reflect
        the broken blue skies of Peter de Wint
        in peacock hue upon proud neck
        and tail-feathers arched like the firmament.

Birds collect in formation for winter flight
        while the train shuttles across
            the lighted landscape of ridge and furrow.
And it is All Souls' Day, bright
        as a day shimmers in summer.

In New York it is still night:
An only light glimmers under a green shade
        where a girl lies sleeping,
            a smile upon the clever sensitive lips,
Those lambent eyes closed for ever,
The flower-like face shut up in night,
        a tulip cut upon its slender stalk,
The shapely head fallen to one side,
The light now extinguished quite.

Adam

All my life I've always been frustrated
By envious human beings, inspired by jealousy
Of an evident and honest superiority
(See Milton) at school and at the university,
In literary life, the snake-pit of society:
If they could checkmate, frustrate, keep out,
Reject one already from the hour of birth,
They would, themselves unknowing the inner fact
But intuitively inspired, if they could, to destroy
The growing boy.
In fact, all has worked out very well,
Rid me of any obligation to my kind,
Enabled me to concentrate on the thing in hand,
The assumption being—their loss, not mine.
Quite another thing from the sense of providence
That guided me, the guardian angel at the gate,
Forced me to labour in the sweat of my brow—
Without the distractions of seductive Eve—

At that which from the first I was meant to do.
With split nature, impossible to satisfy,
Gifts on one side, defects on the other
To turn into advantages, eventual triumph—
A pity perhaps—over original good nature
Like Adam's, now become Swift's.
Repent not, nor conciliate: the achievement's
The thing, the ecstasy, the rapture,
Listening alone in the silence for the word,
One apart from others, evening light
On darkening beech and over the threatened city,
Civilisation falling in the sound of bells,
Rising and falling, relishing the thought that
Knowing humans is a waste of time.

The Outsider

Outside, for ever outside of everywhere,
Never within the welcoming walls
Where others are at ease and feel at home,
In their familiar aquarium:
Unaware of themselves in their element—
Fish in water, for ever pursuing each other,
Jaws working, gaping and gawping with fixed stare,
Unaware of where or what they are.
Would one be one of those, warm in the tank,
Or prefer to be well outside on one's own,
Alone, but an observant, sentient being,
Without illusion, knowing the human score?

Knowing

Nobody ever understands anything.
HENRY JAMES

Certainty?
Apparently
They object to my certainty:
But what's the point of writing about
What you are not certain about?
Better to keep your uncertainties
To yourself, retain mysteries
Within the inner shaping self
Until they come clear,
Ready for the light of day,
Sharp as a bugle-call.

As for them all
Living in a never-never land
Of doubt and unclarity—
Naturally
They cannot see
Anything defined or clear.
They should be content with what is,
Thankful for small mercies,
Rendered so
For their benefit, to learn
Since they cannot discern
And never know.

The Scillies: Finis Terrae

The world is uninteresting today:
Too small and cramped, nowhere
That is not already known—
None of the excitement of early explorers
Finding new islands like rain

338

Scattered upon the surface of the seas.
Cramped and cabined and confined
We are here in our murderous crevices
Too well informed of every day's news
Of ambushes, traps, bombs in bars,
Too many people, too many everywhere—
More of them arriving every day at Heathrow,
Turbaned, bearded, living in suitcases,
Swathed in bright-coloured saris,
Saffron, canary yellow, lemon or lavender,
Swamping the silly little island
Where the people have never had it so good.
Nowhere for us to go to, nowhere to go:
We must content ourselves with the Scillies.*

* Adopted retreat of Sir Harold Wilson, Knight of the Garter.

On Being Robbed

Somewhere, wide in the world,
Is an unknown man
Who knows all my intimacies,
Has been through all my things,
My cupboards, closets, cabinets,
Chests of drawers, boxes, desks, papers,
Been into every room, through every thing,
Knows the whole run of my house:
Smashed three windows, forced two doors
To break into this locked and barred redoubt,
Leaving a bloodstain to remember him by.

Now he knows me through and through,
This unknown man two hundred miles away—
No starlight lit his lonesomeness,
Just a few matches thrown about
Here and there, until he found
My phallic torch.

Then all was not difficult—to make away
With delicate blue-john urns, their ormolu swag
Having an allure for this old lag—
Or more likely young. Which was he?
How much I long to see
Him by the light of day.

Unknown prowler while I was away,
I long to see you face to face,
Hug and hold in a thief's embrace.
Mysterious intruder, my life
Has no mystery for you—
All laid bare in my rare possessions,
Snuff-boxes, card-cases, *étuis,*

Porcelain, agate, tortoise-shell, mother-of-pearl,
That have accompanied me over the years
Since, I, a boy from the working class
Not far removed from you,
Used to come here and long to enter in—
No thought of shivering the glass—
This lonely paradise, no longer now alone,
For you have penetrated.

Everywhere I look I see you here,
Lurking on staircase, in corners,
Behind curtains, in bedroom and corridor,
A shadow in the night's alarms.
O thug and thief, my robber and lover,
Come forth, take me in your arms!

Modernist Verse

The verse of Sylvia Plath
Is too esoteric for me;
And yet there's no doubt at all
It's authentic poetry.

Her poetry shows very clear
    She was obsessed by suicide,
Drug-haunted, dream-tormented,
    Swung by every moon and tide.

Such fine-spun intellectual drift
    He may catch and hold who can:
Verse so exotic can never speak
    Clearly to the heart of man.

New Poems

VII

For more than thirty years I have wanted to write this poem. The local story of Charles Rashleigh of Duporth has lain all that time in my mind—but not inactively: I have often thought of this remarkable man to whom our landscape here owes a lot to remind us of him, and of his mysterious story, of which so much is missing. Only the outlines have come down to us, with attachments of folklore and superstition in the creative way that the older unconscious or subconscious life of the people added to their memories. With an historian's respect for the past, I have taken few liberties with it: the truth about people, if one can only find it out (as with Shakespeare's Dark Lady), is always more interesting than people's conjectures.

Born and brought up in Cornwall, I am fortunately old enough to remember the folklore, the unconscious memories, of my early village and parish life. It has been a perpetual source of inspiration, as readers of *A Cornish Childhood* will know. I always meant to make a poem of the Duporth story, but could never get forward with it until a fortunate chance placed in my hand some letters and fragmentary material which helped to fill in the shadowy background. I am grateful to Elizabeth Sparrow for thus helping me to clinch my intention after so many years.

The poem is written in the blank verse I find appropriate to narrative, which comes nearest to the form into which English speech falls naturally—witness the whole of Elizabethan drama. But my verse is never all that blank. The attentive reader will notice constant alliteration, along with occasional rhyme to vary and decorate it, often internally as well as at the end of lines.

A fellow poet, W. R. Rodgers, was always alive to the continuous creative inspiration of folklore, folk tales and speech—alas, sadly eroded and fragmented in today's nondescript, shiftless, demotic civilisation.

346

Duporth

(I)

There is the house upon a southward slope
Looking to the sea, sheltered by leafy flanks
Of stunted oak and beech, lateral screens
That open wide their arms to embrace the shore.
'The House of the Doomed Shore' I used to call it
Romantically in my childhood story
(Now I seek but history and the truth).
This afternoon all is jewelled, clear,
Translucent like the water that but sips
And saps upon the shore below. And here
Am I ensconced in the lane the smugglers trod,
A pebbled lane where a little silver stream
Makes music all the summer afternoon:
A place now choked with purple thistle, ragwort
And rank cow-parsley. At the end of the road
A camouflaged gunpost, covered now
With feathery grasses, red sorrel and a few
White cornets of convolvulus. Beyond
There lies the bay of Neapolitan blue
Today, the Gribbin our Posilippo.

The sun gleams through the trees, making patterns
Of leaves and light, the gulls, contented, laugh.
The wrinkled hide of the Gribbin, old sea-monster,
Defines the distance, the four buoys stand out clear
As if to mark the drowned lads of the seventies.[1]
There is the tall white target-float for the planes.
Looking up the lane a war-time notice:
'W.D. Admission on Business only.'
All is quietness and *Wohlgemut*,
The war over; the mingled oats and barley
Whisper and ripen under the summer sky.

[1] See, 'The Old Cemetery at St Austell'.

The gate clangs: I am reminded by
The cheerful cheap accents from the neighbourhood
Of Birmingham, Walsall or Surbiton
The place is now a holiday resort.

But I know it in quite different moods:
The sea-mists drifting in upon the land
Blanketing it with whiteness and with silence,
Blotting out the landscape and the house,
The sifting mists caught and hung on the branches
Like shrouds—veiled and hollow presences
That watch round the house, grey and lowering clouds
That sit on the smokeless chimneys where the owls
Hoot hollowly through the winter nights
Answered only by the Há-ha-ha of gulls.
From the muffled coast one hears the beat and surge
Of the sea upon the rocks, and then remembers
The old forgotten meaning of the name.

Dúporth means dark beach against white Gwéndra—
Anything sinister in that? A strange fate
Befell the place: I always wanted to tell
The story. The place itself possessed my mind
All the years of my youth—a Naboth's Vineyard.
Living an impoverished life in the village above
I would come down to the coast and from the cliffs
Look longingly up to the grey, deserted house—
No-one ever appeared at window or door,
No sign to betray the mysterious life of the gentry
The bookish boy had read of but never knew
And, envious, resentful, longed to penetrate,

Only once did he succeed—at a sale
At fifth or sixth generation from the founder,
Successors, but not of his family.
A dull November afternoon filled
The house with the sense of sadness, the youth thought
Of Chekhov's *Cherry Orchard*, the old retainer—
The family departed—shutting the shutters up.

348

Here were the shutters, the musty bookcases,
The Regency library looking down to the sea,
Dark dining room, the heavy portraits in gilded
Frames: several portraits of earlier Rashleighs
Years later I saw in the auctioneer's villa
At Tregarne Terrace in the town: noone would buy.
I hadn't a penny to buy anything.
Amid the flotsam and jetsam, an account book
Of the Duchy Stannary of Tywarnhayle
Has remained in my memory over thirty years.
Had he been steward? And in which among the portraits,
Bewigged and Georgian, was he who created it all?

Not only the house, but planted the estate,
Formed the grounds and filled the southward ravine
With flowering shrubs, early rhododendrons
Brought from the Himalayas, camellias
When the gorgeous East was still in fee, gold dust
Of mimosa, magnolia from America.
He threw a granite wall around his park,
A belt of beeches down Brick Hill to his port,
Calling it Charlestown after his name—
A piece of hubris asking for nemesis.
Not content, the miners' village he called Mount
    Charles—
After all, he'd called it all into being—
Broke in the moor around the monolith,
The prehistoric menhir by the barrows
He obliterated to make a road:
A rational Georgian gent having no use
For superstition. Yet was it wise to affront
The unknown powers that lurk under the earth,
Tempt fate, an unpropitious destiny?
Particularly on setting forth, the first
Of a new line, though sprung from old historic stock?

How much I longed to know more about
This mystery man, banished from popular

349

Memory, no one remembered him, and yet
He has left the mark of his hand on all the land.
Who was he? For thirty years I've been in search
Of information, suppressed and relegated:
A more respectable 'In Quest of Corvo',
Not less rewarding, but no less difficult.

(II)

Arrived at All Souls kind old Oman said,
'You come from St Austell? That's the place that had
The 18th century landscape wall-paper,
A fine specimen, now in the V. and A.'
I'd never heard of it. The idiot people
See nothing, know nothing, and never understand
Anything: it may be imagined how much I resented
Being born among them, who should have been born
At Duporth, heir to all that elegance.
In the vacation I hurried to the White Hart Hotel—
The house Charles Rashleigh built, of silvery granite,
For town residence and law offices.
There was his dining room, Adam fire-place
And chimney-piece, tall Venetian window,
And behind a panel a piece of the paper
To show what once had surrounded the room
With imaginative grace: a marine scene,
Turreted castle, a shore-line like Duporth itself.
Across two centuries I recognised
A kindred spirit, of sensibility,
A man of taste. This glimpse into his life
Inspired research. What kind of man was he?

Charles was the fifth son of Jonathan Rashleigh
Of Menabilly, that rose-red Queen Anne house
At the other end of the bay, behind the Gribbin,
The long peninsula a world of its own
—Made famous by my friend as 'Manderley'

350

In *Rebecca* and, later on, *My Cousin Rachel.*
The pretty park sinks down to the beach at Pridmouth,
And so around the coast to the harbour of Fowey.
There the Rashleighs made their fortune in trade
And shipping: John Rashleigh sailed his little ship
The *Francis of Fowey* up to serve under Drake
At Plymouth against the Armada, in '88.
They moved their wealth before the Civil War
Into that delightful land with its combes,
Cornish elms, ilexes, cork-oak,
Its fields and pastures running to the sea.

A century later, a fifth son needed to move
For himself, make a career in army or law
Or the Church. Young Charles made a start as a soldier
—Nothing of this is known, or how he came out.
We hear of him first as a lawyer, a country attorney
Setting up in the town of St Austell, a junior
Partner in the firm of elderly Polkinghorne,
Then pushing him out to form his own, Rashleigh,
Coode and Kempthorne, all good county names.
Ambitious, full of energy, never at rest,
One sees him reaching out for office and place,
Under-sheriff of Cornwall, year after year.
His elder brother, Philip, in Parliament
Holds the family seat: no place for him
With far more brains, initiative and drive.
He must cut a swathe for himself, harvest
The innings, accumulate stewardships
Of others' estates, until he can found his own.

We have a letter from dear Fanny Boscáwen,[2]
The Admiral's admirable wife and widow,
Accepting Rashleigh's candidature for hers.
He became steward of her remote estates
Near Land's End, Dormynack of my friend, Derek
   Tangye,

[2] Pronounced Boscó-wen.

351

Boscawen-ros, of that ancient family
The original *Ursprung*: 'the dwelling by the elder tree
On the heath'. A friend of Mrs Delany sets out
For Cornwall in the summer of 1774.
Makes for Mount Edgcumbe and Boconnoc of the Pitts;
After that, all is strange and foreign.
'From Lostwithiel seek directions to St Austle,
Which may possibly be out of the way
Of the direct road to Land's End. But there's *a mine*
Near St Austle better worth seeing than any,
By reason of the close resemblance it bears
To the Duke of Bridgewater's underground navigations.'
This must be Polgooth, the making of the town,
Its fortune in those distant days, Rashleigh
Had a lucky share in Polgooth Mine,
The beginning of his mining interests:
In which he came to conflict fatally
With the Carlyons of Tregrehan, who held the land
Rich in tin and copper, from the coast
At Crinnis to Wheal Eliza and the rest.

'Mr Rashleigh is a very worthy man,
His brother a member of Parliament,' wrote Fanny
In days when that was thought a recommendation.
'He is my steward and, as I have some farms
Near the Land's End, will be useful in giving your friend
Passports to the farmers for hospitality
And lodging, for there is nothing of a town that way
Beyond Penzance.' You see how wild we were
In those forgotten days, how very *outré*
To Fanny's friends, the blue-stocking ladies
Of George III's distant metropolis.

Debarred from that intended for the heir
To the family, he fancied a career for himself
Building his own empire around the bay.
I don't know whether he was Whig or Tory,
Or, if a Whig, followed Fox or Pitt—

He had something more valuable to do than that:
Hence there's nothing about him in the books.
Before the American war, he set work going
For the poor folk around St Austell growing,
Opening up the mines. Polmear was the name
Of the place before overlaid by his own:
A valuable vein of copper, the tip
Of disused detritus below my house,
Covered by golden gorse in bloom through the year,
Where Peter my cat loved to play all day,
The levelled drive the former old mine-road.
Opposite the gate was Dally's mine,
A villa promoted now to Soulsbyville.
(I thought to call mine All Soulsbyville,
But was contented to revive Polmear,
Suppressed by him hubristically for Charlestown.)

Polmear too was the name of the tiny haven,
A mere crevice in the cliffs with a couple
Of fishing boats, seines and nets on the wall,
A very few families that lived thereby
Before he began his operations.
On the ledra above he opened Appletree,
The mine in which my grandfather worked below
The sea, in the bad air from which he died
Of miners' phthisis, before attaining fifty,
Leaving a mass of sons, all miners too,
Cheerful, gay and drunken, all musical.

Charles Rashleigh's genius set these folk on work,
All this and more he called into being.
The population multiplied by ten,
People moved in from surrounding villages:
The mines prospered while prices soared upwards.
In those days, for a quarter of a century,
Cornwall produced half the world's copper.
Rashleigh was on a rising market, but whence
Did he raise the money for his rash speculations?

A fifth son had little from the family:
A speculative spirit, he was ready
Ever to take any and every risk.

(III)

The strange story I've only lately learned.
I always sensed he was not a marrying man:
Then why did he marry, and what were the conditions?
Of course, marriage was in the order of things
For a would-be founder of a family;
But his came about in a peculiar way.

Down Pentéwan Valley from the town
—Beyond Nansládron of the Arundells—
Was the gate to the long drive of a mile or more
To Heligan of the Tremáynes, in the time
Of Elizabeth, stewards to the Catholic
Arundells, and so had come by the estate;
Conformed, became lay-rectors of St Austell,
Got the tithes of the large and populous parish,
And so built their house in a fine position
Looking down the valley to Mévagíssey.

Here lived Rashleigh's friend, Hawkins Tremayne,
Euphoric, easy-going, and charitable,
With money to spare, and also a sister to marry.
Grace was getting on, no happy prospects
Offered, Charles a regular visitor
To bachelor brother—not known what terms they were
    on:
Fanny Boscawen says, 'the closest affection'.
Charles found himself engaged to Grace, with less
Affection, we may suppose. A cool affair—
To judge from the letter he wrote on April Fool's day
In the fatal year 1776—
Declaration of Independence and all—

To elder brother entrenched at Menabilly.
'I paid a visit to Heligan yesterday
With a view to settle my future happiness,
And give up the idle life of a bachelor.
With pleasure I acquaint you that my offer
Was well received by Miss Tremayne; they all
Seem well pleased by the intended connexion.
I hope that you too will approve the match,
Which I assure you is the result of long
Acquaintance and sincere regard. I trust
It ties the knot of friendship so long subsisting
Between the two families. I wish
This not to be the common conversation
Of all companies; nor publicly
Announced as yet.'
                    Why ever not? What
Difficulty had he in making up his mind?
What was his reluctance in tying the knot
So appropriate to both families?

He delayed, Grace became anxious.
(Could he not face the joys of the marriage-bed?)
Did he mean to break his plighted word?
Withdraw? Mrs Boscawen had not thought so:
'Of his integrity can be no question—
I need not mention it, as his name is Rashleigh.'

Secretly, unbeknownst from that day to this,
Charles had borrowed £10,000 from Tremayne,
And now was unable to pay. All had gone
Into the mines . . . perhaps at a later day
All might yet be well, when prospects cleared.
Meanwhile no word of marriage.
                        Then in June
A sudden arrest committed the prospective,
But reluctant, brother-in-law, dragging his feet,
To debtors' Marshalsea. A case was heard,
Or perhaps fixed up, for by the middle of the month,

355

Charles was back at Heligan for the night.
The formal arrangement made: Rashleigh conveyed
All his property to Hawkins Tremayne
For a nominal five shillings, and rented it back
For a peppercorn rent. The marriage settlement
Followed immediately: Grace to have,
On husband's death, all household goods
And chattels, gardening and husbandry,
Carriage and horses, and an annuity.

The wedding took place in virtual privacy
In their church of St Ewe, of the splendid rood-screen
That survived the horrid Reformation—beasts
And birds, dragons, tendrils and flowing vines,
The masterpiece of some long-vanished craftsman—
Looking down on the pair that summer day,
The first of July, 1776.
(Three days later, Independence declared
By the Colonies, in the week Charles lost his.)

Grace must have known how her marriage had been
    made,
To a friend she put the best face on it:
'I was married with the greatest prospects of happiness.'
Let that be as it may be. 'Only my brother
And sister and Mr Rashleigh at the wedding—
The elder brother of Charles, who was best man.'
The local newspaper gallantly wrote of the bride:
'A young lady no less justly admired
For the known amiableness of her disposition
Than for her charity and benevolence
To the needy, and being endowed with every virtue
That can adorn the mind.' All in a cool
And temperate key, nothing of person or beauty
To excite passion in one so unresponsive
To the sex as Charles.
                    Oddly enough, when so much
Has been lost, all gone down in the fall of his house,

356

Her wedding dress is still entire in existence,
A cream damask brocade woven in France.
No dance, no honeymoon tour: the couple stayed
A fortnight at Heligan, then moved into house
At St Austell. There they entertained freely,
Grace refurbishing, and spending a lot
On clothes, for assemblies regular in the town:
Dances before tea, and cards after tea.

The years rolled on, but brought no hoped-for heir,
Only pallid daughters, to the number of three.

(IV)

The years rolled on, full of historic events,
The American Revolution the demagogues
Of Boston brought on—Sam Adams and John Hancock.
Intolerable as their Puritan ancestors,
Rabble-rousers who destroyed the Empire
To rebuild an imperialism of their own,
Too evident throughout the world today
Despite their smoke-screen of democratic cant.
Or Patrick Henry, shooting his mouth off—
'Give me liberty, or give me death!'
No-one was restricting his liberty—
Mere Irish verbiage—and as for death,
All he asked for was a horse-whipping,
This sea-green incorruptible tribune
Of the people ended a reactionary.

All the same, these folk made the bloodshed
Of Lexington and Bunker's Hill, created
The myth of an oppressed people—as if anybody
Ever oppressed Americans, except
Americans, as the North oppressed the South!
Once blood was shed the dreary conflict went on—
Lying propaganda all the way—

Through victory and defeat, Brandywine
And Saratoga, the winter in Valley Forge,
Until the last surrender at Yorktown:
Britain fighting not only colonials
But half the world: France and Spain and Holland,
The Armed Neutrality of the North,
Facing a world of enemies at sea,
In the West Indies and India alike,
Holding besieged Gibraltar through the years.
Such was the background of those heroic years
To the life in Cornwall, when the war came near.

In January 1779, the last
Month of Grace's pregnancy, Charles left
For London, leaving her brother to fetch her back
To Heligan, where the first belated child
Was born. She did not return till April.
(Four blissful months scot-free of churning out
The dreary chores of domesticity.)

That summer the combined Franco-Spanish fleet
Was in command of the Channel, for the first time
In history. Up the coast they sailed
In full view from the Cornish cliffs to make
Their attempt on Plymouth, ill-garrisoned, defences
Unprepared. The fleets anchored off Cawsand:
Crowds of women came in from the country arrayed
In their scarlet cloaks to man the heights of the Hoe.
The French made no attempt to land their troops.

The invasion scare continued all that summer.
At Heligan Grace was alarmed for Mevagissey,
Apt for a descent upon the quay.
'The company of volunteers then formed
Have just begun to learn their exercises.'
Francis Basset, a game bantam-cock,
Raised his own regiment of miners,
Trained them, marched them up the county to Plymouth.
'I am sorry to find he's made a baronet.'

He led the opposite party in the county
To the Boscawens, on his way to a peerage,
As they won theirs a generation before
For borough-mongering, like all the Cornish peers.

A new-raised regiment marched into Launcèston,[3]
County capital then: 'among the officers
To make the winter gay, Lord Waldegrave's[4] son;
But the men are the most shocking creatures that ever
Was, picked out of all the jails and lighters.'
That winter Rashleigh's hands as under-sheriff
Were pretty full of urgent public business.

Grace's cousin, Betty Wallis, married
To the discoverer of Tahiti (in the *Dolphin*),
Was always on the verge of a nervous breakdown
When ever Captain Wallis went to sea.
Grace suggested someone to live with her;
Mrs Boscawen thought 'better to bring her
Up to the cheerful society of Heligan
Instead of someone catching her melancholy.
Why will she always fancy the French are coming?
Perhaps you will say is not Heligan near
The sea? Certainly it is. But there
Are many stout men at Mevagissey.'
The widow of the victor of Louisbourg
And Lagos had no terror of the French.

A cousin of Grace at Trebártha to her husband:
'You terrify us with your lamentations
Over poor old England: how can we be worse
Than we are already? A rebellion at home
Would be a most dreadful affair; there is,
I think, a greater prospect of one in Ireland' . . .

The country, after the mutiny at the Nore,
Reached the nadir in its affairs. The worst,
As in 1940, heralded an upturn

---

[3] Pronounced Láns'on.   [4] Pronounced Wálgrave.

In morale. Charles as sheriff viewed
A procession of independent companies
At Penryn to consecrate their colours.
('Had such a thing ever been before?')
The colours were held before the altar, prayers
Said over them as in sacramental days,
Church crowded with all the gentry of Falmouth,
And for the people fireworks in the evening.

These were busy prosperous days for Charles.
War was good for the mines, prices went up,
Copper and tin in good demand: his debts
Were all paid off. In 1791
He was able to build the quay at new Charlestown,
Make a harbour, the port for his mines and incoming
Produce, coals and lime for the moors and downs
He was breaking in for arable and pasture.
Where prehistoric barrows had been he formed
Two ponds to flush the inner basin out;
The outer, tidal beyond lock-gates, a pretty
Octagonal watch-house with weather-vane—
A recognisable Regency touch—
Above, the Harbour Terrace you see today,
Washed orange and tawny, cherry-pink and blue,
The end one the harbour-master's: in my time
A Héndra, who relished my poems about Charlestown.
Around the ponds a bosky wilderness
Filled with fragrant musk-smelling ferns,
One *Osmunda regalis*, or Royal Fern.

In course of the French Revolutionary war
He set up the Foundry, second oldest in Cornwall,
To turn out swords and bayonets, flintlocks
And muskets, wagons and gun-carriages
For the Peninsula—as it continued
To serve the country in its last heroic
Phase, the struggle against Germany, in which
Its long history came proudly to an end.

(V)

In his prime of life and fortune a strange thing happened.
Charles had never known what love was. All
Had been ambition, a consuming drive,
His only happiness in his creation.
Love came to him in unexpected guise.
In the village he had built, shaded by beeches—
Glinting sun in summer with a glimpse of the bay—
Warm colour-washed, butter-yellow and cream,
There one family stood out for looks.—Still did
Till recent days: one of the handsome Dingles
Married my cousin Violet, beautiful,
Care-free and sexy she was, and insolent.
She captured her man; they came by an early end
Skiing or tobogganning in Canada.
No children to continue the looks of either line.
But, earlier, there had been one of the Dingles
The image of Violet's man: tall and slim,
Of mercurial grace, and irresistible
Combination of black hair, and eyes
Blue as the sea they looked out upon.

What attracted Charles in bleak middle age,
Bleak family life, unintelligent wife
And daughters, was the promising intelligence
Of this young man, helpful, responsive, willing,
Able to take a line, in contrast to
His ladies, inert and very conventional.
Having no son and heir, he thought of adopting
Dingle, educated him to that end,
At one moment even suggested it.

They grew closer, were always together about
House and grounds, now taking shape. The youth
Would often linger after the day's work
To help and sort papers and documents,
File them away in the double cabinet.

Of Charles II's time, which Rashleigh had bought
At a neighbour's sale. Dingle would strike a match—
An old-style loud, malodorous lucifer—
To light the new patented lamp for the master
When together they worked late into the night,
Like Dutch William and his young friend, Keppel,
In the private suite at Kensington Palace.

No-one knows whether they retired together,
Any more than whether William and Keppel did.

Relations became so close and intimate
That people talked. Partly to put them off,
Partly to provide incentive and reward,
With the vague possibility of succession—
A half-formed scheme of a forward-looking mind—
Charles thought to qualify his friend: to make
A gentleman J.P. of him at least.
For this, necessary to draw up a deed,
In case of his demise, making over
His property, as years before he'd done
With friend Tremayne: an empty formula.

Dingle's father had been lost at sea.
What was the nature of the youth's own feelings
For Charles? Who can ever tell when there's
A whole generation lost between? Perhaps
He sought in Charles a father's protection;
Perhaps a natural pride in such a patron
(Here lay an unconscious element of danger:
Such patronage could both turn a head
And unaware, inspire a dumb resentment.)
A genuine admiration entered in,
With a faculty for social imitation
That comes easily to the ambivalent,
The familiar desire to move higher up
The social scale.
                    How much of sex, who knows?

362

I suspect willing enough when the stars came out
Over the bay, in all the harvest heat,
The phosphorescent sea slumbering lay
Beyond the harbour: so in the moonlight they.

On Rashleigh's side, what accounted for it?
In this honeyed youth he saw the youth
He'd never had, his complex character
Had never been realised or quite fulfilled.
A good deal of a gambler, he'd take a risk,
A last chance for belated happiness.

The war went on and on: Admiral Howe
And 'the glorious First of June' had long gone by,
Cape St Vincent and Camperdown: in the West
The war meant the war at sea. Copenhagen,
And Nelson at Trafalgar put paid to that.
A well-read man, an intellectual,
But always too much *affairé* to write himself,
He thrilled to read of naval victories,
Bought each ode of Campbell as it came:

> Ye mariners of England!
> That guard our native seas:
> Whose flag has braved, a thousand years,
> The battle and the breeze!
> Your glorious standard launch again
> To match another foe.
> And sweep through the deep,
> While the stormy winds do blow;
> While the battle rages loud and long,
> And the stormy winds do blow.

These verses still inspired my schooldays: not
Today. We read 'The Battle of the Baltic':

> Now joy, Old England, raise!
> For the tidings of thy might,

363

By the festal cities' blaze,
Whilst the wine-cup shines in light;
And yet amid that joy and uproar,
Let us think of them that sleep,
Full many a fathom deep,
By the wild and stormy steep,
Elsinore!

Dingle's father had been one of these.

At last the war on land woke up, and took
A turn, brought Cornwall into the front line—
Moore's campaign in the Peninsula—
Commented on by Jane Austen in Letters
To Cassandra and their sailor brothers at sea.
Falmouth harbour filled with transports, ships
And men, the hub of much activity,
Privateers off shore, packets coming
And going for Portugal. On one of them
Byron playing about with the boys in harbour,
Plucking his 'hyacinths', much too busy
To pay a visit to his ancestors,
The maritime Trevanions at Caerhays.
Moore's death—'Not a drum was heard, not a funeral
    note'—
The retreat to Corunna, Wellington's return
To hold fast the lines of Torres Vedras—
Vimiera, Talavera, Busaco.
Young Dingle could not but volunteer in time
For Fuentes and the bloody Albuera—
To be invalided home a changed man:
Like 'The Changed Man' of Thomas Hardy's tale.

The years, the strain, the sickness of hope deferred,
Somewhat changed Charles too: a harder man,
Disenchanted with the foolery
Of human beings, ready to ride rough-shod
Over the petty foibles by which they live,

364

No respect for what they *think* they think,
Impatient, inconsiderate, and vain.

Over the years he'd made enemies,
His success elicited jealousies;
I detect a patronising note even
When he meant to be kind. He had a kindness for
Old Samuel Drew, the cobbler-metaphysician,
Whom visitors came to the town to see;
Something of a prodigy, untaught,
Unschooled, he wrote his theological
Works on the bellows by the kitchen fire.
A pretty good reply to egregious
Tom Paine the cobbler wrote, who better knew
The facts of life than any radical
Stuffed full of humbug about the Rights of Man.

I often think of good old Samuel Drew
As my precursor: he too began to write
With a poem on the churchyard at St Austell:
He gave the place a name in literature.
In the only letter of Rashleigh to survive—
—What has become of all his correspondence?—
He complimented Sam in lofty tones:
'Your favour I received on my return
From Menabilly—hence unforeseen delay.
The additions and alterations to your book
Improve it, and should give satisfaction.
I thought your answer to Tom Paine the best
I've read. If my good opinion of you
Has been of service I am very glad:
A justice to your character and conduct.'
I should not like such a missive to receive;
Shoemaker Sam was a humbler man than I:
A resigned spirit, a Christian gentleman.

Only one more scrap of Charles remains:
In the Bodleian, for the antiquary Gough,

A drawing of the fifteenth century sculpture,
The Pelican in her Piety, feeding her young,
Over the south porch of our parish church
Opposite Rashleigh's house: often must he
Have looked up, as he entered church, to see
The work of the long-dead sculptor, whose masterpiece,
Magnificent rendering of the Trinity,
Should draw all eyes to the western face of the tower.

Charles had no time to pursue antiquities—
Consoling study for a conjured spirit—
Involved in one more complicated suit
With the Carlyons of Tregrehan over mineral rights.
The veins of copper and tin-lodes criss-crossed
From Charlestown to Crinnis—now Carlyon Bay
(God save the mark) complete with swimming pools,
Lido and squash courts, everything to delight
The hearts of the people bent on holiday
All the year round: no thought of earning it.
The lawsuit was to delimit mineral bounds,
Correct and compensate infringements made
Below surface, in addits and sunken levels.
Once more Rashleigh emerged with the chief spoils
Of victory.
          The Carlyons bided their time.
With larger resources they could afford to wait:
Revenge is sweet: opportunity would come.

Recorder of the town Rashleigh became
Receiver general of the Duchy of Cornwall.
He had reached his apogee, when the blow fell.

(VI)

On Dingle's return something had been lost
Out of his golden nature, Charles observed.
What a charming boy he had been, innocent

366

Yet willing, clinging to him like son to father—
Sons and lovers. He never could forget
A midnight coach-ride when the lad's dark head
Had fallen asleep on his shoulder, comfortably
With childlike confidence nestling into his neck.
He had been touched at such a mark of trust
Who never could have given such trust himself.
Now he noticed a coarsening of response:
Had such a brief experience of soldiering
Made him cynical? He now took for granted
What Charles had done for him—and *should* do more.

Rashleigh was never one to be taken for granted,
His pride affronted at this attitude
In former *protégé*. Nor could he make out
A curious discontinuity of mind
That declared itself—all the former charm
At times, at others a strange casualness:
Not always there—a screw loose somewhere?

Unable to diagnose the trouble, Charles
Lost confidence. Was he intemperate?
Had a younger friend come to occupy
His place, understandably enough?
The anguish was that Charles had not ceased to love,
But, seeking to impose a test, withdrew
As if indeed he had ceased to care.
The simpler nature drew the wrong conclusion:
Suspicion entered in, fatal to love—
The man concluded he was thrown over,
That Charles had loved him only for his looks
As a boy, had now no further use for him.
The complex situation was otherwise,
But could not be explained between them. For
Rashleigh decided not to make him heir,
But leave things to take their natural course.

All this was an inextricable mistake.
Dingle's failing was weakness of character:

Feeling himself cheated of support,
On learning he was not the destined heir
He turned elsewhere, to Rashleigh's enemies.
There were plenty of them round about,
A rival lawyer to head a combination
To back Dingle's legal claim. He knew
Where in the double cabinet the deed
Reposed. One night at precisely ten o'clock,
In Rashleigh's absence, he abstracted it.
It made a fine foundation for a case.

A mighty law-suit took them all to London:
A Chancery suit, like Jarndyce v. Jarndyce,
Occupied months and months, witnesses
By the score on either side were called.
Lawyers' fees, expenses accumulated,
Till at the end, to extricate himself,
Rashleigh had to mortgage the estate
To his London lawyers for £40,000:
The price he paid for the privilege of dying
In what he had created, no longer his own.

A last look-round, the spring before he died:
Gardens and grounds matured, park grown up,
Rose-buds of japonica against
Regency cream-washed stucco (now dirty grey),
Red blood of camellias spilled on greenest grass,
Flourishing clumps of laurestinus in bloom,
Scented daphne, viburnum on the air,
Magnolia blossoms beneath open windows
Looking south to the sea, in sheltered corner
Butter-yellow of sophora to vie
With fallen gold-dust of mimosa over.

All was well, and all was very well.
No one knew what he thought or suffered
In mind or heart, or if he had a heart:
This secret man took his secret to the grave.

He died in the summer of 1823,
Buried in the old graveyard of St Austell.
I've never even seen his grave—headstones
Removed to make a public park of it.
Was it the Regency monument with urn
I used to see as a boy overtopping the wall
Under the melancholy ilexes?

Strangely enough, or corroboratively,
Dingle never married. Perhaps he had loved
The master after all? No-one knew.
I never even heard his Christian name.
The suit was lost, and he had lost the game,
But ruined Rashleigh.

                        A kind of censorship
Came to be imposed by the town upon
The fall of its most eminent citizen;
A hoo-doo on the place and all concerned.

Dingle was shunned, became impoverished,
A recluse, and ever more eccentric, lived
A solitary bachelor in a poor
Cottage at Trevárrick upon parish pay.
He too kept his secret to the end.

(Hence the job I've had to wrest the truth
Of the tale: it's taken more than thirty years.)

Intruding Londoners were not popular—
No one ever felt that they *belonged*—
No roots, no Cornish name, nor did they settle
On unlucky Duporth for a country seat,
Merely held on to the profitable port,
Absentee landlords, Duporth put up for auction.

Once more a strange thing happened, as before.
An unknown purchaser appeared at the sale—

At 'The White Hart', which had been Rashleigh's
   house—
Made his bid and bought, left his deposit,
A substantial sum, and was never seen again.
Hue and cry was made for him in vain.
Folklore said he was a murderer
Who had thus obtained the money, blood-money,
Subsequently convicted. The auctioneer
Went up to the prison to identify
The unknown purchaser, but—shaven crown
And convict clothes—could not swear to him.

Hence the place was sold again for less
Than its value, with the condition in the conveyance
That if the unknown bidder should return . . .
He never did.

                    Some things went with the house:
Those eighteenth century portraits I saw as a youth,
The double cabinet in the drawing room.
The local people said the house was haunted.
Far into the Victorian age, the loud
Striking of a match would be heard in the hall:
When one went out to check, no one at all
Was there or had been. At precisely ten o'clock,
On one night of the year, the cabinet door
Would open with a click—no loud report,
But as if fingers familiar opened it
Unseen. Again, no one ever there.

The family who bought, poor as church-mice,
Were sold up in the end: the sale I went to.
The house became sadder and sadder, grey
In the swirling sea-mists as I used to watch—
Always the desolate cry of wheeling gulls—
From the lane below, along the coastguard walk
By the hedge of sloes, bullards in the autumn,
In spring the blackthorn white against the bay.
Never a glimpse of direct sun on the house—

Sometimes a pale gleam at end of day.
The mellow chime of the stable clock still came,
When the wind was southerly, up to the village,
As in my childhood. Now for ever silent.

In the social revolution of our time,
With all things bright and beautiful about—
(Without pride of ancestry and all
Too much hope of superfluous posterity)—
A garish cheer eradicates memories:
Nothing like it for overlaying the past.
Only one ruminative observer sees
Beneath the cheap bungalows, the bijou
Residences, the villas, the hideous flats,
The crazy paving, decorative gnomes,
Rabbits, fairies, horrors in front gardens,
All round the margins of the park to the cliffs.
The heart, if that's the word, around the house
Given up to huts and noisy caravans,
The apparatus of popular enjoyment,
In a time when the people have never had it so good:
The ancient granite piers, pink-coated cement,
Beckon the roadster to—a Butlin's Camp.

VIII

Autumn in the Thames Valley

O the beauty of the world as I grow older
Assails me with sharper and sadder sense:
Early autumn evening in the Thames valley,
The river holds up its leafy mirror to the sky,
The pasture green and chocolate-coloured arable
Alternate on either side the glass ribbon
Where summer boats are laid up, hug the bank
Under the Chinese willows, funereal and still.
Lights come out in the clearings of the Chilterns,
The eye follows the sleeping reaches of the river
To the further foothills gathering the dark,
While the pale continent of cloud reflects
Lost worlds of childhood, innocence and dream.

Peopled Sleep

My dreams are peopled by those in life I loved—
What a happiness then to sleep, perchance to dream,
Since they come back and are with me again
Whom once I knew, along with whom my life
Was lived, but are now no more. The great
Unhappiness of living long is missing them.
But in sleep they are as formerly they were,
Speak to me with no sense that they have gone
Out of life and I can no longer communicate.
By day I think it illusion that I do
And sometimes talk as if they answer me.
As if! But at night, in dream—a miracle—
They speak and look, a wonder still,
As once we were, and life was at the full:
The tide now ebbing from the familiar coast,
The scene now lonelier, ghostly and chill.

The Cherished Dead

October bells are ringing
        —and Bruce is dead.
The Sunday sky wheels by
        —and Richard is dead:
There under the berberis, orange under the sun,
There between the grey buttresses he lay
        —life ebbing away.
The clouds reveal a sliver of moon
Over the Roman volutes of stone
        —and Charles has been long dead.
The weathervane swings gold in the wind,
Shadow of bird crosses the face of the dial
        —*Pereunt et imputantur:*
No soul about the bright morning,
No soul about within the empty walls—
Emptiness echoed by birds in the cold breeze—
Peopled by shadows of the more cherished dead.

A Dream

In my dream I saw you once more
As in old days at Oxford: you were
Packing up to go away for vacation.
I thought all was well again, and I was glad.
But I was wrong.
Never a word came, never a letter
Or any message to renew former kindness.
As I was waking I felt again
The familiar ache of unhappiness,
And knew that grief is still alive,
Has taken the place of love
Once known.

Married Happiness

I am possessed by an image from my youth
A girl leans over her garden gate as I pass,
Golden haired, blue-eyed and dimpled
I remembered her as a boy from my schooldays—
Now married. She has her man in the background—
Mystery lurks in his masculine sex,
Dark and lean, silent as a fox.
She, all contentment, arms spread wide
Leans over the gate, the kindly superior smile
Of a few years older at the growing youth,
Never to be initiated into the secret of life.
A golden radiance from the harvest moon
Bathes all the valley—Boscoppa, Bethel:
Each awaits the happy moment for bed,
Expectation in her eyes, he darkly watching her.
The youth goes on his way
In accustomed solitude,
Having understood.

In Vain

I know now, but after half a century
Why she wept at her boy's recovery.
She should have been glad: why not,
He wondered. He rose from bed of sickness
A ghost, to see the recovered world anew:
The miracle of light on the ivies opposite,
The old house looking strangely at him;
Gone to bed a boy, he rose a man:
The ghost of the man she had long ago known
And lost, come back to reproach her,
Handsome and tall as he, a stranger.
She wept, he could not think why,

When she should have been glad.
In place of the chubby boy, the man
Stood before her, a living reproach,
A reminder of lost love, the only one
She had ever loved. The years were rent,
Rent the veil she had drawn before her eyes:
Her fault stood there before her, her love, her grief.
For her I weep fifty years after,
In vain, in vain.

All Clear

Obsessed by beauty in the lithe young man
Who comes up to ask about his boy's
Passion for astronomy, I am touched
More by my own esoteric response to him,
At my late age, to this erect pillar
Of youth and fatherhood: a decade
Of domestic happiness for him,
Never for me.

Beneath the exterior of the public man
The woman's soul opens a bud, a flower:
Unaware, unsuspecting the disguise,
Eager and inquiring,
He knows not why.

Going to sleep, and even at the hour
Of dawn, awaking, the image is still there:
The brief experience, the momentary touch,
Brush of wing between two unknowns,
Never to meet again, he never to know
The secret. When, after a lifetime
All is clear to me,
All clear.

Episode in the Train

O, how lovely my country, end of September,
Everything turning to colour, lemon and umber—
I have to put down my book—when down in the seat
Opposite flops a flaxen floozie with great
Breasts, heavily uddered as a cow.
Plenty of seats in the compartment now.
A sexy slut—I cannot concentrate,
Collect my thoughts, or even read or write.
I point to the vacant seat on the other side.
She doesn't take the point, looks up. 'I said, "There *is* a
    seat over there".' Arousing herself
From drowsy hangover or menstrual sloth,
Sits up. I point: 'There's a *beautiful* seat.'
She heaves up heavily, forward out of my sight.
I do not want her to confer her favours on me:
I want peace to write, intent to see
The first autumnal clouds over the Glyn
Valley, the light and shade shuttling within
Green glades of pine, fronds upturned at end,
The river below Restormel beginning to wend
Its way to harbour at Fowey, the grey walls
Of Trematon, now that the sunlight falls
Direct and clear. She is gone. I am at peace.
A withered old lady promptly takes her place.

Suburbia

They have mouths, and speak not:
eyes have they, and see not. They
have ears, and hear not: noses
have they, and smell not.

Psalm CXV

Look at the idiot people at their games—
I see them as so many baboons in a zoo,
Their own local zoo among the tenements,

A patch graceless as a monkey's bare behind:
Playing games of moving chairs about,
Standing in self-conscious attitudes
To catch each other in the eye of the camera—
As in the cold eye of the observer in the train,
Watching their infant idiosyncrasies.
Now one comes up behind another to put
Arms around bulging breasts or hips,
With inevitable strings of kids attached,
Unselfconscious, unknowing, unaware:
Slaves of nature, just like other animals,
Copulating, conceiving, giving birth,
Their own animals but simulacra of them.
See the summer acreage of ugly flesh,
The borborygmic joys of family life!
Not one observes the beauty of the world,
The panoply of may along the river banks,
Explosions of golden gorse and broom
Amid the arrested suburban greenery,
Chestnuts coming into flower, and lilac
Above the squalor of the human scene.
Nor notices that the honeysuckle's out.

'Le Pape est Mort'

Overcast September sky,
    The flags are flying at half-mast:
A mere matter of a month—
    A brief pontificate has passed.

A momentary gleam of sun
    Lights up the leaden-clouded place,
Reflects a transitory smile
    Upon a kind, benevolent face.

The little boy of Daudet's book
    In old Provence preferred to stay

Out among the vines all day
    To amuse himself in game and play.

Home arriving late at night,
    When he should long have been in bed,
To escape punishment he said:
    'Le Pape est mort'—'The Pope is dead'.

Next morning when the household woke,
    So pleased to find it was not so,
The young delinquent was forgiven,
    Misconduct passed without a blow.

Today the case is otherwise;
    Unwittingly the child spoke true:
Posters and drooping flags confirm
    Words more veracious than he knew.

Shelley

Shelley saw in Prometheus his own fate,
Rose up to contest the power of fear and hate,
In his own youth saw imaged the cruel strife
Between his wishes and the decrees of life:
The delightful liberties of sexual desire
Without their obligations to enmire
The free enfranchised soul in human mud;
The aim to enjoy the fullest solitude
While engendering children, fathering a family.
But human wishes cannot liberty
Command. Love betrayed him and soon fled
Abandoned, lighted upon another head—
Inconstant the human heart. The children died.
The poet the power of Providence defied,
Still stood a man courageous to delate
The criminal injustice of man's fate—
Erect, cursed God, the Deity who frowned
On human happiness. The poet drowned.

Louis MacNeice

How clever you were, Louis,
With your metrics, your virtuoso
Words, your parasangs, mynas, kebabs,
Striking, but unmoving—when I
Remember you as a handsome boy,
But sullen, loping and sloping about the quad
After a pig-tailed schoolgirl. That
Youthful idyll ended comically,
With Marie's mama threatening to hire
A pugilist at the water-side before
The ship that carried her errant daughter,
Absconding with Lithuanian-American boxer
Who ran through women like a knife through butter.

Leaving you a desolation, shortly filled
By other scents and trips to Cannes.
But how desolating, unsatisfactory
It all was, moving from cockstand to cockstand,
Breast to breast against the gates of Doom,
Hoping to know each other better
When the tunnels meet beneath the mountain.
There is no hope that way, no life nor love—
Nor anything to show
We passed this way. While you
Were clever enough to know
Such sophistication
Is the enemy of creation.

Requiem for Benjamin Britten

When I hear your music I seem to see
You, whom I last saw in the chapel at King's—
In sombre September, candlelight flickering—
The colour of ivory, hardly recovered from illness,

382

Carefully kissing a lady, a considered gesture
Before your life-long friend looking on,
Silvery and spectacled, with archidiaconal air,
There to sing the Passion according to St John.

Your life is more real to me now you're dead:
No oppression of envy, nor thought of rivalry
Between East and West, yourself gregarious,
Happy and extrovert, giving yourself to life—
As against the soul dedicated to solitariness.
Flight of seagulls over the widowed house,
Burst of March sun and shower, a splash of rain
Trembles in tiny chalices of anemone.
Kyrie Eleison, Christe Eleison, Kyrie Eleison:
The tenderness of the old superstition
On its way out, this Good Friday,
The three hours of the Passion unobserved—
Or perhaps they are, in their different way?

What fun they had, making music and making
Love—Ben and Peter and Wystan:
No melancholy life like mine—theirs
Fulfilled, topped up like wine.
Sea and spray, Aldburgh, Ellen and Grimes,
Youth and gaiety, in those pre-war times
Now a world away: this tribute from another
Sea, softer and deeper blue,
But no less true, this Good Friday
Of remembrance, hearing and seeing you
In the inner world of sound and sea.

'Instead of thy fathers, sons are born to thee'—
No sons were born to you, but the children
Of music and song, proliferation of ear
And mind and heart, along that other coast,
From childhood touched by the Holy Ghost,
Imagination opening like a flower:
No fear of life or hostages to fortune,
Filled to the brim with pleasure given and taken.

When I left home in despair, hearth forsaken,
The world was then their oyster, theirs—
Though I was there before them: now
Their survivor, no friend, whose life has gone
Another way to its appointed end.
Waves of sound, the music you made
Surround me, mind and heart, like the waves
Of this other sea, whence my prayer
Goes up for you—'O rose, thou art sick'—
(Open my heart, closed most of life to life
At strife with itself, as it never was with you.)

Dear Ben, whom I never knew,
And yet see clearly now, if not too late:
We therefore pray Thee help Thy servants
Whom Thou hast redeemed with Thy precious blood;
And Christ receive thy soul.

Shostakovich: Last Word

These lonely voices in the night
Of terror and cruelty—
The springs of sympathy
Are dried up in me
Not yet wholly
When I hear the voices of suffering
Reaching to me in the night,
The night of my own trial approaching:
A sea of terror and cruelty—
How far was it not avoidable?
O why, O why
Must it always be
Thus?

In the strings I hear
The human discord
Unresolved, always unresolved.

How can one find faith
In a world without faith
Where faith has become impossible,
Nor is there any apocalyptic hope?

Only these lonely voices
Speaking not each to each,
Neither answering each other,
Each offering his own suffering—
Intervals of ecstasy amid the pain,
Yet still the marching threat
Of terror and cruelty,
The knock on the door at night,
Knock, Knock,
In the darkness of the soul.

At the end of all
The prison bell,
The knell,
The sharpening of knives
And the cry of protest
In a woman's voice.

Plymouth: A Memory

Here is sleeping Plymouth
Under a lowering sky,
Grey and dank October:
Here the sailors lie

Hand in hand, face to face,
After the night's carouse,
For this is Sunday morning.
Do not them arouse,

Though sad and sober citizens,
All in their Sunday best,

Straggle along the streets
After their Sabbath rest,

Ready to lift up voices
In unison, begin
With willing heart and mind
To censure others' sin:

United and Disunited
Methodists at prayer,
Plymouth Brethren, Baptists,
Primitives all there.

On my way I pass
The Sailors' Hospital,
Devote a thought to the men alive
Caught in that doomed nightfall.

The Church at Withiel

How to put into words the ache of heart
When one enters a deserted country church
And sees upon the walls the memorials
Of those who once lived here lives gay or sad?
See here the sons of the Victorian rector,
Who went from this sequestered place to advance
The bounds of Empire. The one, a young lieutenant
In the Royal Welsh Fusiliers, died at Lucknow;
The other, lieutenant in the old D.C.L.I.,
Died at Mandalay. I see them bright-eyed boys
Restless at sermon-time, father in pulpit,
Mother's eye on them in family pew,
When they'd rather be out about the fields,
Birding or squirrelling in Costislost,
Chasing across the downs at Hustyn Gate,
Roaming the lanes, full of foxgloves and ferns,
Climbing the Cornish elms around the rectory,

Huddled under the lee of St Breock Downs
From Atlantic howlers swirling from the coast;
The winter heights sometimes white with snow.

Today the sheep crop peacefully in the place
Where these might have lived useful lives, rearing
Their families in turn, instead of leaving
The childhood hearth desolate, an ache of heart
For their folks growing old, keeping their vigil
For the fine grown fellows who will not return.
Did their last thoughts turn, I wonder, in the fever
And alien heat to these familiar lanes,
Stepping the runnels down to Ruthernbridge?
Did they think of Polmorla Wood, and the way
Up through September hedges of hips and haws;
Or winter closing in, and Christmas bells
Ringing their chime from Withiel to Roche,
Coming faint over the hillside from St Breock
To Winnard's Perch and westing to St Wenn?

Lanhydrock

The cobwebs are swept away: the dream remains.
Here I am in the house of my ancient friends.
Eva, upright châtelaine, eye on everything,
Acidulated version of Queen Mary, kind
At heart, but—'I suppose you know *every*body?';
Or—'When did you first become a celebrity?'
Violet, violet-eyes, always the ungrown-up girl,
Demure in the corner, still—'the light of our eyes'.
Gerald himself, last of his race to inhabit
The house—'Lordy' they called him—sad, unsatisfied
Smile, life denied, dedicated to good works.
Last time I saw him, visibly dying, I was made
To go on my knees to receive a formal blessing
For what I had done with my own so different life.
They had been born with silver spoon in mouth—

Here were the evidences: the grand gallery
Of the halcyon time before the Civil War,
The learned library of the politic first Lord,
The vast fortune made from tin and usury—
The maker lying in state on his tomb at Truro;
Portraits on the walls of subsequent descents,
Tapestries, Brussels, or Soho, or Mortlake,
The gilt Kent furniture from far-off Wimpole.
Gone from the gallery the portrait of the children
They were, six happy innocent faces, frilled
And flounced in Edwardian fashion, in spring sun.
Now spring sun, cold and clear through lattices,
Chequers the honeyed boards from the park,
Falls on Turkey carpets and the bindings of books.

But they are no longer here, the former occupants
But shadows, flickering motes in the eye
Of the faithful visitor, alone with his thoughts
As he remembers the ruin of war, death of the heir
Rescuing a comrade on the Western Front,
The catastrophe on the pavement of Grosvener Square;
Friendly George, the footman, repository
Of the family story; the sage and silent butler:
A handsome page-boy, holding open the gate
Of the Barbican, for the favoured visitor to enter
From the avenue of the time of the Commonwealth.
Trees have fallen, and have to be renewed—
But not renewed the life of those three,
Huddled in the hall, wraps on arthritic knee,
Screens to keep out the draughts of centuries;
Yet still they maintained state and dignity.
The cobwebs are swept away: the dream remains.

Luxulyan Church

How much I longed earlier to write a poem
About Luxulyan church, which never came
At the right time into my reluctant mind.
The grey vicarage was my Naboth's Vineyard
Lying sculpted in the granite hill,
A rim of beeches and, strewn all around
The fields, mammoth boulders heaving their flanks,
Prehistoric monsters out of the soil.
The lodestar of long solitary walks
Through china clay villages, Carclaze,
Trethurgy, Sterrick Moor, past Methrose
With memories of Wesley and the Knights,
Tudor hall and coloured coats-of-arms,
Walled forecourt and, within, a friendly welcome.

Arrived in the church, after the long hot walk
A green coolness in the quiet interior—
A holy place, where silted up the prayers
Of many generations who have had their day
And all is now as if they had never been—
As it will be for me when my time comes.
Sitting there in the church waiting for what,
Listening to silence as if a revelation
Might open the shut door to the unseen.

The minutes mark the beating of the heart,
No sound—and suddenly in the hamlet outside
A cock crows, and I remember the Gospel:
'And Peter went out and wept bitterly.'

But that was Easter-tide; now it's high summer—
It's always high summer in my memory
Of Luxulyan, bright sun coming through the panes,
The honeyed sun of afternoon spattered
Through lattice and window, lying on the pavement
Of the porch—one step down into the church.

I enter the solitude of the sanctuary
Wishing that I too might be able to pray
Like the simple folk of the farms of this parish
On the edge of the moors and the deep riven valley,
Bodiggo of old Trevail the councillor,
Menadue, Tregantle, Rosemellon in the heath.

Silence and sunlight, yet I cannot pray.
I think of the vanished generations, the sense
Of their presence is all around me; though they
Can no longer be here, is something of them left?
Light comes and goes, glows and fades. No-one
Enters, I am always here in the church alone.
Ivy scrattles on a pane, and suddenly
A rustle of wind on the roof, a veil withdrawn.
Time stops. It is as if all time were one,
An arrested moment of eternity.

Summer's End

The lanes of Withiel and St Wenn
When shall we see together again?
As signposts Brown Willy and Rowtor
Beckon to tell us where we are:
The hooded monk's cowl of the one,
The other's spine in September sun.
Berries of mountain ash announce
Summer's end, and now renounce
The flourish of August, though there is still
Honeysuckle by Ruthern Mill;
Hollyhocks by cottage door;
Early heather bursts on the moor.
Over the pastures a plane rides by
Peacefully under a mackerel sky;
Murmur of reaper borne on the breeze,
Below, the gathered rectory trees
Around the sunlit granite tower,

Grey in quiet afternoon hour;
Like parson in pulpit upon his perch
A pigeon is posted beside the church.
Up to Trewollack and Trewollack Vean
Across the pattern of varied green
Pastures crop contented sheep.
Already the young ferns shooting peep
From the shaven and straw-strewn hedge
Along the lane from Ruthernbridge.
At Rosenannon a wise old horse
Looks over his stable door at us;
A farmer halts his tractor the while
To greet us with apple-cheeked rustic smile.
The harvester passes, the chaff is shed,
Even as we shall be harvested.

St Endellion

The little tower stands sturdy on the dead
Looking out to sea, to Kellan Head
And over Atlantic miles away to Lundy.
Here came the faithful forbears Sunday by Sunday
From farms of hereabouts, Trelights, Tresunger,
From the labour of their lives to stay their hunger
With hope of rest and peace: who now lie here
Beneath their headstones to tell us who they were
When they were alive. They do not cease to be
When the bells ring out over the land and sea
Calling us to church and festival,
Music and lights. Around us the prebendal
Houses, crouching from Atlantic wind,
Mottled and mossy from time out of mind,
Huddle like cattle on the distant moor
Southward to Brown Willy and Rowtor.
Through the summer hedgerow lanes we come
Over the hills and valleys from our home—
Honeysuckle, campion, August flowers,

Meadowsweet and ragwort to tell the hours,
Until time to enter, group by group;
We pass Roscarrock's holy-water stoup,
Genuflect to Endellion's elvan shrine,
Borne to burial here by eight white kine.
The congregation safely gathered in,
Subdued air of excitement, a friendly smile,
The faithful greet each other across the aisle—
While Nicholas Billing, a grey slate on the the wall,
A white surround, looks down to bless us all,
And we are lost: the music has us in thrall,
Voices and violins make festival.
Time passes with the music's cadences,
The sense of ebb and flow of centuries . . .
Night falls; and we come forth from the Requiem,
The crowding gravestones nod, Remember them.

Trenarren towards Christmas

How to describe the stillness, the planetary
Perfection of this moment caught and held;
The face of the moon meshed in the branches
Beholds me; quartz sparkles in the ground,
Latticed shadows on white gravel,
The skeleton of the insignis pine;
Billowing clouds move eastward
Out over the bay under a resplendent
Three-quarters moon and one attendant
Star. In the west the screen of trees
Filters the light, and the world moves on
Towards Christmas, as my life moves on
To its term. The thought of those here before me
Inhabits the moonlit scene—the taciturn
Colonel, pacing the terrace with his gun,
The former peacocks with their raucous cry,
And all those visitants who now have gone,
The farmer's boy, handsome as Antinous,

Moody and sullen, drowned in his bravery
Upon the beach. Ghostly *revenants* mostly
Appear on the terrace in the white moonlight,
Present themselves to the mind to punctuate
The vanished irrecoverable years;
The shelving lawn, the signal pine,
The bay all silver in the moon, in beauty
More rare than ever in its solitude.
All that is wanting is love fulfilled.

Something of Myself

Everything has always been denied me—
So what wonder I hate humans as I do.
So did Swift for a much similar reason—
He took it out of them in consequence.
And so would I—horsewhip them if I could
For refusing or frustrating at every turn
Whatever I wished, or only half required.
Out of his hatred came the Houyhnhnms,
Humans he depicted as Yahoos.

For such indeed they are. I've not done that.
But out of my detestation a lot of good
Work has come, contempt the sovereign mood—
As all through Hobbes, see the *Leviathan*:
One hears it in the accents of his style
As in the natural rhythms of my voice.
I follow him rather than Swift in withdrawal,
Who could not do without society.
I can, and always have withdrawn, the assumption
Clear in 'that proud head': *Their loss, not mine.*

The Normal

Life has left its scars on me—
Perhaps I should not allow
That, but how could that not be,
Beginning with questionable paternity,
And hating to have been born
Amid the alien corn
Of a home without books, music, art,
Or any promptings of the heart?

Child of the one skin too few,
Always exposed to the view
Of unfavourable eyes,
Holding their inevitable surmise,
Making their unkind comment
On what was more evident
To lascivious adult than to the innocent
Child, yet too intelligent
Not to suspect what they meant.

Thus the seeds of distrust
Were all too early sown,
Which flowered into disgust
With much that's human,
Man or child or woman,
And fixed in the grown
Man a preference
For the innocence
Of object or animal,
Rather than the common, the usual,
The inane, the normal.

Desire is Dead

Desire is dead: no longer the alert
Of eye and heart at what passes,
Beauty whether of women or of men,
The wish to penetrate
The secret of their lives,
To be one with them, one of them.
I accept the difference—
With some surprise
To be no longer stirred
By light of the eyes
Or winged word
To disturb the sense—
Ever awake, ever ready
To respond, a flake
That leaps to set the flame alight,
Whether welcome or unwelcome
To the stranger.
No matter now.
All is alike, indifferent
To the challenge of what is
Different and strange.
I note the change,
No longer interested,
Yet still surprised that all
Desire is dead.

Poetry at Bay

All my life I have been keeping
Poetry at bay, like madness.
Work, work, work put in the way
All day and every day. If it had
Been poetry I'd have been mad
With midnight apprehension and suspense,

Fear and apprehension, like my dreams.
There is the long shadow of the murderer,
My half-brother, or is it myself?
There is the woman with the appalling face
Lying extended, who touches me
With her thigh, seeks to seduce me—
Whence I fly out to the open sea.
I could not give myself to such thoughts,
Allow them to overwhelm me
With their burden, drag me down
Into the depths. But for the discipline
I should drown.

Hound of Heaven

Nothing that I touch can succeed,
Whether an attempt to help another,
Or advantage my own interest:
Some perversity in the heart of things,
Some determination to withhold
What it might so easily give,
And do me good. Instead it makes me mad.
But would it do me good? Sometimes not.
A guardian angel stands in the wanted way
With 'This is not for you.'—And he was right,
It subsequently transpires. And yet
It would be nice to have one's own way:
Frustration is not the best of medicines
For an ambitious mind, wishing to create
Its own fate, its proper course in life,
Come what may, one hardly knows which
The better way. Sometimes denial, rejection
Worked out very well, but one can hardly
Cherish the whiplash across the face
As Hopkins did, submit the will to more
Subjection—that was his way: not mine.
Sometimes, ungrateful spirit that I am,

I am tempted to think my guardian angel malign,
Knowing me well, seeing me at every moment
Of the night and day, watching and waiting
To trip me up—Hound of Heaven? Or Hell?

No Regrets

I've had a wonderful life,
　　All things considered,
Coming through stress and strife—
　　Could it be bettered?

Most that I meant to harvest
　　I have managed to garner,
Over every obstacle
　　At length been a gainer.

But why did *they* wish to make
　　It an obstacle-race?
Perhaps they did not like
　　The look on my face:

In an envious world of
　　Supposed 'equality',
The recognisable look
　　Of superiority.

After all the set-backs
　　There is little to rue,
And still remains something
　　More to do.

Reproaches

Poor Philip, how can it have come to this?
I fear I never took you seriously,
Never for a moment considered
Your offer of love, if that were it,
Or rather of your embodied self.
Perhaps I might have saved you—if anyone could—
You had no friend, no friend at need—
The lonely life shared with mother:
Mother dead, no one at all to make
Life go on worth living.
What could I have done
If I had given thought to it,
And realised your desperate need,
What step to prevent the deed
Irremediable, irrevocable:
Lying dead in your flat alone,
After a life so unfulfilled,
So ill a start. And such an end—
As I might have known it would be.
But I would never take responsibility.
And even now, in the hour for reproaches,
In the still watches of the night,
When I would,
I find I do not grieve,
As I should.

In the Street

Too happy am I: can it last?
Too well, as never in the past.
How to account for it?
Age, fulfilment, sticking to my last—
So that a young woman, passing in the street
Today should say,

'I cannot speak to one I so much admire.'
Too late, yet it brought a smile
In the same street where I
Was often greeted with a scowl.
I had not forgotten.—Strange:
How to account for the change?
Passage of time, a lifetime now,
Fulfilment in work, having stuck to my last,
An old public man
Surprised in the street.

Te lucis ante terminum

Reading high up in my New York room,
My eye falls on the words in Dante,
Te lucis ante:
The years fall away, and I hear
The voices of the youths we were
Lifted up towards the end of day
In that same hymn in lighted choir
At Oxford; I sense the spirit we put in
The ancient words for compline
In unison, gallant and surpliced,
Under the vigilant eye of bird-like Dean
And gathered dons—Julian, Tom and I.
Julian, who was to face a charge of treason,
Tom, mathematical and pious, against reason
Would submit to medieval discipline,
And I remain, dedicated to memory.
The day over, full of eager activity,
Night closing down on cloister and hall,
Light reflected in plashing Mercury—
I hear our vanished voices in the room,
Te lucis ante terminum,
And recognise from far away
The closing of our day.

Intimations of Mortality

I am haunted by the idea of this poem,
Intimations of Mortality—
Haunted by visions of what I once did see
From early childhood, years of innocence,
Moments when the envelope of experience
Was broken to reveal images
To remain constants in my life and heart,
Terms of reference to which to return:
Mirrors to reflect eternity?
I do not know: only the images
Remain, inhabit a secret world unchanged.
The years do not blemish them, neither decay
Nor any stain deface their purity.

Before the poor cottage of tumbled thatch
Stood a group of straggling apple-trees,
The child beneath looked up through criss-cross branches
To catch a glimpse of blue sky unseen
Before—and saw a vision of the Civil War:
No angels ascending and descending like Jacob's
But the feeling he had seen it all before,
The strange sensation that he had been there—
But where?—as if it were a shaft into
The secret heart of the universe withheld,
Withdrawn—and now revealed unto a child.
That moment saw his first awareness flower
And, like a flower, the mystery closed upon
The blue depths of unfathomable sky.

But earlier still, so early he could never
Be sure whether experience or dream,
He stood in the summer dawn upon the shore
Of long Crinnis beach, when the seines were drawn
And, behold, a miraculous draught of fishes,
A myriad scales shone silver in the sun;
The whole inner bay shimmered and spun

With movement, as if the sea itself were alive,
The drawn fish thronging the golden sand.
The child was there with the men and fisherfolk:
It was no dream, the experience was real.
As years passed, the memory was blurred—
He knew no longer what the vision meant.
Was it Crinnis or the Sea of Galilee
Where it happened, and who were the men among whom
He was a stranger, unrecognised and alone?

A growing boy, a more familiar scene:
Leading his beloved 'Neddy'—in the dark before dawn
Under a firmament of stars—to be shod
At the smithy before the day's work began.
Suddenly he was aware as never before
Of the granite cottages asleep, the starry
Silence and the great canopy of lights
That spanned the village, the darkness visible,
And all things were clear as they shall be made clear
At the latter day. For that moment time stood still.
Yet the memory of that moment lasted
All his life, into unquesting age.

Then, coming home from church, breasting the hill,
Breasting the keener air from Carclaze downs,
Turning he saw the harvest moon would fill
The bowl of the bay, brimming with luminous gold.
Perfection of the scene would stir the sense
Strangely with unease—wherefore, and why?
He stood at the gate, the threshold of mystery,
A return of the self upon the self, a voyage
Into the bidding night, upon seas strange
Yet familiar, as if visited before:
Enticed, yet always voyaging alone.

Other such moments have accompanied him
Upon the journey of years, the ladder of life:
War-time evensong when the summer sun

Transfigured the western window of the church
To coloured glory and the Apostles shone;
While down below service of intercession
For men's lives went on. We prayed in vain.
The revelation was in the glow of light,
The sense of a world halted and transformed.

Nor less in later life, an eldering man
Was he the visionary consolation
Denied. In the toil and moil of daily work,
All unbidden, at the corner of the eye
Would come the visitation to announce
Time standing still: the copper-beech there
For ever, the frozen eagle with spread wings
Eternally poised for flight into the unknown,
The invitation of the Italian sky.

What to make of it? I cannot say.
Here and now we cannot know. I know
Only that these moments have sustained me,
Given food to the spirit, nourished mind
And imagination in the forlorn spaces,
Shafts of light into the heart of things
Though the mystery remain immutable.

IX: Children's Verses

Roseland* Year—A Children's Calendar

Come to Lamorran Woods
When the snowdrops are all out,
And the February birds
With gladness begin to shout:

For the winter is now over
In the valleys of the Fal,
And spring comes very early
By Grogoth and Tresawle.

In March or early April
Go down the banks of Gare,
When the primroses are there,
And sniff the earthy air.

In sequestered lanes of Ruan
In May or late springtime
Bluebells crowd together
To ring their gallant chime.

Honeysuckle, foxgloves,
Set the summer scene
All around Tresillian,
Trencreek, Goviley vean.

The Council men in autumn
Cut back the summer growth:
The ferns put forth fresh shoots
In the hedges of Trelowth.

Brown is October bracken
Where the squirrels revel
In hips and haws, the nuts
And mast of St Michael Penkevil.

* Roseland means the land of the promontory, between the Fal and
the sea.

About the church at Creed
Not a bud does peep:
The roses have lost their leaves
And sleep their winter sleep.

And all around the parish
The ways are white and weird:
Frost and rime on boughs
Hung with Old Man's Beard.

The Rooks at Trenarren

When the rooks descry me
'Caw-Caw-Caw' they say,
In the morning quiet
At the dawn of day,

When I go out at door
To unbar the outer gate,
And up the unswept gravel—
Whether I'm early or late

'Caw-Caw-Caw' they say,
Sending the message round,
Giving the alert
With their barbaric sound—

As if I'm an interloper
In this ancient place,
Where they for generations
Had bred their corvine race.

They took a sudden fancy,
After many a year,
To build their noisy nests
Upon the treetops here.

They chose the common conifers
With their ragged line,
Ignoring beech and chestnut
And the great insignis pine.

No children in the house—
The rooks all fly away,
Desert their lofty nests,
So the old folks say.

This year they're back again—
And what does that portend?
A prolific year for poems,
The children of the mind?

A raucous row they keep,
Building their nests on high,
Rearing their silent young,
With many a warning cry,

Teach them to leave their nests,
Encourage them to fly—
Till, on a summer morning
With lyric ecstasy,
Out they sail their black ships
Across the waiting sky.

Charlestown Church Bells

Noel, Piran, Petroc,
    Michael, Morwenna, Paul,
To the church above the harbour
    Sweet and silvery call.

They send their message outward
    Across the crystal bay,
And bless the passing seasons
    From New Year to Christmas Day.

Ring out around the coast line
　　　From the Gribbin to Black Head
Summoning the living,
　　　Remembering the dead:

Who once lived in these places,
　　　Porthpean, Charlestown, Duporth,
The miners of Wheal Eliza,
　　　The farmers of Kilmarth;

And inland to Tregrehan,
　　　Along the sands of Par,
At morning and at evening
　　　They send their message far

To remoter Menabilly,
　　　The grey quay of Polkerris
Under its grove of trees,
　　　And over the cliffs to Crinnis:

Speaking their living language
　　　Alike to the quick and the dead,
For all are one communion
　　　For whom Christ's blood was shed.

These are his saints they're named for,
　　　With one who answered their call*
Noel, Piran, Petroc,
　　　Michael, Morwenna, Paul.

* Nöel Coward, who loved Charlestown, gave the bell named for
him.

408

The Pleasant Places of Devon

Do you know Maristow,
Bridestowe or Virginstow?
O come to Brimmacombe,
Dunchideock or Challacombe,
Broadswoodwidger, Tetcott,
Ellacott or Priestacott.
Though we've no Toller Porcorum
There's Buckland and Zeal Monachorum.
From Thrushelton and Kelly
Take the turning to Bratton Clovelly;
Nor is it far to seek
Germansweek or Bramford Speke.
We're contented here
With Larkbeare or Rockbeare;
All is very well
At Sampford Peverel or Sydenham Damerel.
Come to Dittisham in cherry time
Or Gittisham at any time.
O Lovadon and Livaton,
Caddaford and Baddaford,
St Giles-in-the-Heath and Strete
Are very hard to beat.
Shuttaford and Shallowford,
Harford and Bittaford,
Owl's Rattle and Rattery,
Woolfardisworthy* and Ottery,
Doddiscomleigh and Throwleigh—
Through which you must drive slowly,
The road is so narrow,
As at Ugborough or White Barrow—
Petertavy and Marytavy
Are surely,
With Cruys Morchard
And Whimple with its cider orchard,

* Pronounced Woolsery.

409

Torbryan and then
Sampford Courtenay and Ipplepen,
Sampford Spiney and Manaton,
Bagtor and Ilsington
Broadclyst and Clyst Honiton,
Lamerton or Coryton,
Collacombe or Hayne,
The pleasantest places
In sun
Or rain.

Apollo, Glorious Labrador

Apollo, glorious labrador,
Of golden coat and amber eyes,
Of your regal looks and gentle ways
We have so many memories.

What a kingdom you had here:
Trevissick Turn to Hallane Mill,
Trenarren village and Ropehawn,
Along the headland to flagstaff hill.

All the beaches here were yours,
Porthtowan, Gwendra, Silvermine,
When you were young and frolicsome,
In summer days, of sheen or shine.

Following your master into the sea,
Close on his track, treading the waves,
Bounding across seaweed and rocks,
Under the Vans, exploring the caves.

You toss your treasure trove in the air,
Flotsam and jestsam, wrack of the sea,
Pieces of spar, a cellophane square
To protect from the birds his cherry tree.

What days you had of bliss and joy
Splashing in the valley stream;
Back to the shelter of Rose Cottage
All the night, perchance to dream

How once you chased my favourite cat;
Peter, the white Persian, spat
Fury from the safety of a tree
At such a breach of his dignity:
Nor was I wholly pleased thereat—

But forgave you for your charming way
Of welcoming me, a visitor,
With a present of your bone or toy,
A shoe or slipper at your door.
You became with advancing age
A wise old dog, a sober sage,
Couchant before the friendly fire
Of the ever hospitable squire

Who made Rose Cottage what it is—
A haven of all felicities.
How much we miss you: there's not much fun
At your home now you are gone.
Yet, on reflection, I am glad
To think what a golden life you had.

Retiring to Cornwall

Retiring to Cornwall
You can always play games
With odd Cornish names:
For example, there's ample
Room to ramble
At Chapel Amble.
Do you feel a hunger

411

To live at St Ingunger,
Or would you prefer Tresunger?
Or a positive ache
For a quiet life at Landrake?
Would you quake
At the thought of a journey
With a forgetful attorney
To remote St Erney?
If so,
Consider Davidstow,
Or moorland Michaelstow,
Petrockstow or Perranzabuloe.
Express no scorn
For Ruan Lanihorne
Of Epaphroditus, former vicar, all forlorn.
You could do worse than put
Your funds into a house at Herodsfoot,
A roadside stall at Trerulefoot;
Or share a boat with a boy-
Friend at Fowey,
With a nice ingle-nook at 'The Ship-Ahoy'.
Do not join the blimps
Or hope to catch shrimps
At Ventongimps.
You might have reason for ruth
To leave a good thing at Redruth
In hopes of a better at Ponsanooth;
One might well feel lazy,
Or at least a little crazy
At demotic St Blazey,
While the crowds at Mevagissey*
Are enough to make one dizzy—
Better retire to inland St Issey.
You could take a boat from Polruan
And cautiously ribbon
Around Point Gribbin

* The proper pronunciation is Mevagizzey and St Izzey: these
Cornish s's are z's.

412

To land at Pentewan.
Just as one arrives
To take a lease for three lives,
In the old Cornish manner, at St Ives:
But abstain from three wives—
Nor take one at all
In the parish of Paul,
Better to catch lobsters off Prawle.
What kind of a dance
Would you lead at Penzance?
You could prance practically to Kynance,
Or, replete with Cornwall, retreat to France.